Grant Writing For Dummies®

Steps for preparing your first-ever request for funds

- ✔ Assess your needs.
- ✔ Prioritize — decide what needs funding first.
- ✔ Design a funding plan and identify the kinds of funds you need. (Take a look at Chapter 4.)
- ✔ Create a planning team representing everyone who has a stake in the project.
- ✔ Assign research and writing tasks.
- ✔ Find out when grant applications are due.
- ✔ Determine what kind of application format is required.
- ✔ Develop a draft funding-request document for critique and review. (Chapter 10 is your guide.)
- ✔ Polish your document to a high luster. (Check the two grant narratives in the Appendix for examples.)
- ✔ Submit your request and hope for the best.
- ✔ Follow-up with funders and team members.

Reasons never to stop seeking grants

- ✔ The need for funding is eternal.
- ✔ Getting grants means learning to exist on grants — you will always need grant monies to keep programs running.
- ✔ Even when your most recent grant request is funded, you have to start looking for future funding immediately.
- ✔ New grant funding opportunities are announced every day. (Flip to Chapter 2 for examples.)
- ✔ If your grant application isn't funded the first or second time, don't succumb. Reapply. Some funding sources look for tenacity — the grant applicant who never gives up!
- ✔ Your stakeholders are depending on you.
- ✔ Your constituents are depending on you.
- ✔ Your staff or coworkers are depending on you.
- ✔ Your grandmother told you over and over that when you fail, you need to try, try, and try again!

Resources to keep you up-to-date on funding opportunities

- ✔ Catalog of Federal and Domestic Funding: www.cfda.gov
- ✔ Federal Register: ocd.usda.gov/nofa.htm
- ✔ The Foundation Center: www.fdncenter.org
- ✔ The Taft Group: www.taftgroup.com
- ✔ Fundsnet: www.fundsnetservices.com

For Dummies: Bestselling Book Series for Beginners

Grant Writing For Dummies®

Cheat Sheet

Writing a riveting request

- ✔ Study and carefully follow the funder's grant application guidelines.
- ✔ Begin writing by introducing the organization seeking funding.
- ✔ Write a compelling needs statement with current data on the problem and the demographics of the people to be served.
- ✔ Describe how grant funds will be used.
- ✔ Develop long-term goals.
- ✔ Create measurable objectives that answer who is being served, when, and for how long.
- ✔ Tell how long the project will take — use a timeline.
- ✔ Staff the project with experienced people. (See Chapter 14 for guidance.)
- ✔ Show lines of authority — who reports to whom.
- ✔ Talk about equity for staff and participants.
- ✔ Emphasize the basic, beneficial changes the project will bring about.
- ✔ Develop a budget summary and a detailed budget narrative. (Chapter 16 contains details.)
- ✔ Include the right attachments.
- ✔ Package the grant request properly.
- ✔ Write with vigor and style! (Chapter 9 shows you how.)

Your turn: Ten projects for grant requests

I've emptied my brain and opened my heart in *Grant Writing For Dummies* to give you the most up-to-date information on grant seeking and grant writing. Now it's your turn to brainstorm the top ten funding needs for your nonprofit organization. So get started!

1. _____
2. _____
3. _____
4. _____
5. _____

6. _____
7. _____
8. _____
9. _____
10. _____

Hungry Minds™

For Dummies: Bestselling Book Series for Beginners

Praise for Grant Writing For Dummies

"Bev Browning is the national guru on grant writing. She has an incredible record of obtaining grant dollars! Bev has taught this topic for my organization for ten years. Her clear, concise instructions led many nonprofit organizations and agencies to funding for critical projects. Now everyone can follow her guidance by reading this book and using her grant writing tips. She is awesome and well-respected by both grant writers and grant makers."

> — Joan Hutchison, Director of Education, Michigan
> Municipal League, Ann Arbor

"*Grant Writing For Dummies* takes the intimidation out of the grant writing process. This book is for both the novice grant seeker and seasoned grant writer who want to increase their rate of funding success. Be prepared for the thrill, excitement, and relief of having your project funded."

> — Vanessa Buhs, CEO, Renaissance West, Inc., Grant
> Writing/Grant Management, Manistee, Michigan

"This book will prove an invaluable tool for novice and experienced grant writers alike. Bev Browning has used her years of experience in this field to provide an in-depth look at grant writing, from beginning your research to getting funded. Her depth of knowledge on the subject is seemingly endless, as she takes a complicated subject and makes it easy to understand and even easier to follow."

> — Mara Gerst, Grants Officer, Phoenix Art Museum

"What a wonderful resource — comprehensive, clearly written, and to the point! There are no assumptions made by the author, who includes information that everyone needs, from the rank beginner to the more experienced grant writer seeking to improve his or her success rate. I found this book highly organized and particularly welcome the notes, tips, rules, and cross-referencing."

> — Louise Yohalem, Executive Director of Development,
> Union County College, Cranford, New Jersey

"Exciting, informative, and welcome, this step-by-step guide is a tool of empowerment that will benefit millions of nonprofits and community agencies who have consistently struggled with grant writing!"

> — Brenda K. Patrick, President/CEO, Write Spirit

"Bev Browning is a master grant writer and her newest book informs, encourages, and inspires you to write and win your funding request. The book's easy-to-use format, thorough approach, and clear and experienced advice make it seem as if Bev is providing a one-on-one tutorial."

— Arlene Krebs, Author, *The Distance Learning Funding $ourcebook,* President, New Orbit Communications

"Of course it's Bev Browning who writes a book that will be considered a mandatory *must read* by anyone thinking about becoming a grant writer! Whether it's matching funders with seekers, writing an infallible grant proposal, or defining (and refining) the business of grant proposal writing Bev knows it all. Her ability to break down the most complicated situation into very palatable bits is gold to anyone starting out in this business. For the new or even veteran grant writer, this book is the next best thing to having the real, live Bev by your side...and I should know. From the time I was a "newbie" grant writer to this very day, I have been fortunate to have the one-on-one mentorship of this incredible woman. Buy this book and thank me later."

— Kimberly Contreras Mosher, Owner, The Marketing Department, Phoenix

"Bev Browning, student of grant writing who never missed a class, now becomes the teacher who lets us peer over her shoulder to absorb years of experience and knowledge bound in one book, *Grant Writing For Dummies.* I'm honored to sit in her classroom to learn the mastery of money — where to find it, how to get it, what to do with it when it arrives."

— Rebecca Hardcastle, Spirituality Via the Arts, Fountain Hills, Arizona

Grant Writing

FOR

DUMMIES®

Grant Writing FOR DUMMIES®

by Beverly A. Browning

Hungry Minds™

Best-Selling Books • Digital Downloads • e-Books • Answer Networks • e-Newsletters • Branded Web Sites • e-Learning

New York, NY ◆ Cleveland, OH ◆ Indianapolis, IN

Grant Writing For Dummies®

Published by
Hungry Minds, Inc.
909 Third Avenue
New York, NY 10022
www.hungryminds.com
www.dummies.com

Library of Congress Control Number: 00-110911

ISBN: 0-7645-5307-0

Printed in the United States of America

10 9 8 7 6 5

1B/TQ/QR/QS/IN

Distributed in the United States by Hungry Minds, Inc.

Distributed by CDG Books Canada Inc. for Canada; by Transworld Publishers Limited in the United Kingdom; by IDG Norge Books for Norway; by IDG Sweden Books for Sweden; by IDG Books Australia Publishing Corporation Pty. Ltd. for Australia and New Zealand; by TransQuest Publishers Pte Ltd. for Singapore, Malaysia, Thailand, Indonesia, and Hong Kong; by Gotop Information Inc. for Taiwan; by ICG Muse, Inc. for Japan; by Intersoft for South Africa; by Eyrolles for France; by International Thomson Publishing for Germany, Austria and Switzerland; by Distribuidora Cuspide for Argentina; by LR International for Brazil; by Galileo Libros for Chile; by Ediciones ZETA S.C.R. Ltda. for Peru; by WS Computer Publishing Corporation, Inc., for the Philippines; by Contemporanea de Ediciones for Venezuela; by Express Computer Distributors for the Caribbean and West Indies; by Micronesia Media Distributor, Inc. for Micronesia; by Chips Computadoras S.A. de C.V. for Mexico; by Editorial Norma de Panama S.A. for Panama; by American Bookshops for Finland.

For general information on Hungry Minds' products and services please contact our Customer Care Department within the U.S. at 800-762-2974, outside the U.S. at 317-572-3993 or fax 317-572-4002.

For sales inquiries and reseller information, including discounts, premium and bulk quantity sales, and foreign-language translations, please contact our Customer Care Department at 800-434-3422, fax 317-572-4002, or write to Hungry Minds, Inc., Attn: Customer Care Department, 10475 Crosspoint Boulevard, Indianapolis, IN 46256.

For information on licensing foreign or domestic rights, please contact our Sub-Rights Customer Care Department at 212-884-5000.

For information on using Hungry Minds' products and services in the classroom or for ordering examination copies, please contact our Educational Sales Department at 800-434-2086 or fax 317-572-4005.

Please contact our Public Relations Department at 212-884-5163 for press review copies or 212-884-5000 for author interviews and other publicity information or fax 212-884-5400.

For authorization to photocopy items for corporate, personal, or educational use, please contact Copyright Clearance Center, 222 Rosewood Drive, Danvers, MA 01923, or fax 978-750-4470.

Hungry Minds is a trademark of Hungry Minds, Inc.

About the Author

Beverly Browning is the founder of BEV BROWNING & A$$OCIATE$. Through contracted grant writing, workshops, internships, and publications, she shares her years of experience in winning public- and private-funding requests for her clients. Bev has demonstrated expertise in securing foundation, corporate, state, local, and federal grants for municipalities, state agencies, associations, homeless shelters, health care institutions, Chambers of Commerce, libraries, schools, and numerous other organizations. She has secured educational grants for science and mathematics projects, telecommunications planning and program development, computer and technology training (Goals 2000 and technology literacy challenge programs), early childhood development, performing arts programs, environmental education, and various youth-directed programs including university-level student support programs.

Bev is the author of six self-published grants-related publications, including audio and video products. In 1999, she published *Getting Grants Funded in Your Community,* and in 2000 she released an audio book, *Fundraising with the Corporate Letter Request.*

Since Bev started consulting in 1986, she has assisted clients throughout the United States in receiving awards of more than $45 million. In October of 1995, Bev relocated to Chandler, Arizona, after residing for 47 years in Flint, Michigan. She holds a BA in organizational development from Spring Arbor College and a master's degree in public administration from the University of Michigan.

In her spare time, Bev teaches for the University of Phoenix in Arizona, where she is approved to facilitate over 20 undergraduate Business Management and General Studies courses.

Annually, Bev travels throughout the United States to conduct grant writing workshops for local, regional, state, and national nonprofit organizations. She has trained many grant writing interns.

Dedication

To the thousands of nonprofit organizations with little or no financial or human resources who struggle to find grant opportunities and write effective and winning grant applications. You are truly the shining stars for those falling through the widening gaps of disparity. You are the people Booker T. Washington, educator and reformer, spoke of when he said, "The world cares very little about what a man or woman knows; it is what the man or woman is able to do that counts."

Author's Acknowledgments

I would like to thank a number of earth *angels* who have helped me by believing that this project was possible. First, thanks go to Margot Maley Hutchison, my literary agent at Waterside Productions, and Joan Hutchison, Margot's mother-in-law. When I conceived the idea for this book, it was Margot who climbed to the top of the manuscript mountain to make a vision a reality. Joan was the ever-present bridge that linked me with Margot.

Next I would like to thank the dedicated professionals at Hungry Minds, Inc. In particular, Holly McGuire, Norm Crampton, Ben Nussbaum, and Maridee Ennis, for guiding my efforts from an idea to the most comprehensive grant writing reference book of the millennium.

A special thanks is in order for my family. To John, my loving husband, who fed me, encouraged me, and stayed up all night to share my deadlines, tears, and smiles. He became my coach and head cheerleader. To my daughter, Lara, for whom I strive hard to be a role model. She eased my grant writing and training load by taking over some of the more time-consuming projects. To Keith, my brother, whose awe and amazement that I was writing a *For Dummies* book renewed my energy when it was needed the most. To the remarkable women who are also my cousins: Sara Shopkow, Dr. Leah Shopkow, Dr. Faith Mitchell, and Atty. Kathie D. Dones-Carson. Your lifetime achievements have defined the role for our family's women.

Finally, to my dad, Sherman Mitchell: Your tenacity to always march to a different beat, your creativity, and your pursuit of excellence continues to make a difference in my life.

Publisher's Acknowledgments

We're proud of this book; please send us your comments through our Online Registration Form located at www.dummies.com.

Some of the people who helped bring this book to market include the following:

Acquisitions, Editorial, and Media Development

Project Editor: Norm Crampton

Acquisitions Editor: Holly McGuire

Copy Editor: Ben Nussbaum

Acquisitions Coordinator: Erica Bernheim

Technical Editor: Lanny Carmichael

Editorial Manager: Pam Mourouzis

Editorial Assistant: Carol Strickland

Production

Project Coordinator: Maridee Ennis

Layout and Graphics: Amy Adrian, Jackie Bennett, Brian Torwelle, Erin Zeltner

Proofreaders: Dwight Ramsey, York Production Services, Inc.

Indexer: York Production Services, Inc.

Hungry Minds Consumer Reference Group

Business: Kathleen A. Welton, Vice President and Publisher; Kevin Thornton, Acquisitions Manager

Cooking/Gardening: Jennifer Feldman, Associate Vice President and Publisher

Education/Reference: Diane Graves Steele, Vice President and Publisher

Lifestyles/Pets: Kathleen Nebenhaus, Vice President and Publisher; Tracy Boggier, Managing Editor

Travel: Michael Spring, Vice President and Publisher; Suzanne Jannetta, Editorial Director; Brice Gosnell, Publishing Director

Hungry Minds Consumer Editorial Services: Kathleen Nebenhaus, Vice President and Publisher; Kristin A. Cocks, Editorial Director; Cindy Kitchel, Editorial Director

Hungry Minds Consumer Production: Debbie Stailey, Production Director

Contents at a Glance

Introduction 1

Part I: Powering Up with Grant Basics 5
Chapter 1: Getting Smart, Getting Money 7
Chapter 2: Searching for Government Grants 23
Chapter 3: Federal Grant Application Kits and Tidbits 35
Chapter 4: Using a Funding Plan to Raise Your Hit Rate 49
Chapter 5: Harvesting Critical Information on Foundations and Corporations 63
Chapter 6: Talking the Talk of Grant Writing 71

Part II: Understanding the Rules of the Grants Game 83
Chapter 7: Preparing for Review Criteria of Government (and Other) Grants 85
Chapter 8: Writing to Meet the Review Criteria of Government Grants 93
Chapter 9: Words that Work and Win Grant Funds 101

Part III: Putting Together Your Grant Application 111
Chapter 10: Fashioning the Little Essentials: Cover Letters, Abstracts, and Such 113
Chapter 11: Putting the Spotlight on Your Organization 123
Chapter 12: Conveying Your Need for Grant Funds 133
Chapter 13: Demonstrating How Grant Funds Will Be Used: The Plan of Action 141
Chapter 14: Profiling Personnel, Resources, and Equity 155
Chapter 15: Writing the Evaluation Plan Section of the Narrative 167
Chapter 16: Presenting the Budget 179

Part IV: Reaching the Finish Line with Your Grant Application 195
Chapter 17: Counting Down to Deadline: What to Check before Launch 197
Chapter 18: Submitting Your Information Electronically 209
Chapter 19: Cleaning Up and Following Up 215
Chapter 20: Win or Lose — How to Play the Next Card 223
Chapter 21: Using a Letter to Ask for Goods or Services 229
Chapter 22: Exploring for International Funds 233

Part V: The Part of Tens 237

Chapter 23: Ten Ways to Personalize Your Request 239
Chapter 24: Ten Grant Writing No-No's 245
Chapter 25: Ten Data Collection Tips 249
Chapter 26: Ten Tips for Organizing Your Writing 255
Chapter 27: Ten Tips for Handling a Rejection Letter 259

Appendix: Two Complete Examples of Grant Application Narratives 263

Index 289

Cartoons at a Glance

By Rich Tennant

page 195

page 111

page 237

page 83

page 5

Cartoon Information:
Fax: 978-546-7747
E-Mail: richtennant@the5thwave.com
World Wide Web: www.the5thwave.com

Table of Contents

Introduction 1

Why You Need This Book 1
The Best Ways to Use This Book 2
How This Book Is Organized 2
    Part I: Powering Up with Grant Basics 3
    Part II: Understanding the Rules of the Grants Game 3
    Part III: Putting Together Your Grant Application 3
    Part IV: Reaching the Finish Line with Your Grant Application 4
    Part V: The Part of Tens 4
Icons Used in This Book 4

Part 1: Powering Up with Grant Basics 5

Chapter 1: Getting Smart, Getting Money 7

Defining a Grant 7
Describing an Application or Proposal 8
Describing Who This Book Is For 9
Thinking about Full-time Grant Writing 9
Separating Grant Writing from Fundraising 10
Planning for Grants 12
Knowing the Language 12
Connecting Your Needs to a Governmental Source of Funds 14
    Government funding — cashing in with your richest uncle 15
    Seeking public funds closer to home 15
Looking at Foundation and Corporate Funding —
    the Other Pot of Gold 15
    Looking at the foundations 16
    Visiting the public foundations 16
    Finding corporate funders — the real angels 16
Getting Started on a Proposal 17
    Federal, state, and local units of government 18
    How a federal grant shapes up 18
    Foundations — lean, clean funding machines 19
    About the Regional Associations of Grantmakers 20
    Corporations — just get to the point! 21

Chapter 2: Searching for Government Grants 23

Looking at Home 23
Finding Federal Jackpots 24
   Advantages of direct grants 25
   The disadvantage of direct grants 25
   Advantages of pass-through grants 26
   The disadvantage of pass-through grants 26
Checking Out the Money Catalog 27
Finding Money Now in the Register 29
Taking Your Best Shot at Federal Grants 31
   Calculating the odds — taking cautious steps 31
   Calling all legislators — making critical connections 32
Weighing All the Funding Options 32
   Auditing preparedness 33
   Understanding family rules 34

Chapter 3: Federal Grant Application Kits and Tidbits 35

Touring the Federal Information Highway for Money 35
   Federal Emergency Management Administration (FEMA) 36
   Institute of Museum and Library Services (IMLS) 37
   Legal Services Corporation (LSC) 37
   National Aeronautics and Space Administration (NASA) 37
   National Endowment for the Arts (NEA) 37
   National Endowment for the Humanities (NEH) 38
   National Science Foundation (NSF) 38
   Small Business Administration (SBA) 38
   U.S. Department of Agriculture (USDA) 38
   U.S. Department of Commerce (DOC) 38
   U.S. Department of Education (DOED) 39
   U.S. Department of Energy (DOE) 39
   U.S. Department of Health and Human Services (HHS) 39
   U.S. Department of Housing and Urban Development (HUD) 40
   U.S. Department of the Interior (DOI) 40
   U.S. Department of Justice (DOJ) 40
   U.S. Department of Labor (DOL) 40
   U.S. Department of Transportation (DOT) 40
   U.S. Environmental Protection Agency (EPA) 41
   U.S. Institute of Peace (USIP) 41
Figuring Out the Forms 41
   The cover form 42
   Budget information forms 44
   Assurance forms 44
   Certification forms 44
   The lobbying-activity disclosure form 47

Chapter 4: Using a Funding Plan to Raise Your Hit Rate 49

Creating a Complete Funding Plan 49
Rules for making the plan 50
Structuring the plan 50
Funding plan for the Jefferson County Regional
Health Care Consortium 51
Improving Your Odds of Getting a Grant Award 56
Following the steps to sure funding 56
Meeting the request for a letter of inquiry 58
Handling Good Fortune 60

**Chapter 5: Harvesting Critical Information
on Foundations and Corporations** 63

Knowing the Secrets of Successful Grant Seeking 63
Clicking in the Right Places 64
Web sites worth visiting (just a sampling) 65
Looking at selected print resources 66
Scanning the Most Important Information Fields 67
Taking the Next Step — Prioritizing the Funders 69

Chapter 6: Talking the Talk of Grant Writing .71

Understanding "Grantlish" — Your Second Language 71
Speaking of your qualifications 71
Filling in the blanks with style 74
Learning the lingo for the main event 75
Defining the parts of the narrative 76
Wrapping Up the Grant Request 80

Part II: Understanding the Rules of the Grants Game 83

**Chapter 7: Preparing for Review Criteria
of Government (and Other) Grants** 85

Detailing a Federal Grant Announcement — the Early Steps 86
Deciding whether the timing is right 86
Knowing whether this is the right grant competition for you 86
Terms you need to know 87
Calculating money and chances 88
Gathering eggs for your grant basket 88
Gathering Research for Your Request 89
Identifying Other Players and Bringing Them in Early 90
Making Sure You're Eligible 91
Making Contact at the State Level 91

Chapter 8: Writing to Meet the Review Criteria of Government Grants 93

Passing the Pre-Review Process 93
Understanding the Peer Review Process 94
Reading and Writing the Federal Way 95
    Addressing the program goal for funding 95
    Using federal or state announcement language to your benefit ...96
    Pushing the point for your needs 96
    Aiming for a strike with goals and objectives 97
    Project design — in words that look familiar 97
    Evaluating your objectives 97
    Showing that you're capable 98
    Connecting numbers to words 99
Getting Help from the Feds to Score Higher 99

Chapter 9: Words that Work and Win Grant Funds 101

Doing the *"You"* Stuff Right 101
    Winning example: Application from a religious organization 102
    Winning example: Special training grant request 103
Knowing the Important Steps to Remember
    When Talking about Yourself 104
    Step 1: Who and where 104
    Step 2: The bad stuff 104
    Step 3: Use a thesaurus 107
Doing the Request Stuff Right 107

Part III: Putting Together Your Grant Application 111

Chapter 10: Fashioning the Little Essentials: Cover Letters, Abstracts, and Such 113

Setting the Tone for Your Request with the Cover Letter 114
Creating the Common Grant Application Cover Form 116
Filling In Federal Cover Forms 118
Writing the Abstract or Executive Summary 119
Where, Oh Where Is Everything? 120

Chapter 11: Putting the Spotlight on Your Organization 123

Explaining Your History and Accomplishments 124
Describing Your Programs 127
Defining the Target Population 128
Writing about Your Work with Local Groups 130

Chapter 12: Conveying Your Need for Grant Funds **133**

Telling and Selling — Making It Compelling 133
    Explaining the problem that grant funds will solve 134
    Integrating charts and tables into your narrative 134
Knowing When You've Written the Right Stuff 136

**Chapter 13: Demonstrating How Grant Funds
Will Be Used: The Plan of Action** **141**

Describing Your Vision to the Funder 141
Expressing Your Organization's Purpose 142
Writing Goals and Objectives 142
    Writing great goals 143
    Writing super objectives 144
    Making the connection between goals and objectives 147
Describing Your Strategies 148
Making a Timeline That Tells the Story Accurately 150
Making an Impact Statement 151
Formatting the Workplan 152

Chapter 14: Profiling Personnel, Resources, and Equity **155**

Making the Right Choices for Project Personnel 156
    Starting the personnel selection process 156
    Integrating the management plan into key personnel 160
Identifying Resources That Will Be Available to the Project 164
Showing Equity in Your Personnel and Participant Selection 165

**Chapter 15: Writing the Evaluation Plan Section
of the Narrative** **167**

Getting Comfortable with Evaluation Terms 167
Finding Evaluation Plan Ideas Online 170
Choosing to Conduct an Internal Evaluation 172
Choosing an Outside Evaluator 173
    What to look for in an external evaluator 173
    What to ask a prospective evaluator 174
Writing a Stakeholders Evaluation Plan 174
Writing a Third-Party Evaluation Plan 176
Getting the Word Out When Your Project Is a Model for Others 177

Chapter 16: Presenting the Budget **179**

Walking through the Terms 179
    Allocation and budget summary 179
    Budget detail 180
    Personnel 181
    Travel 181
    Equipment 182
    Supplies 183
    Contractual 183

Construction 183
Other 184
Direct costs 184
Indirect costs 184
In-kind 185
Linking Dollars to Activities 186
Scouring Up Matching Funds 187
Hard cash match sources 188
Soft cash match sources 188
Projecting Multi-Year Costs 189
Using a Fiscal Sponsor 190
Crunching the Numbers Ethically 191
Using conservative and accurate cost figures 192
Including all possible program income 193

Part IV: Reaching the Finish Line with Your Grant Application 195

Chapter 17: Counting Down to Deadline: What to Check before Launch 197

Using a Checklist for Assurance 197
The final check-off 198
Introduction to your organization 198
Problem or needs statement 199
Program design or plan of operation 199
Key personnel, organizational and partner resources,
and equity statement 199
Evaluation and dissemination 200
Budget summary and detail 200
Putting Your Attachments in Order 200
Using a Postcard to Track Your Application 204
Increasing Your Chances with a Few Finishing Touches 205
Bindings, staples, and clips 205
Paper — the magic touch 205
Mailing the right way 208

Chapter 18: Submitting Your Information Electronically 209

Streamlining the Grant Seeking Process 209
Talking to the Feds after Your Grant Is Funded 212

Chapter 19: Cleaning Up and Following Up 215

Housekeeping 101 215
Finding Tracking Software 216
Debriefing and Sharing with Your Lead Partners 217
Tracking Your Request at the Funders 218
Foundation and corporate grant requests 218
Federal and state grant requests 221

Chapter 20: Win or Lose — How to Play the Next Card **223**

Accepting Grant Monies 223
Hitting the Grant Jackpot 226
Knowing Your Rights When a Rejection Letter Arrives 226
Picking Up the Pieces and Starting Over 227
    Transforming failed federal or state grant applications 227
    Transforming failed foundation or corporate
      funding requests 228

Chapter 21: Using a Letter to Ask for Goods or Services **229**

Brainstorming the Possibilities 229
Asking for Small Stuff in a Small Way 230
Following Up after the Letter Is Mailed 232

Chapter 22: Exploring for International Funds **233**

Gathering Information on International Funders 233
Knowing Application Protocol 234
Preparing Budgets in Euros 235

Part V: The Part of Tens **237**

Chapter 23: Ten Ways to Personalize Your Request **239**

Include Photographs 239
Incorporate Color Graphics in Strategic Places 240
Make a Statement with Color 240
Include Handwritten Letters of Support 240
Use Brightly Colored Envelopes 241
Use the Same Buzzwords That the Funder Uses 241
Mimic the Funder's Corporate Colors 242
Use "We" instead of "It" 242
Create a Watermark Theme 242
Grab Their Hearts with the Visual Results of Previous Grants 243

Chapter 24: Ten Grant Writing No-No's **245**

Don't Forget to Get Permission and Input 245
Don't Look Stupid by Makng Errors 246
Don't Overlook the Importance of Stakeholders' Input 246
Don't Include Audio or Visual Attachments 246
Don't Do a Show-and-Tell Too Soon 246
Don't Submit a Rejected Grant Application
  without Making Major Changes 247
Don't Assume the Funder Has No Changes from Year to Year 247
Don't Ignore the Printer 247
Don't Get Caught by Murphy's Law — If It Can Happen, It Will 248
Don't Celebrate for Too Long; the Funding Ends Soon 248

Chapter 25: Ten Data Collection Tips 249

Look at Data from the U.S. Census Bureau First 249
Look at Data from State and Local Government Agencies Second 250
Use Data That Builds Credibility with the Funder 250
Use Current Data 251
Compare Statistics from the Same Family of Problems 251
Don't Ring if You Can Click 252
Organize Your Findings 252
Look for Free Research Reports and Newsletters 252
Share with Others and Experience the Bounty That Flows to You 252
Allocate Time Daily to Search for Best Practices
   in Your Service Area 253

Chapter 26: Ten Tips for Organizing Your Writing 255

Build a Mountain of Ideas to Write a Molehill 255
Collect First, Write Second 256
Identify and Pull Attached or Appended Documents Early 256
Sort Information by Grant Application Narrative Sections 256
Take Stock of What You Have and Don't Have 257
Write Front to Back 257
Write Like the Wind is Blowing You at 90 Miles an Hour 257
Make and Use Templates 257
Complete Each Section before Moving to the Next 258
Save the Worst for Last 258

Chapter 27: Ten Tips for Handling a Rejection Letter 259

Don't Cry 259
Don't Give Up 259
Open the Post-Rejection Discussion with Private Sector Funders 260
Request the Grant Viewers' Comments for Public Sector Funders 260
Don't Take It as a Personal Rejection 260
Read the Letter Carefully and Look for a Window of Opportunity 261
Play Their Game and Win 261
Track the Results of Your Efforts 261
Do It Again 261
Use Your Connections — a Miracle Can Happen 262

**Appendix: Two Complete Examples
of Grant Application Narratives** 263

1. Government Grant Narrative 263
2. Foundation Grant Narrative 279

Index 289

Introduction

• •

*B*ack in third grade, when your classroom had career day, did you dress up as a grant writer? For show and tell day, did you bring a grant writer to class? Probably not! The occupation of grant writing is not one that most small children, teenagers, or even young adults list as one of their life goals. Most grant writers start out in a field of their choice, like nursing or education, but along the way are dragged, sometimes unwillingly, into helping a nonprofit organization find money — mostly in the form of a grant award.

Almost two decades ago, when I first started writing grants, there were no formal college degrees in grant writing and very few, if any, books on how to write a grant. The process of learning how to write a grant was mostly trial and error, sort of like indoctrination by fire or ice. Fire, meaning your efforts were funded and everyone celebrated. Ice, meaning you efforts fell by the wayside when a rejection letter arrived in the mail, courteously stating that your grant application or proposal was not selected for funding — but try again next year!

Today, the art or skill of writing a grant request is no longer a process of trial and error. Grant writing has become an occupation. It is a science — a skill that reflects a precise application of facts or principles. *Grant Writing For Dummies* begins with the steps to take to discover exactly what it means to write a grant and ends with full examples of winning government and foundation grant applications.

Why You Need This Book

The information in this book is intended for nonprofit board members, administrators, and staff members who find themselves in the position of having to go out and secure grant funds in order to keep the agency's doors open for business. This book is for every individual who was hired for one job, like an executive director, program coordinator, marketing specialist, and so on, and asked to take on the additional role of grant writing. This book is also for the extraordinary volunteer who agreed to serve on a board of directors and help out when needed. For many of you, the challenge of learning a new skill is just too good to pass up. So you say, "Yes, I'll write that grant for you," before you realize the magnitude of the job that lies ahead. This book flattens the mountain of mystery to a plateau of knowledge, delivered systematically in every chapter.

This book is also for every person who always wanted to learn how to write grant requests, but didn't know how or where to get started. It is for the curious, the inquisitive, the hesitant, and the fearful. Once you see how easily each chapter flows and how the order of the information appears in just the right sequence to answer your questions, you won't be able to put *Grant Writing For Dummies* down. Eagerness and tenacity will surface and be the driving forces as you either learn how to write your first grant application or learn to write better grant applications that get funded more often.

This book speaks to the both the novice and the veteran grant writer. It helps you to organize your thoughts and writing into a proven format for winning grant awards. This book gives you the most up-to-date, accurate information on how to find grant funding opportunities and how to write appealing and compelling grant applications and proposals. Finally, this book is the heart and soul of an individual who started writing grants as a board volunteer and ended up as an international grant writing consultant, author, and expert for nonprofit organizations around the world.

The Best Ways to Use This Book

First, make a list of the ten burning questions you have about writing a grant. Then look through the table of contents for the chapters that contain the information to answer your questions. As you reach each chapter, make a list of more questions and look for the chapters that contain the new information you seek. Keep this book on your desk for easy and quick accessing. It will be your daily guide, whether you look up one specific answer and then go back to working on your grant writing project, or whether you stop and read an entire chapter at one time. Let each chapter come naturally and in response to your need at the moment.

Use this book before you start writing a grant. Don't wait until you've written a grant the same way that you've been writing for eons and find out you've been rejected, again. Use these chapters to re-energize and renew your research style, writing approach, and other skill areas. Highlight the tips that are most important to you in your own writing area and put sticky notes in the chapters that you find yourself returning to day after day.

How This Book Is Organized

Grant Writing For Dummies is organized into five different parts, with chapters arranged to walk you through the process of planning for, organizing, writing, mailing, and following up on your grant request. The underlying message throughout the chapters is creativity and tenacity — to always be fresh in your thinking and writing and to *never, ever* give up if your grant request is rejected. So come and walk with the author — be bold, be daring, be very, very successful at grant writing.

Part I: Powering Up with Grant Basics

Part I is all about the basics of grant writing. It answers your questions with enough detail to remove the mystery and open up the secrets. What is a grant? What is a grant writer? What are the areas of grantmaking? How do I get started? This part of the book shows you how to search for all types of grant funding using the Internet and the library. It also tells you how to talk "grantlish," the language of the world of grants. So get ready to roll up your sleeves and get started with the basics.

Part II: Understanding the Rules of the Grants Game

Part II introduces you to the review criteria for government grants. It also shows you how to write competitive language to meet the review criteria — to get all of the review points and beat out the other grant applicants! This part includes the kinds of words that work to win grant funds, and presents a winning recipe for formatting your grant request.

Part III: Putting Together Your Grant Application

Don't let a stack of papers or guidelines overwhelm you. Figuring out how to assemble your grant application is as easy as 1, 2, 3. In this part, you learn how to prepare the cover forms, write abstracts and executive summaries, and develop tables of contents. The way to introduce your organization as the grant applicant and to convey your need for grant funds is presented in common lay terms that guide you in every detail. You will be able to talk about how grant funds will be used, present key personnel, resources and fair practice statements, create evaluations, and present a clear and understandable budget section. This part is the meat and potatoes. So enjoy your grant morsels to the fullest.

Part IV: Reaching the Finish Line with Your Grant Application

Just writing a great grant application is not enough. Part IV gives you the finishing touches needed to grab and hold the grant reviewer's attention. It also addresses the follow-up tasks that will make your next grant writing project much easier. This part includes a chapter on electronic grant submissions, what to do if your grant is not funded, and how to explore international funding sources.

Part V: The Part of Tens

This part of the book presents several collections of ten or so items, grouped around a particular subject. Some are tongue-in-cheek, others are vital. Whichever the case, be sure to read through the ones that suit you best. You may want to start with "Ten Grant Writing No-No's." You may already be committing these acts of grant suicide. It's never too late to learn how to avoid the deadly pitfalls of grant writing.

Icons Used in This Book

The little pictures I place in the margins are designed to flag information that's special and important for one reason or another. Here are the icons I use in *Grant Writing For Dummies* and what they mean.

A good idea, trick, or shortcut that can save you time and trouble.

A piece of information that you shouldn't forget.

Information that can help you avoid disasters.

Things you can do to make your grant application stand out from the crowd.

Part I

Powering Up with Grant Basics

"The next part of your grant writing test is designed to determine your sense of humor."

In this part . . .

Before you jump into the ocean of grant writing opportunities, you need to know the basic preparatory steps necessary to write successful grants. Grant writing involves more than just having a good idea and putting it down on paper. In this part, you begin at ground zero. What is a grant? What is a grant writer? What areas are grants awarded in? Who has the money? How do you find out about government grants? How do you wade through the pages and pages of instructions? Who else has money to give besides the feds? What terms are critical to understanding the grants game? This part helps you answer these early questions and puts your grant writing in order.

Chapter 1

Getting Smart, Getting Money

. . . .

In This Chapter

▶ Starting at ground zero

▶ Discovering the field of grant writing

▶ Sorting out the types of grants

▶ Finding the funding

▶ Using the right format for the right funder

. . . .

*W*hen I first decided to pursue grant writing for a living, my colleagues in the field told me that I needed a day job — that I'd never make a living, because there simply wasn't enough work for a full-time freelancer. Some 14 years later, I still chuckle at the naysayers. I followed my heart and stepped off the ledge without a parachute. I'm still floating.

I started out with a 50 percent success rate. About half of the grants that I wrote actually got funded. Fifty percent may sound okay — at first. But think about a baseball team that wins only half its games. You can be sure that some player is going to be traded before the next season starts. Likewise, you cannot survive for long as a development officer, grants specialist, or grants consultant as a halfer! You must push yourself harder to make the hard work and long hours of grant seeking and grant writing pay in a big way.

Now that I've achieved a 90 to 95 percent success rate, I assure you that you can have great success, too. Dozens of grant announcements and grant application opportunities are published every day. You can get smart — and get the money — almost all of the time.

Defining a Grant

A *grant* is a monetary award given by a funder. Some of you may think that the only grants are those that pay for college tuition. You're in for a surprise. Grants pay for all kinds of things. And pursuing grants is one of the most interesting occupations in the world.

A *grant application* is a written request asking for money from a government agency, a foundation, or a corporation. Most grants go to organizations that have applied to the Internal Revenue Service for nonprofit status and received the IRS's blessing as a *501(c)(3) organization,* although a few grants do go to individuals. Since I've been writing grant applications, I've seen a growing number of grant awards made to cities, villages, townships, counties, and even state agencies. While none of these governmental units are IRS 501(c)(3) designees, they are still nonprofit in structure and can apply for and receive grant awards from the federal government, foundations, and corporations.

Grants are bestowed upon, awarded to, or just plain given to a nonprofit organization that has written a winning grant application to a funding source. Some grant applications are a mere three to four pages long. This is usually the case when the funding source has created its own grant application form and you just fill in the blanks. But 90 percent of the time, you won't be lucky enough to get away with only a three- or four-pager. Federal grant applications are often 20 to 40 pages of blood, sweat, and tears. Foundations and corporations can be sold on your worthy idea in 10 or fewer pages. Of course, that's with a lot of supporting documentation attached.

Describing an Application or Proposal

The terms *grant application* and *grant proposal* mean — more or less — the same thing. A distinction does exist, though. The term *application* is used when the funding source hands you — you guessed it — an application, either on a piece of paper or in electronic format. Cover forms, budget forms, and other information-gathering forms may be included for you to fill in and return with the grant application narrative by a specific due date.

A governmental unit (federal, state, or local) generally issues a grant application kit and guidelines for completing each required section. A foundation or a corporate funder may develop its own grant application form simply to avoid having to read a zillion different writing formats from a zillion creative grant writers.

A *proposal* is usually a more free-flowing grant request. It's you putting your ideas on paper about your organization and the program that you want to fund. You can dash off a proposal foolishly, simply writing what you're thinking as it pops into your mind. Or you can create a proposal the smart way, using a national or regional *template format* (I explain that term elsewhere in this chapter). So whether you're writing a grant application or a grant proposal, both types of funding requests require planning, organization, good research, and writing skills.

Describing Who This Book Is For

This reference book is targeted to two main users.

The first group is made up of people who've been assigned the task of writing grants (in addition to their many other backbreaking duties). Careers that often include grant writing among their other duties include grants specialist, grants manager, development officer, project specialist, executive director (usually a very small nonprofit organization has its executive director do *everything*), project coordinator, volunteer, volunteer coordinator, program manager, teacher, professor, and on and on. At any given time, anyone could find themselves in the position of having to learn what a grant is and then having to write a grant application.

But this book can also help people who want to make a career of freelance grant writing. Most folks who decide to strike out on their own usually refer to themselves as *grant writing consultants*. A zillion opportunities are out there for freelance grant writing. But before you hang out your shingle, make sure you know the ins and outs of what it takes to win a grant. This book is your guide and ever-ready reference.

Thinking about Full-time Grant Writing

If you're thinking about becoming a full-time grant writer, you should know that you've got many options. You can become a freelance grant writing consultant and write grant applications for more than one nonprofit organization. Or you can seek full-time employment in the nonprofit sector and have one employer. Or you can develop your present job, whatever and wherever that may be, into a grant writing specialty. Deciding which way to go may be easy — or already decided for you. Or it may be hard. Think about these matters:

- Mobile or stationary — what type of work environment is right for you?

- Do you want to write grants for the same organization every day or would you rather write for a different organization every month?

- Do you need the stability and routine of a 9-to-5 job, or are you looking for a chance to write your own paycheck?

- Do you work better under someone else's supervision and direction, or would you rather call your own shots and supervise the project, from research to writing to submission?

- Can you equip your home office with all of the necessary grant writing tools and technologies, or would you rather simply go into someone else's office every day?

What type of grant writing is right for you?

Often, you won't have the luxury of deciding what grants to pursue. You'll apply for every grant that you've got a chance to win! However, if you make a long-term commitment to grant writing, you'll find that you have to start exercising your discretion when it comes to deciding what grant competitions to enter. You'll also have more room to allow your personal predilections to affect what types of grants you write. Some factors to consider:

✔ Are you a procrastinator? If so, you may want to specialize in writing requests in which grant applications can be submitted any time during the year. Another option would be to enter competitions with rolling deadlines; if you miss the first deadline, you can always write the grant application and mail it in for the next deadline. Some competitions have deadlines three to four times per year.

✔ Are you looking for a slow and easy start with less pressure? If you answered yes, then you may want to specialize in writing corporate grant requests — less writing can still result in large monetary rewards.

Corporate givers tend to allow submissions at anytime.

✔ Do you like to be challenged on a daily basis? Does the thrill of a clock ticking closer and closer to the midnight hour make you work harder and faster? If you answered yes, then you may want to specialize in the more complex types of grant applications — federal and state — with dozens of writing hours required, short notices of funding availability, application deadlines less than 30 days away, and forms, forms, and more forms.

✔ Do you like constant change? Do you like to do something different each time you start a project? If so, then generalizing may be the key to your grant writing success. If you're a generalizer, you're like me. You will take on any grant writing project, any topic, any type of funder, and make headway fast. Deciding not to specialize in the types of grant applications that you write and taking a broader approach instead may be your cup of tea. It's certainly mine!

Grant writing doesn't necessarily require a specialized degree; but having good research skills, writing skills, and critical thinking skills is essential to successful grant writing — that is, to getting your grant proposals funded on a regular basis.

Separating Grant Writing from Fundraising

Before going any farther, I want to underline the big differences between two occupations that sound a lot alike. Some grant writers also do *fundraising*. And, yes, some fundraisers also write grants. It's sort of like wearing two hats. But you know how you look wearing two hats — like you've gone slightly mad. From my own experience, writing grants and achieving a high funding success rate takes daily practice and full concentration. I can't imagine adding the stress of fundraising — planning special events, meeting with individual donors, and worrying over all the other nitty-gritty on a fundraiser's to-do list.

Using one person to write grants and do traditional fundraising can be overwhelming, even to a hardened veteran. In both fields, fundraising and grant writing, burnout occurs faster than in other professions because of the daily deadlines and the long work hours.

My advice: Think long and hard before accepting a position that requires you to chase grant monies as well as run around day and night planning this and that. (Did you know that when someone wears two or more hats in an organization, but only gets paid for wearing one of the hats, the Human Resources guru often gives her the title of *Project Specialist?* If that's your title, tough luck!)

Just so we understand each other very clearly on this two-hats business, I summarize the difference between grant writing and fundraising in Table 1-1.

Table 1-1	Fundraising versus Grant Writing
Fundraising	**Grant Writing**
A fundraiser spends a lot of time researching people to approach for big bucks and deciding what they are interested in putting their money in — that is, what social cause Mr. Moneybags may contribute to at the moment.	A grant writer finds a specific project needing monies, and then identifies government agencies, foundations, or corporations to approach. The asking is done in the form of a written request, referred to as a *grant application* or *proposal.*
Organizing special events to raise money. For example: selling raffle tickets, getting sponsors for a 5K race, having a silent auction, and on and on and on!	Writing a precisely formatted grant application or proposal to a specific funding entity asking for money.
Having the ability to know how much money you have raised immediately after the sponsored event.	Waiting up to 12 months to find out if your request has been funded.
Working on a project for months before it actually happens.	Researching a project for up to six months before actually writing the funding request.
If freelance, often hired as a consultant and paid in part on a commission or a percentage of funds actually raised.	If freelance, hired in a consulting capacity and paid an agreed-upon fee, either at the start of the project or in stages, until the grant application or proposal is ready to submit to a funder.

Most states require that fundraisers be registered and have a license number. Why? Fundraisers often handle large sums of money, have access to the money people, and may even visit a wealthy person's home to discuss a fundraising event or to appeal for a contribution. The fundraiser could leave that afternoon tea with Mrs. Moneybags' blank check. The fundraiser is looking for big bucks in a big way. Usually, the more she can raise; the more she makes for her efforts.

A grant writer is like any other writer and does not need bonding, special licensing, or errors and omission insurance. A grant writer can be compared to a technical writer who writes computer books or electronic instructions or to a fiction writer who plugs away at chapter after chapter to produce a book. Grant writers do not handle money other than the money they are paid to write a grant application or proposal.

Planning for Grants

Rule number one is that you don't ask for a grant without thinking first.

You'd be surprised how many nonprofit organizations lurch from one crisis to another. They never plan ahead in terms of grant seeking. They lack a planning tool to give them direction. What they lack is a *funding plan,* an internal examination of the organization's strengths, weaknesses, opportunities, and threats. It answers questions like:

- ✔ What programs are strong and already have regular funding to keep them going?
- ✔ What new programs need funding?
- ✔ What opportunities exist to find new funding partners?
- ✔ What existing grants will run out before new funding is found?

When you answer these questions with the counsel of a grants planning team, you can begin to look at the multitude of areas where grants are awarded and begin to prioritize the type of funding that you need. (I write more about funding plans in Chapter 4.)

Knowing the Language

Before you jump into the grants fire — I call it a fire because the competition is hot — you need to be sure that you speak the language. These are the terms and phrases that grantmakers use.

Annual campaigns: Money to support annual operating expenses, infrastructure improvements, program expansion, and, in some cases, one-time only expenses (like a cooling-system replacement).

Building/renovation funds: Money to build a new facility or renovate an existing facility. These projects are often referred to as *bricks-and-mortar* projects. Building funds are the most difficult to secure; only a small percentage of foundations and corporations award these types of grants.

Capital support: Money for equipment, buildings, construction, and endowments. These types of large-scale projects are not quickly funded. It often takes 2 to 3 years for the total funding to be secured. This type of request is a major undertaking by the applicant organization.

Challenge monies: These funds act as leverage to secure additional grants from foundations and corporations. They're awarded contingent upon your raising additional grant funds from other funding sources.

Conferences/seminars: Money to cover the cost of attending conferences and seminars, planning them, and hosting them. Funding may be used to pay for all of the conference's expenses, including securing a keynote speaker, travel, printing, advertising, and facility expenses, such as meals.

Consulting services: You may want to secure the expertise of a consultant or consulting firm to strengthen some aspect of organizational programming. For example, if you bring in a consultant to do a long-range strategic plan or to conduct training for a board of directors you're paying for consulting services.

Continuing support/continuation grant: If you've already received a grant award from a funder, you can return to apply for continuing support. Be aware that many funders will only fund an organization one time.

Employee matching gifts: Many employers match the monetary donations their employees make to nonprofit organizations, often on a ratio of 1:1 or 2:1. If you have board members that are employed by large corporations, have them check with their Human Resources department to see if their employer has such a program. It doubles or triples the original contribution.

Endowments: A source of long-term, permanent investment income to insure the continuing presence and financial stability of your nonprofit organization. If your organization is always operating in crisis-management mode, then one of your goals should be to develop an endowment fund for long-term viability.

Fellowships: Money to support graduate and post-graduate students in specific fields. These funds are only awarded to the institution, never to the individual.

General/operating expenses: Money for general budget line-item expenses. These funds may be used for salaries, fringe benefits, travel, consultants, utilities, equipment, and other expenses necessary to operate a nonprofit program.

Matching funds: Grant funds that are awarded with the requirement that you must find other grant funding that matches or exceeds the initial grant's matching-fund stipulation. Matching funds are a type of leverage grant.

Program development: Funding to pay for expenses related to organization growth, the expansion of existing programs, or the development of new programs.

Research: Money to support medical and educational research. Monies are usually awarded to the institutions that employ the individuals who will be conducting the research.

Scholarship funds: Scholarship awards to individuals. Remember that any time funds are awarded to an individual, they are considered taxable income.

Seed money: Most often, these types of grants are awarded for a pilot program not yet in full-scale operation; hence the term *seed money*. Seed money gets a program underway, but other grant monies are needed to continue the program in its expansion phase.

Technical assistance: Money to improve your internal program operations. Often, this type of grant is awarded to hire an individual or firm that can provide the needed technical assistance. Alternatively, the foundation's personnel may provide the technical assistance. For example, a program officer from a foundation may work on-site with the applicant organization to establish an endowment development fund and start a campaign for endowment monies. In some instances, the funding source identifies a third-party technical assistance provider and pays them directly to assist the nonprofit organization.

Connecting Your Needs to a Governmental Source of Funds

Grants, grants, everyone wants a grant! You are constantly hearing about other organizations winning grant awards, but no one tells you how they found the money. Is your organization being left out in the cold — no money, no luck, and no clue? Once you realize how easy it is to *find* and *get* the money, you'll rejoice and sing praises like everyone else.

Conducting a funding search leads you to the money. You need to know what type of grant money will fund your idea, project, or program.

Government funding — cashing in with your richest uncle

The first place to look for money is with Uncle Sam. You always knew that you had a long-lost relative somewhere with money, right? The money (government funding) originates from the federal, state, and local levels. Using the Internet and your local public library, you can cash in on the dollars.

The *Federal Register* and the *Catalog of Federal and Domestic Assistance* are two excellent and free government publications. Using both of these funding sources to find and win federal grants sharpens your grant seeking skills. In Chapter 2, I give you the scoop on using these funding tools.

Seeking public funds closer to home

Each state receives grant monies from the feds. After they take their fair or unfair share, they regrant it to eligible agencies and organizations in the form of competitive grants or formula grants.

Examples of some state agencies that regrant federal monies are agriculture, commerce, education, health, housing development, natural resources, and transportation.

Contact your state legislator at their local office or at the state capitol for assistance in identifying grant opportunities within your state.

Looking at Foundation and Corporate Funding — the Other Pot of Gold

The rainfall of private-sector grant money is continuous. Let me name the ways for you: foundation and corporate.

Where can you find out more about these-no-strings attached grants? You can locate sources by visiting a Foundation Center Cooperating Collections site (usually at a state university library, community foundation, or other non-profit information center) or on the Internet. The Foundation Center's Web site address is www.fdncenter.org.

Using technology to find money is a good idea — you'll see lots of Web sites throughout this book.

Looking at the foundations

Private foundations get their monies from a single source, like an individual, a family, or a corporation. Here are a few sources of funding. Check them out to whet your appetite:

- PGA Foundations: `www.paulallen.com/foundations/main.asp`
- The Arthur Vining Davis Foundations: `jvm.com/davis/FND.HTM`
- The William Randolph Hearst Foundations: `fdncenter.org/grantmaker/hearst/index.html`
- The Henry Luce Foundation: `www.hluce.org/`
- The Pew Charitable Trusts: `www.pewtrusts.com/`
- Turner Foundation: `www.turnerfoundation.org/`

Visiting the public foundations

Public foundations are supported primarily through donations from the general public. That's is a no-brainer, right? They also receive a great deal of their funding from foundation and corporate grants. For starters, take a look at these:

- Arts Midwest: `www.artsmidwest.org`
- The Enterprise Foundation: `www.enterprisefoundation.org`
- Independent Television Service: `www.itvs.org/home/index.html`
- Local Initiatives Support Corporation: `www.liscnet.org`
- Nonprofit Facilities Fund: `www.nffusa.org`
- Touch'em All Foundation: `promotions.yahoo.com/promotions/garth`
- Kristi Yamaguchi's Always Dream Foundation `promotions/yahoo.com/promotions/kristi/adf.html`

Finding corporate funders — the real angels

All of this time that you were out there patronizing big businesses, I'll bet you didn't know that many of them set 5 percent or more of their profits aside for grants. The term of the millennium is *corporate responsibility*.

Corporate responsibility is the approach a successful business takes when it decides to make a financial commitment to the community where its head-quarters are located or where it has operating locations.

Corporations that award grants have a Web site link labeled: *community, community relations, social responsibility, local initiatives, grants,* or *corporate giving.* Some corporate Web sites to visit are

- Exxon Mobil: `www.exxon.com/community/index.html`
- Kellogg Company: `www.Kellogg.com`
- Metropolitan Life Insurance Company: `www.metlife.com`
- AT&T: `www.att.com/att`
- Ben & Jerry's Foundation: `www.benjerry.com/foundation/index.html`
- Toyota USA Foundation: `www.toyota.com/times/commun/feature/founhome.html`
- Fannie Mae Foundation: `www.fanniemaefoundation.org`
- Philip Morris: `www.philipmorris.com/pmcares`

Getting Started on a Proposal

The first step in getting started is to learn the different types of formats and when to use them.

Some funders require more information than others. Some funders have reams of forms that must be scanned before typing. Some funders insist that their forms not be replicated. That means you pull out that old typewriter and fret about typos. (Stock up on correction fluid.)

Determine the writing format for each funding source that you identify. Call or write each funding source and ask for their guidelines for submitting a grant application or proposal. Governmental agencies have their own application kits and they only let you submit the application at certain times in the year. Foundations and corporations may have their own form. If not, they may have you use a regional grant application format or they may ask you to simply submit a two- to three-page letter of initial inquiry.

If getting grant money were too easy, everyone would already have a grant and there wouldn't be any money left for you!

Federal, state, and local units of government

The format for government grants changes from agency to agency, but some common threads exist in the highly detailed, structured, military-like regimen that's commonly referred to as an *application kit*. The basic parts:

- ✔ Application cover form
- ✔ Program summary or abstract
- ✔ Table of contents
- ✔ Program narrative
- ✔ Budget and budget narrative
- ✔ Assurances and required forms
- ✔ Appendices

How a federal grant shapes up

A sample table of contents from a federal grant (Table 1-2) gives you an idea of how much writing is involved. The *Federal Register* guidelines for this program limited the narrative to 30 double-spaced pages.

Generally, federal grant applications have page-limit guidelines. The page limit changes from one program to another and from competition to competition. Read the instructions closely so that your grant application isn't disqualified on a technical point.

Table 1-2	Sample Federal Grant Table of Contents
Narrative Section	**Page(s)**
Competitive Priorities	1
Need	1–8
Significance	8–14
Project Design	15–24
Personnel	24–25
Resources	25–26
Management Plan	26–28
Evaluation Plan	28–30
Section 427 Provision Requirements	30

In addition to the main narrative sections listed in Table 1-2, the application would include Assurances, Certifications, Lobbying Disclosure, and Appendices. The appendices may include letters of support and partnership information, congressional support letters, resumes and job descriptions for project staff, and resumes of evaluators (internal and external).

Foundations — lean, clean funding machines

Large or small, foundations like to have a cover letter, a regionally or nationally accepted cover sheet or cover form, and a narrative that includes a description of your organization and a description of your request. The attachments are what count with this group of funders. They may ask for the evaluation plan, your organization's structure/administration, your finances, and other supporting material.

My favorite format is the one developed by the National Network of Grantmakers (NNG). It can be found on the NNG's Web site, www.nng.org. The Common Grant Application (CGA) is a labor-saving device for groups seeking grants for social and economic justice work. First created in 1995 by the NNG's Philanthropic Reform Committee, the CGA is now accepted by over 40 grantmakers. To determine if using the CGA is appropriate, check the funder's guidelines. Contact them directly to obtain the guidelines or seek information in one of the many available directories of funders.

The CGA format has a cover sheet, narrative (two main sections and a total of nine response areas), and attachments (see Table 1-3). I use the CGA format for 90 percent of the foundation grant requests that I write. It works because it contains all the essentials. Even if the funder requests a different order of information, you can do a lot of cutting and pasting from a grant application written in the CGA format to create a non-CGA grant.

Table 1-3	CGA Format
Informational Components	*Brief Overview*
Cover letter (One page)	Introduction to grant applicant, purpose of request, amount requested, and closing.
Cover sheet (One page form)	Organizational identification page with key contact information, a glance at finances, mission statement, and summary of grant request.

(continued)

Table 1-3 *(continued)*

Informational Components	*Brief Overview*
Narrative (Five pages, maximum)	Part I: Introduction and background of organization that includes: history, accomplishments, current programs, activities, demographics on your constituency, overview of the constituents' involvement in your project, and how they will benefit from your program and/or your organization.
	Part II: Description of your request that includes: problem statement, description of the program for which you seek funding, goals, objectives and activities, timelines, equity statement (how you address diversity), and description of the change you are trying to achieve.
Attachments	Evaluation, organizational structure/administration, finances, and other supporting material.

About the Regional Associations of Grantmakers

The Forum of Regional Associations of Grantmakers (RAGs) can be found on the Internet at www.rag/org/about/whoare.htm. The regional groups of foundation grantmakers you can find at this site have each designed their own specific grant application format. Before you start writing in a generic format (like the National Network of Grantmakers format) check to see if the region you live in requires using a different format.

As an example of a regional form, the New York Regional Association of Grantmakers (NYRAG) and the Council of New Jersey Grantmakers have developed a common application form (refer to Table 1-4) that is accepted by more than 60 funders in the New York/New Jersey area. It can be printed from the Web site www.nyrag.org/for_grantseekers/cafcrf.htm.

Table 1-4	NYRAG Format
Cover sheet	
Proposal summary (one-half page, maximum)	
Narrative: background, funding request, and evaluation (five pages, maximum)	
Attachments (financial information and other supporting materials)	

Corporations — just get to the point!

For corporations, you repeat the foundation format, only in five or fewer pages. You also attach your proof of nonprofit status. Table 1-5 shows you the lineup, with my helpful hints thrown in.

Curious about what to put in the postscript? Here's an example: "The likelihood of our organization providing these needed services to our community at this proposed level is slim without your support. Please consider becoming our partner."

In many instances, corporate funders state in their guidelines to submit only a two- or three-page letter proposal. Yes, it can be that simple!

Table 1-5	Corporate Proposal Format
Date line, contact name and address, salutation (Dear Ms., Mr., Miss, Mrs.)	
Introduction to your organization (limited to ten or fewer sentences, with a fact sheet or a program brochure attached)	
Problem statement (be thorough and build the case that you deserve the money you ask for at the end of the letter)	
Problem solution (briefly include the goals, objectives, timelines, and benefits to the target population that the grant money will enable)	
Cost of solution and how much you want from this funder	
Emotional and appealing closing (like closing a sales pitch)	
Personal signature	
Postscript (another chance to further close the sale)	
Attachments: IRS 501(c)(3) letter, full project budget, organization fact sheet or brochure, other supporting documentation (keep the attachments light!)	

Chapter 2

Searching for Government Grants

- -

In This Chapter

▶ Looking for government monies

▶ Figuring out whether you've got a shot

▶ Preparing for success

▶ Choosing the right funding opportunity

- -

*I*nformation on government grant monies (monies originating from our nation's capital that trickle down to the local level, directly to you or to a state agency) is not as elusive as you may think. Information on government grants is free at your nearest reference library, government-documents library, or on the Internet. But without knowing where to look and what to look for, finding government grant opportunities that match your program needs can be like looking for a needle in a haystack. This chapter shows you where and how to look for federal grant programs.

Looking at Home

Since mega dollars travel from the federal government to your state, searching for state-agency grant opportunities on a regular basis is critical. Most states do not have a *one-stop grant shop* where you can get on one mailing list and be notified of all grant opportunities from every state agency or department — meaning you must surf the Web weekly to look for competitive grant announcements.

State grants are usually less money and just as much paperwork as federal grants, but the odds of winning a grant are better at the state than federal level. Fewer grant applicants are competing for the monies.

To find grant opportunities at the state level, you should:

✔ Search for your state government's Internet site. If you can't find anything that lists all the grant opportunities, then call the governor's office to see if it can direct you to the various agencies that give grants.

✔ Contact each agency and get on its mailing list.

✔ Get to know at least one person in every government program that you plan to seek grant monies from. Set aside one day, each year, to travel to your state capital and visit your new grant friends. Invite them to visit the program you're seeking funds for.

You have to be aggressive when it comes to finding grant monies. Don't be shy when it comes to making contacts.

Finding Federal Jackpots

Federal grant monies come in the form of either *direct grants* — meaning that you apply directly to the federal government for a grant — or *pass-through grants* — meaning that your state applies to the federal government for a grant, receives the grant, and then passes the federal monies on. Pass-through monies are still considered federal monies, even though they're distributed by the state.

Now it gets complicated: Federal monies are also classified as either *competitive* or *formula*.

To win a competitive grant, you must compete with other grant applicants for a limited amount of money. Your application is reviewed and points are assigned to each section of the request. The applications scoring the highest are recommended for funding.

When you look for federal grant competitions to enter, look for grant competitions that are both direct and competitive.

A formula grant is money that's disbursed by a state agency to a grant applicant based on some kind of a preset standard or formula. Say that your community receives a formula grant to increase the foot patrols by the police department in a certain neighborhood. In order to access the formula grant monies, the police department had to fill out a very simple formula grant application that included the number of crimes that occurred in the designated block watch areas in one year. The neighborhood experienced a high level of crime (say 100 crimes over a one-year period), so the department got the money. Simple.

The state agency awards $500 for each crime committed in a one-year period. Your community is automatically eligible for a $50,000 grant, based on the formula of 500×100 crimes. You do not have to compete against other communities for this money. Every community that's eligible to apply receives an application and instructions for how to fill in the information and calculate the formula. Every eligible community is awarded a grant.

When you see federal grant monies designated as formula, keep looking. These monies are most likely pass-through formula grant monies, which means that you must look for your share at the state level, not the federal level. (Although looking for these monies at the state level may not be such a bad idea, of course.)

Formula money is easy money, but it doesn't come in high amounts. Every community or organization that's eligible must be able to receive funds, meaning that no one community or organization is going to strike it rich. Whether your grant writing is good or not so good, you still get a formula grant award if you meet the criteria.

The two publications that harbor bountiful information about federal grant opportunities are *The Catalog of Federal and Domestic Assistance* and the *Federal Register*. Both publications carry similar information and describe grant-giving programs as either competitive or formula.

Advantages of direct grants

Some advantages to applying for a direct grant award exist, including:

- ✔ Direct grants have no middleman and no extra layers of red tape. You apply directly to the feds for a grant in response to their announcement of the availability of funds.

- ✔ When you compete for a direct grant, you communicate directly with a program officer in a division of a federal agency. Don't plan on getting too chummy, but you need to try and win this person over. You want to have a question a day about the grant application requirements. Leave a message on voicemail. Do this every day until you receive a call back.

   The more you call, the better your chance of developing a lifelong grant friend in the right place — where all the money is being held hostage.

The disadvantage of direct grants

You need to know the one major disadvantage to applying for a direct grant award: They're tough to win. You compete with other grant applicants in 50 states and all the U.S. territories. If the feds are only going to award give money to five grant applicants, your chances are slim, even with the best grant writing.

And it gets even worse. Urban areas and U.S. territories with high pockets of poverty are usually designated a *federal empowerment zone, federal enterprise zone,* or *colonias community.* All three of these hard-earned federal designations give communities a competitive edge over a nondesignated area. If you're not proposing services in one of these areas, your chances of getting a federal grant from a competition that gives extra review points to applications from one of these designated areas are reduced to almost nothing.

Advantages of pass-through grants

Three advantages exist to applying for pass-through grant funds:

- ✔ Pass-through monies are waiting for you in the state capital at the state agency that administers federal grant monies in a specific area.

- ✔ When you apply for grant funds at the state level, you're only competing against other grant applicants in your state. There's considerably less competition than at the federal level.

- ✔ Driving up, down, or over to your state capital to make a personal appearance before state agency program staff is pretty easy. While you're there, ask for the insider's perspective, a list of grants funded previously (grant recipients and award amount), and a copy of a successful grant application from a previous competition.

  Most state agencies don't require Freedom of Information Act letters before they share award information. The feds do require the letter, and you may have several birthdays while you're waiting for the information you request from them.

The disadvantage of pass-through grants

The only disadvantage to applying for pass-through grants that I've seen is that your grant award will be a lot smaller than if you applied directly for a federal grant and received an award. Larger pots of money are at the federal level, although the heavy competition reduces the odds of your getting those big awards.

Pass-through grant awards are significantly smaller than direct grant awards because the state takes money off the top of a federal grant for administrative costs. The amount that's left must be divided geographically and politically. Grants go to certain areas of a state because that area has not had many grant awards lately or because the state senator or representative has a lot of power and influence with a state agency. Yes, Virginia, politics does affect grant monies — at the state and federal level.

Checking Out the Money Catalog

You can find all sorts of information about where the money's at and what it can be used for in *The Catalog of Federal and Domestic Assistance* (CFDA). Information about every program administered by departments and agencies of the federal government can be found in this single publication. It's available from any public library or online at www.cfda.gov.

When you want to know what's out there for you at the federal level, the CFDA is where you start. Once you find grants that you're interested in applying for, you track grant announcements in the *Federal Register*. See the section on the Register later in this chapter.

Programs in the CFDA are grouped into 20 categories and more than 170 subcategories that identify specific areas of interest. Listed below are the 20 basic categories into which all programs are grouped:

- Agriculture
- Business and Commerce
- Community Development
- Consumer Protection
- Cultural Affairs
- Disaster Prevention and Relief
- Education
- Employment, Labor, and Training
- Energy
- Environmental Quality
- Food and Nutrition
- Health
- Housing
- Income Security and Social Services
- Information and Statistics
- Law, Justice, and Legal Services
- Natural Resources
- Regional Development
- Science and Technology
- Transportation

The entry for each federal program in the CFDA includes information on the:

- Federal agency administering the program.
- Authorization upon which the program is based. (This means the federal legislation that created the program.)
- Objectives and goals of the program.
- Types of financial and nonfinancial assistance offered under a program. (A grant is financial assistance. Just skip over the nonfinancial talk.)
- Uses and restrictions placed upon a program.
- Eligibility requirements.

✔ Application and award process.

✔ Amount of obligations for the past, current, and future fiscal years. (This means how much money Congress allocated to this program.) The federal fiscal year starts October 1 and ends September 30.

✔ Regulations, guidelines, and literature relevant to a program.

✔ Information contacts at the headquarters, regional, and local offices.

✔ Programs that are related based upon program objectives and uses. (Use this section of the CFDA entry to find other federal programs that award grants in your project's area.)

✔ Examples of funded projects. (You know you're looking at the right program when you see a funded project that sounds like the project you're seeking grant monies for.)

✔ Criteria for selecting proposals.

✔ Individual agency policies and federal management policy directives pertaining to a program.

Programs in the CFDA are classified by the General Service Administration (GSA) as either *formula* grants or *project* grants. Formula grants are explained earlier in this chapter.

A project grant is funding for a specific period of time. Grant funds must be used to deliver the specific services that you outline in the grant application narrative. Project grants include fellowships, scholarships, research grants, training grants, traineeships, experimental and demonstration grants, evaluation grants, planning grants, technical assistance grants, survey grants, construction grants, and unsolicited contractual agreements.

The CFDA is full of confusing terms and numbers. Here's a brief explanation:

Numerical coding: When you look in the CFDA, you find that each federal agency has a section and that each section is numbered with a five-digit code. The code is assigned to an agency's programs. The first two digits identify the federal department or agency that administers the program, and the last three numbers are assigned in numerical sequence, beginning with program number 001 through program 999.

Program titles: Each program also has a title, the descriptive name given to a program.

An entry in the CFDA looks like this:

84.334 Gaining Early Awareness and Readiness for Undergraduate Programs (GEAR UP).

The entry lists the name of the federal agency, the act that authorized the grant monies, the objectives of the funding, type of assistance (project or formula), allowable grant money uses, eligible applicants, the application and award process, total dollars allocated for a fiscal year, and contact information at the federal level. Log on to the Internet or take a trip to your local public library to spend some time learning how to use the CFDA.

Finding Money Now in the Register

The *Federal Register* is the primary resource for locating information about available grants. You can pay for your own hard copy of the Register by contacting the Government Printing Office (GPO) or you can use the Internet (free) to look at the daily Register announcements. Of course, you can also use what we all used before the Internet, that is, the public library. Most public libraries that store government publications have the Register in their reference department. You can't check it out, but you can read through it to look for grant announcements and then make copies of the pages that provide the information you're looking for, including where to call for a hard copy of the grant application kit.

The Internet carries the full text published in the Register.

The Government Printing Office Web site address is `www.access.gpo.gov/ su_docs/aces/aces140.html`. The Register is published every weekday except for holidays. It's the direct road map to federal grant monies that are available to apply for *now*.

Web site addresses change almost daily. If you run into a "Web site not found" message after you type in one of the addresses that I give you in this book, try doing a search with the federal or state agency's name to find the new Web site address.

When you visit the GPO Web site, you see a whole assortment of federal documents to choose from. Here are the steps you should take the first time you visit the GPO on the Web.

1. **Click on "Federal Register."**

2. **Click on the box next to the current edition; in other words, the 2000 *Federal Register*, the 2001 *Federal Register*, and so on.**

   You should see a check mark next to the edition you selected.

3. **Scroll down and click the "Notices" box.**

4. **Enter a date range for the announcement you're looking for.**

   I usually enter the current month (use two digits), the first day of the month (entered as *01*), and the current year (use four digits).

5. **Enter the word *grant* in the "Search Terms" box. Click on Submit and see what your search results are.**

   You will see a box for the number of entries you want to review at one time. I recommend viewing 40 entries as a good start.

6. **When you see a grant announcement that looks interesting, click on it.**

   You can read it in three forms: HTML, PDF, and Summary. If you don't have Adobe Acrobat Reader loaded in your software collection, don't select PDF. Use HTML (Web page view) or Summary (text view).

The announcement gives you information on how to retrieve the full grant application (guidelines and forms) online or how to order a hard copy of the application kit. (When I use the term *hard copy,* I mean a paper copy.)

When you access the Register online, you can click on links that take you directly to the Web site of the federal agency that has authored the Register announcement.

Each federal grant competition has different guidelines, review criteria, funding priorities, competitive priorities, deadlines, and amounts awarded. To find grant funding opportunities at the federal level, you must research federal funding every weekday. If the funding is pass-through (meaning that a state agency is the only eligible applicant for bringing these monies into your state), then start monitoring your state government's Web site to look for competitive grant opportunities closer to home.

Using the Register to get a sneak peek

One good reason to read the *Federal Register* every weekday is to find glimpses of federal money before the grants' application guidelines are published and before the grant deadline clock is ticking. The Register publishes a "Call for Public Comments" announcement for every federal program that awards grant monies. The call for comment gives you a preview of the program's guidelines and encourages you to submit written comment on any requirements or restrictions that you feel are unfair (those that eliminate your organization from getting its fair share of federal grant funding).

The monies may not have been allocated by Congress when the call for comments is published. However, the federal department is anticipating that these monies will *come down* (the federal term for the allocation of congressional funds to a specific federal agency). Call your congressperson in Washington and ask him or her to track the bill that authorizes the expenditure. (The bill or act is referred to as the *authorizing legislation.*) Also ask your congressperson to keep you updated on when the grant announcement will be published in the *Federal Register.*

Taking Your Best Shot at Federal Grants

Once you find several federal programs in the Catalog that fit your organization's mission and purpose, it's time to start tracking *notices of funding availability* in the Register. Remember that when applying for federal grant monies, you're competing with eligible applicants from the 50 states and the U.S. territories. What should you look for in the Register announcement? How do you know when your chances for receiving a grant award are good or not so good? What's the key?

Calculating the odds — taking cautious steps

Before you apply for a federal grant, doing your homework is important. Knowing the critical areas to focus on in the Federal Register announcement saves you time and grief. Don't even start the writing process until you go through these four internal, organizational, prequalification steps.

1. **When you find any grant announcement, quickly scan the first few pages to find the *Eligible Applicants* language.**

   This is where you look to make sure your organization is eligible to apply for the grant funding. Before proceeding to the next step, make sure that your organization is eligible. You'll become good at speed-reading when you see how long grant application announcements are and learn to focus in on the key phrases.

2. **Next look for the *Deadline for Transmittal of Applications.***

   This is when the grant application must be in the hands of the agency issuing the grant announcement. You will find the deadline in the first few pages of the announcement. Make sure that you or your grant writing team can make the application deadline.

3. **Next look for the *Estimated Average Award Size.***

   This is the average amount of a grant award that this federal agency intends to make. It's important that you calculate your anticipated project cost and compare that total sum to the Estimated Average Award.

   If you've already started to prepare a draft budget and it totals $300,000 for the first year, then this Federal Register entry is very important. If the average award is only going to be $125,000, where will the rest of the funding you need come from?

4. Determine the chances of having a federal grant award occur in your state by looking closely at the *Estimated Number of Awards*.

If only 35 grants are going to be awarded in this competition, your odds may not be that great. There are 50 states, plus seven commonwealths and territories. That means dozens, even hundreds, of grant applicants from each of the 57 geographic areas are eligible to apply for 35 grants. Unless your organization has a one-of-a-kind idea, a fantastic track record with winning federal grants, and a list of very impressive community, regional, and national partners, the odds that you'll get a grant award are not good.

When you find that your chances of getting a federal grant award are negligible, look to other federal agencies that fund in the same area and look at other types of grant monies, like state monies or foundation and corporate monies. Chapter 4 shows you how to diversify your grant options.

Calling all legislators — making critical connections

Does it really make any sense to search for federal grant monies without calling your elected legislators? Overlooking these critical contacts on Capitol Hill could make the difference between finding out about a federal funding opportunity before it's published in the *Federal Register* and not finding out until you have 15 days (or less!) to write a major grant application.

You elected these individuals to serve *on your behalf* in the nation's capital. Use your leverage. Make a telephone call to the local or regional office for your state's congressional legislators. Ask for a meeting or simply state what your funding needs are in the initial telephone call. Let them know that your organization critically needs their support in identifying federal funding.

Weighing All the Funding Options

Trying to determine when you will need grant funds, how much you will need, and how many times you will have to seek grant funds for your program is an ongoing issue with grant writers and program directors. When you receive a grant award, your problem is solved if you only wanted to implement one solution to solve one problem. But if you need to solve many problems, you may need monies to implement many solutions.

Grants are awarded in yearly time frames. You can apply for a one-time, one-year grant or for a multi-year grant. Multi-year grants usually last for two to five years.

You should weigh several factors when you decide to fund a program with grants. Considering the following factors before actually beginning to write your federal grant application is essential. They help you consider the pros and cons of applying for and being awarded grant monies from any type of funder: federal, state, foundation, or corporate.

- ✔ **Total funds needed.** If you need hundreds of thousands of dollars for a one-year program, look for funding at the federal level. If your needs are under $100,000, look for foundation grant opportunities. Foundation grant applications require less writing time. However, foundation grant seeking is just as competitive as federal grant seeking.

- ✔ **The number of years funding is needed for.** If you need program support for two or more years, look for funding at the federal level. While many of the larger foundations may consider multi-year funding requests, most foundations fund for one year at a time.

- ✔ **The eligibility criteria and review criteria.** If you want to have the best possible chance of getting a federal grant award, you must follow the grant application guidelines exactly. If you are required to have partners from the private sector, then you must find eligible partners. If you must demonstrate socioeconomic thresholds (demographics for disadvantaged populations), then start calling state and local government agencies for statistical reports. If you have a program design in your mind and you're trying, in vain, to remold it to fit the federal limitations, then a federal grant that puts restrictions on program activities may not be the best route for you at this time.

- ✔ **Freedom to make line-item changes in the budget.** Once your grant is funded at the federal level, moving one dollar from one line item to another requires written approval. This is not a quick process and could slow down your project's progress considerably. If you're looking for more financial freedom and dread red tape, then maybe government funding is not for you. Foundations have fewer restrictions on line-item changes and written permission is not required as long as you reach your project's objectives by the end of the grant period.

Auditing preparedness

If your nonprofit has a government grant, you can expect an audit eventually. A wise word: Don't spend money from a newly awarded government grant to pay bills that were incurred before the grant was actually awarded or have nothing to do with the grant award you received. Don't move money from one line item to another without written permission from your state or federal funding source.

Understanding family rules

You didn't really think that Uncle Sam would be standing there with his wallet open and no rules, did you? When you go after government funding, expect short deadlines, volumes of instructions to follow (that sometime confuse you), and wheelbarrows of forms to scan into your computer and complete.

Chapter 3 addresses how to access *grant application kits* (a batch of instructions and forms). Federal and state grant awards have strings attached — and require reams of reporting paperwork. You may feel like you're playing Mother May I. Foundation and corporate grants are pretty much hassle-free. Chapter 5 introduces you to the world of foundation and corporate grants.

I have a saying: "Dreams are funded by foundations." It may be worth remembering if you're not willing to make the changes necessary to meet the federal review criteria.

Chapters 7 and 8 talk about how to make your project meet the federal review criteria.

Chapter 3

Federal Grant Application Kits and Tidbits

In This Chapter
▶ Overcoming the intimidation factor
▶ Looking at the branches of government that award grants
▶ Figuring out all those forms

*W*hy do most grant writers remain in the minor leagues their entire career? They fear federal grant applications.

Federal grants are the most difficult to apply for — more difficult than foundation, corporate, or state and local government grants. Federal grants are known for their short deadlines, technically worded writing and review criteria, and zillions of intimidating forms. This chapter takes you on a tour of federal grant application forms. You find out where to download them on the Internet, how to fill them out, what to include in a field, why the assurances and certifications are mandatory, and what it all means.

The federal grant seeking and grant writing process stimulates your mind to its greatest ability and is good practice for other types of grant writing — whether you win or lose. However, if you follow my tips, you'll be on the winning track.

Touring the Federal Information Highway for Money

Normally, all of the federal grant application forms that you need are included in the *application kit.* The application kit is either published in its entirety in the *Federal Register* (both instructions and forms) or it can be retrieved from the specific federal agency's Web site. The Web site address is always published in the *Federal Register* announcement. (See Chapter 2 for the inside scoop on federal grant announcements.)

Remember that each federal agency has its own grant application forms and its own guidelines for filling out the forms. Some agencies have fewer than ten forms (like the U.S. Department of Education), while others have upwards of 20 (the U.S. Department of Health and Human Services). Underestimating the importance of the mandatory forms could result in your grant application being disqualified on a technical point.

All federal grant applications have some kind of a cover form. The information varies slightly from agency to agency, but basically, all federal agencies are collecting similar information on you, the grant applicant. The cover form contains information on your organization, gives the project director's contact information, identifies the federal program that you're applying to by name and identification number, shows the amount of federal funds you're requesting, identifies your congressional districts, and includes a signatory box for your organization's executive director or president. An example of a cover form is included later in this chapter.

Looking at the different cover forms online to get a feeling for how they vary from agency to agency is easy. Some agencies post their forms with the application guidelines, which means they're available electronically, while others simply refer you to the *Federal Register* (meaning you copy your forms from the *Federal Register* at the library).

Visiting the following departments of the federal government on the Web gives you a look at the different funding programs they offer. Becoming familiar with what's out there is important, even if you don't plan to apply for any of these grants. Remember that the main obstacle most people face with applying for a federal grant is fear. Fear because, frankly, these grants are complicated and not very user-friendly. Taking a look each federal agencies' purpose and at its grant opportunities is exciting — there are big bucks to apply for and win at the federal level.

Make sure you familiarize yourself with the federal departments' acronyms. They are used more often than the full names of the departments.

Federal Emergency Management Administration (FEMA)

Accessing online: www.fema.gov

Quick look: Provides grants that allow your state and local government to respond to natural disasters.

Institute of Museum and Library Services (IMLS)

Accessing online: www.imls.gov

Quick look: Provides grants to museums. The IMLS is a division of the National Foundation on the Arts and the Humanities.

Legal Services Corporation (LSC)

Accessing online: www.ain.lsc.gov

Quick look: Provides grants for legal services to the poor.

National Aeronautics and Space Administration (NASA)

Accessing online: www.nasa.gov

Quick look: Provides grants related to space-exploration education and research.

NASA accepts unsolicited proposals. An *unsolicited proposal* is a written request for grant monies submitted to an agency that has not issued a grant competition announcement. It's sort of like showing up for the party before the invitation has been printed and mailed to you. But, sometimes, the early bird actually gets the worm.

National Endowment for the Arts (NEA)

Accessing online: www.arts.gov

Quick look: Provides grants for projects in dance, design, folk and traditional arts, literature, media arts (film, television, video, radio, audio art), museums, music, musical theater, opera, theater, visual art, and multidisciplinary projects.

National Endowment for the Humanities (NEH)

Accessing online: www.neh.fed.us

Quick look: Provides grants for scholarly works with a focus on history, literature, or any other discipline of the humanities.

National Science Foundation (NSF)

Accessing online: www.nsf.gov

Quick look: Provides research and project grants for math, science, and engineering. Funds are directed to colleges, universities, and other research or educational institutions.

Small Business Administration (SBA)

Accessing online: www.sbaonline.sba.gov

Quick look: Provides grants to businesses located in areas of low income or high unemployment.

The SBA accepts unsolicited proposals.

U.S. Department of Agriculture (USDA)

Accessing online: www.usda.gov

Quick look: Provides grants for housing projects in rural areas. The USDA also provides grants to rural schools and health care providers for telecommunications facilities and equipment in rural areas, as well as grants to rural communities for emergency water needs.

U.S. Department of Commerce (DOC)

Accessing online: www.doc.gov

Quick look: Provides grants for job creation, economic growth, sustainable development, and improved living standards. The DOC funds partnership applications for consortiums that include businesses, universities, communities, and workers.

The DOC has nearly a dozen subprograms. I really like to write grant applications for the Technology Opportunity Program (TOP), a grant competition for telecommunication projects for state and local governments, health care providers, school districts, libraries, social service organizations, public safety services, and other nonprofit organizations. Go online to see the list of funding agencies under the DOC.

U.S. Department of Education (DOED)

Accessing online: www.ed.gov

Quick look: Provides grants to schools, colleges, universities and other nonprofits.

U.S. Department of Energy (DOE)

Accessing online: www.doe.gov

Quick look: Provides grants to support relevant research in energy-saving science and technology and has an equipment donation program.

If you're writing grants for a university or K–12 school district, then navigate your mouse to the Equipment Donations Program Web page. Once there, you will find two programs: Energy-Related Laboratory Equipment and Computers For Learning (www.computers.fed.gov).

U.S. Department of Health and Human Services (HHS)

Accessing online: www.dhhs.gov

Quick look: Provides grants to protect our health and provide essential human services related to health care.

HHS is the largest grantmaking agency in the federal government, providing some 60,000 grants per year.

U.S. Department of Housing and Urban Development (HUD)

Accessing online: www.hud.gov

Quick look: Provides grants for decent, safe, and sanitary housing.

U.S. Department of the Interior (DOI)

Accessing online: www.doi.gov

Quick look: Provides grants to local governments for rehabilitation of recreation areas and facilities, demonstration of innovative approaches to improve park system management and recreation opportunities, and development of improved recreation planning.

U.S. Department of Justice (DOJ)

Accessing online: www.usdoj.gov

Quick look: Provides grants for community policing programs, drug-free communities, and law-enforcement related projects.

U.S. Department of Labor (DOL)

Accessing online: www.dol.gov

Quick look: Provides grants to nonprofit and for-profit organizations to help welfare recipients achieve self-sufficiency.

U.S. Department of Transportation (DOT)

Accessing online: www.dot.gov

Quick look: Provides grants to assist state and local governments in the planning, design, and construction of transportation improvements (for example, highway, transit, and airport improvements). This agency also manages the Hazardous Materials Emergency Preparedness grant program.

U.S. Environmental Protection Agency (EPA)

Accessing online: www.epa.gov

Quick look: Provides grants to community groups that are working on or plan to carry out projects to address environmental justice issues. This agency also manages the Sustainable Development Grant Program.

U.S. Institute of Peace (USIP)

Accessing online: www.usip.org

Quick look: Provides grants for projects that educate about, research and promote world peace.

Figuring Out the Forms

Now that you've located the federal program that best fits your needs, and reviewed and downloaded the application kit, what do you do with all of the forms? What order do they go in and how do you fill them out? The answers to these questions, along with examples, complete this chapter.

In order to figure out the forms, you need to know where these forms fit in your overall federal grant application. Table 3-1 shows you the typical order of the forms. As you can see, some are before and some are after the grant application narrative.

Many federal grant applications are not reviewed because of errors or omissions on the grant application forms. Some applicants forget to include the required forms, some don't fill them out properly, and some forget to include their signature. Remember that you're entering a competition where the winner follows the directions to the letter.

Table 3-1	Organizing Your Federal Forms
Form: Application for Federal Assistance	
Form: Budget Information — Section A — Budget Summary for Federal Funds	
Form: Budget Information — Section B — Budget Summary for Non-Federal Funds	
Narrative: Project Budget Detail Narrative	

(continued)

Table 3-1 *(continued)*
Narrative: Project Abstract
Narrative: Project Table of Contents
Narrative: Project Narrative
Form: Assurances
Form: Certifications Regarding Lobbying, Debarment, Suspension and Other Responsibility Matters; and Drug-Free Workplace Requirements
Form: Certification Regarding Debarment, Suspension, Ineligibility and Voluntary Exclusion — Lower Tier Covered Transactions
Form: Certification of Eligibility for Federal Assistance in Certain Programs
Form: Disclosure of Lobbying Activities
Attachments or Appendices to support grant application narrative

All federal forms are downloadable. They can be scanned to your computer, filled in, and printed for inclusion into the final grant application.

The following information gives you an overview of the most common federal grant application forms: cover forms, budget forms, assurance forms, certification forms, and lobbying disclosure forms. Many state funding agencies use similar forms; the required forms are included in the grant guidelines for each funding competition.

The cover form

The cover form is the top page of all federal grant applications. It's what the feds see when they open your application package. The cover form contains critical information about who you are and where you are (fields 1–8), what you plan to do, when you plan to do it, whether your application is subject to state review, whether you're using any human subjects (fields 9–13), how much money you need, how much money you have for this project, and who's authorized to submit the grant application (fields 14–15).

For years, the application cover form has been known as Form 424 (refer to Figure 3-1). Recently, federal departments have customized their own version of the standard form.

Some crucial things to keep in mind:

- ✔ Don't leave any spaces blank.
- ✔ Take the time to read the directions, and be sure to follow them.

✔ The Catalog of Federal and Domestic Assistance number can be found in the Federal Register announcement or at the beginning of the application kit.

✔ Sign the original cover form in blue ink. That way, even after you make the multiple copies that the feds need, you and they will be able to distinguish between the original (the one with the blue ink) and the copies.

OMB Approval No. 0348-0043

APPLICATION FOR FEDERAL ASSISTANCE

2. DATE SUBMITTED	Applicant Identifier

1. TYPE OF SUBMISSION:		3. DATE RECEIVED BY STATE	State Application Identifier
Application ☐ Construction ☐ Non-Construction	Preapplication ☐ Construction ☐ Non-Construction	4. DATE RECEIVED BY FEDERAL AGENCY	Federal Identifier

5. APPLICANT INFORMATION

Legal Name:	Organizational Unit:
Address (give city, county, State, and zip code):	Name and telephone number of person to be contacted on matters involving this application (give area code)

6. EMPLOYER IDENTIFICATION NUMBER (EIN):

☐☐ – ☐☐☐☐☐☐☐

7. TYPE OF APPLICANT: (enter appropriate letter in box) ☐

A. State	H. Independent School Dist.
B. County	I. State Controlled Institution of Higher Learning
C. Municipal	J. Private University
D. Township	K. Indian Tribe
E. Interstate	L. Individual
F. Intermunicipal	M. Profit Organization
G. Special District	N. Other (Specify) _____

8. TYPE OF APPLICATION:

☐ New   ☐ Continuation   ☐ Revision

If Revision, enter appropriate letter(s) in box(es) ☐ ☐

A. Increase Award   B. Decrease Award   C. Increase Duration
D. Decrease Duration   Other(specify):

_____

9. NAME OF FEDERAL AGENCY:

10. CATALOG OF FEDERAL DOMESTIC ASSISTANCE NUMBER:

☐☐ – ☐☐☐

TITLE:

11. DESCRIPTIVE TITLE OF APPLICANT'S PROJECT:

12. AREAS AFFECTED BY PROJECT (Cities, Counties, States, etc.):

13. PROPOSED PROJECT		14. CONGRESSIONAL DISTRICTS OF:	
Start Date	Ending Date	a. Applicant	b. Project

15. ESTIMATED FUNDING:

a. Federal	$	.00
b. Applicant	$	.00
c. State	$	.00
d. Local	$	.00
e. Other	$	.00
f. Program Income	$	.00
g. TOTAL	$	.00

16. IS APPLICATION SUBJECT TO REVIEW BY STATE EXECUTIVE ORDER 12372 PROCESS?

a. YES. THIS PREAPPLICATION/APPLICATION WAS MADE AVAILABLE TO THE STATE EXECUTIVE ORDER 12372 PROCESS FOR REVIEW ON:

DATE _____

b. No. ☐ PROGRAM IS NOT COVERED BY E. O. 12372
   ☐ OR PROGRAM HAS NOT BEEN SELECTED BY STATE FOR REVIEW

17. IS THE APPLICANT DELINQUENT ON ANY FEDERAL DEBT?

☐ Yes If "Yes," attach an explanation.   ☐ No

18. TO THE BEST OF MY KNOWLEDGE AND BELIEF, ALL DATA IN THIS APPLICATION/PREAPPLICATION ARE TRUE AND CORRECT, THE DOCUMENT HAS BEEN DULY AUTHORIZED BY THE GOVERNING BODY OF THE APPLICANT AND THE APPLICANT WILL COMPLY WITH THE ATTACHED ASSURANCES IF THE ASSISTANCE IS AWARDED.

a. Type Name of Authorized Representative	b. Title	c. Telephone Number
d. Signature of Authorized Representative		e. Date Signed

Previous Edition Usable
Authorized for Local Reproduction

Standard Form 424 (Rev. 7-97)
Prescribed by OMB Circular A-102

Figure 3-1:
Form 424.

Budget information forms

In most instances, the budget information form comes directly after the cover form. However, some federal agencies change the order of the budget information form so that it follows the narrative. The budget forms (there are two) are referred to as *Section A* and *Section B*. Section A refers only to the money you want from the feds. Section B is your cash and in-kind match. Treat each form as a separate view of the federal and nonfederal allocation of grant monies and your organization's matching monies. You can see examples of these forms in Figures 3-2a and 3-2b.

Neither of these forms asks for a combined total of federal and nonfederal funds. This total appears in only two places: on the cover form, in the bottom left hand box that says *Total,* and on your detailed budget narrative.

When filling in any form, always read the instructions that come with the application kit.

Assurance forms

The assurances are on two pages and can cover up to 18 items. Basically, it's a prenuptial agreement with Uncle Sam. Don't sweat over this form. Just fill in the requested information and sign.

Certification forms

Expect to fill in two to four pages worth of certifications. The purpose of these forms is to certify your organization's eligibility to receive federal funding. The language on the forms and in the instructions is true legalese; however, a call to the federal Office of Management and Budget (OMB) can clear up any technical questions you have before signing off. The certifications cover lobbying; debarment and suspension; drug-free workplace issues; ineligibility and voluntary exclusion from lower-tier covered transactions; and eligibility for federal assistance in certain programs (for grants from the Department of Education). Fill in the requested information on each set of forms and sign where indicated.

Figure 3-2a:
Section A
of the
Department
of
Education's
budget form.

U.S. DEPARTMENT OF EDUCATION

BUDGET INFORMATION

NON-CONSTRUCTION PROGRAMS

OMB Control Number: 1890-0004

Expiration Date: 02/28/2003

Applicants requesting funding for only one year should complete the column under "Project Year 1." Applicants requesting funding for multi-year grants should complete all applicable columns. Please read all instructions before completing form.

Name of Institution/Organization

SECTION A - BUDGET SUMMARY
U.S. DEPARTMENT OF EDUCATION FUNDS

Budget Categories	Project Year 1 (a)	Project Year 2 (b)	Project Year 3 (c)	Project Year 4 (d)	Project Year 5 (e)	Total (f)
1. Personnel						
2. Fringe Benefits						
3. Travel						
4. Equipment						
5. Supplies						
6. Contractual						
7. Construction						
8. Other						
9. Total Direct Costs (lines 1-8)						
10. Indirect Costs						
11. Training Stipends						
12. Total Costs (lines 9-11)						

ED Form No. 524

Figure 3-2b:
Section B
of the
Department
of
Education's
budget form.

Name of Institution/Organization

Applicants requesting funding for only one year should complete the column under "Project Year 1." Applicants requesting funding for multi-year grants should complete all applicable columns. Please read all instructions before completing form.

SECTION B - BUDGET SUMMARY
NON-FEDERAL FUNDS

Budget Categories	Project Year 1 (a)	Project Year 2 (b)	Project Year 3 (c)	Project Year 4 (d)	Project Year 5 (e)	Total (f)
1. Personnel						
2. Fringe Benefits						
3. Travel						
4. Equipment						
5. Supplies						
6. Contractual						
7. Construction						
8. Other						
9. Total Direct Costs (lines 1-8)						
10. Indirect Costs						
11. Training Stipends						
12. Total Costs (lines 9-11)						

SECTION C - OTHER BUDGET INFORMATION (see instructions)

ED Form No. 524

The lobbying-activity disclosure form

A lobbyist is an individual or a firm that spends a lot of time on Capitol Hill or at your state capitol schmoozing with elected officials. Lobbyists work for for-profit and nonprofit agencies. They're on a (paid) mission to convince legislators to vote one way or another to benefit their client. A lot of pressure is applied and a lot of money flows.

If you've hired a lobbyist to make sure more federal or state dollars come your way, you must fess up by filling out the Disclosure of Lobbying Activities form. The feds want to make sure that no one was paid to propel your grant application into the Funded stack.

The federal grant application review process is supposed to be fair and objective. Every applicant is supposed to have the same chance to reply and get the application in on time. If a poorly-written grant application is reviewed with almost all zeros (or similarly low scores), and that application still ends up on someone's desk for funding consideration, you can bet the Disclosure of Lobbying Activities form is going to get looked at.

Chapter 4

Using a Funding Plan to Raise Your Hit Rate

In This Chapter

▶ Moving your organization forward with a funding plan

▶ Using more than one arrow to hit the funding target

▶ Hitting the jackpot — getting more than one grant for the same project

*I*magine writing a 10- to 40-page grant application narrative, filling out all of the forms, collecting the attachments, and mailing your laborious production off to the funder. "Whew," you say, "it's over!" Does it make sense to work this hard and then wait up to 12 nerve-wracking months only to learn that your grant application is . . . rejected?

Remember what your grandmother said: Don't put all your eggs in one basket! I don't think she was passing down a potato salad recipe. Be realistic and diversify your grant options — bet on all the horses in the race instead of just the favorite.

This chapter assists you in widening your funding vision so that you can increase your funding success rate.

Creating a Complete Funding Plan

You can mix government grants with foundation and corporate grants. Yes — you really can, although many new grant writers seem reluctant to do so. Multiply the power of one grant with another to become the Matchmaker of the Year.

But before you run out and start applying for every grant in sight, create a *funding plan*. Doing so ensures that when money dries up from one source — and it will — you won't see your whole program or special project go down the drain for lack of funding.

A funding plan is an organized, written vision and roadmap that describes the methodology and plots the path your organization will take to bring in grant funds. Plan and write the funding plan with employees and board members.

Be prepared to update the funding plan annually, after rigorous monitoring and evaluation of that year's results (meaning that you compare the number of grant applications going out and the dollars coming in). A well-organized and well-articulated funding plan can help your nonprofit thrive when others fail.

Plan to *do* whatever you write in the plan. Before writing any grant request, make sure that it fits into the plan. If it doesn't, then meet with your administration and other stakeholders and explain that going after every available dollar will come back to haunt you and them. Be organized, stay focused, and follow the roadmap that you create in your funding plan to success and stability.

Rules for making the plan

You and your colleagues need to go somewhere far away from distractions when you craft a funding plan, so that all the members of your team can concentrate.

A retreat setting is an excellent environment for generating a vision and refining ideas on how to make the vision come to fruition.

Here are my rules for success:

- ✔ Everyone participates. Explain at the outset that everyone has something to bring to the table that will assist your organization in identifying priorities and finding ways to fund them.
- ✔ Don't rush through the process because of time constraints.
- ✔ Be realistic.
- ✔ Draw upon everyone's resources. Personal contacts and past professional relationships can pay off. Use your board members and staff as links to potential funding sources.

Structuring the plan

Table 4-1 shows the parts of an all-purpose funding plan. Having a funding plan is the first step to becoming proactive.

Too many nonprofit organizations function in crisis management mode all of the time. They frantically write grant proposals to pay for programs and projects that are already on the downside of funding cessation. Everyone is always in a panic and the threat of layoffs and program closures is a routine fire call. Being *proactive* in grant seeking and grant writing is extremely important, rather than always running in a *reactive* mode.

Table 4-1	Funding Plan Outline
Mission statement	
Assessment of funding needs	
Funding goals	
Funding objectives	
Action plan (long-range, preferably 3 to 5 years; this tool identifies the types of funding you will apply for, the percentage of anticipated revenue from each type of funding, and who will be responsible for identifying the funding sources and writing the funding requests)	
Monitoring and evaluation of funding objectives	

Funding plan for the Jefferson County Regional Health Care Consortium

I include in this chapter an example of a funding plan that follows the structure outlined in Table 4-1. I make comments about some of the sections and let others speak for themselves. Follow the example when you write your funding plan.

Mission statement of the example plan

The Jefferson County Regional Health Care Consortium was formed in 1998 for the purpose of improving health care services in Jefferson County, Alabama.

Assessment of funding needs

Every assessment of funding needs is going to be radically different. For this section, instead of presenting an example, I show you a method that you can use to come up with your assessment.

The first thing the consortium did when it wrote the funding plan was to assess its needs, using *SWOT* analysis. SWOT stands for Strengths, Weaknesses, Opportunities, and Threats. The business world uses this method of analysis a lot. It's an effective tool that you can use for turning your agency inside out and really dealing with critical issues. Following is a guide to the kinds of questions you ask in SWOT analysis.

Strengths: This area of the assessment comes first to bolster your spirits and get the planning brainstorming session started on a positive note. Questions that identify your organization's strengths as they relate to receiving funding may include the following:

- ✔ What are our strengths as an organization?

- ✔ What are some of our premier or stronger programs or services that have high visibility in our target area? (List each program by name; include the numbers of clients served and how the program is currently funded, if it's funded already. Don't talk about insufficient funding in this section.)

- ✔ Who is doing our grant writing, how much is it costing, and what's the success rate — what percent of the grant applications that are written are funded? (A 50 percent or higher rate is good.)

- ✔ What funding sources can be counted on to continue support for five or more years?

- ✔ Have our board members been able to use their community connections to bring in funding from individuals, businesses, foundations, or government grants? (If so, make a list of these connections and make note of when the connected board members' terms are over.)

Weaknesses: This area of the assessment helps you objectively identify gaps in services or general grant seeking problems. Questions that identify your organization's weaknesses as they relate to receiving funding may include the following:

- ✔ What are our weaknesses as an organization? If we have programs that are faltering, is it because of insufficient funding or is it due to staffing shortfalls (the staff's qualifications and abilities)?

- ✔ Has our constituency asked for services and programs that we have been unable to provide? What comments are repetitive on any end-of-service surveys?

- ✔ Have we diligently conducted stringent evaluations of grant-funded programs in the past? What difficulties do you have in collecting evaluation data?

- ✔ Did we meet our stated objectives (in each and every grant application)?

✔ Where does our money come from now? What percent is from the United Way? What percent is from local, state, or federal government? Of this percent, how much are we receiving in formula grants and how much in competitive grants? Of the competitive grant monies, are any multi-year?

✔ Are there any current grants that will not allow second or third year funding?

✔ Is our success rate for getting grant monies lower than 50 percent? What do we think are the causes of this low rate?

✔ If we failed to cultivate one-on-one open communications with previous funders and are unable to reapply for grant funding for any reason, why has this happened and how can communications be reopened?

✔ Are board members helping you identify individual, business, and government funding because of their connections in the community? If not, why not?

Opportunities: This area of the assessment helps you identify possible opportunities that you may have missed thus far. Following are some of the questions that you can ask to identify paths that you haven't yet explored that may lead to future funding.

✔ Where are similar organizations getting their funding?

✔ Are there possible funders at the local, regional, state, or federal level who don't even know of our program?

✔ Are we networking at grantmaker meetings?

✔ Are we inviting elected officials into our organization (at least annually), presenting our funding needs, and asking for their help?

✔ Are we attending meetings with other human and social-service organizations to discuss possible collaborative grant seeking ventures?

✔ Are we subscribing to newsletters (hard copy and electronic) that keep us abreast of any changes that may affect our grant seeking?

Threats: This area of the assessment helps you identify any threats that could drastically alter your current funding structure. Use these sample questions to guide your inquiry.

✔ What funding will be exhausted in the near future and how will those programs be impacted?

✔ Who in our community has taken a negative public position against our agency? In other words, whose toes have we stepped on and how will it impact our local funding?

✔ Have we been buddying up with local politicians to get Community Development Block Grant monies for several years? If so, when will these elected officials leave office? How will their leaving affect our ability to get grants from the city or county level of government?

✔ Are there ongoing feuds between any board members or administrators on staff? Would the sudden departure of a key administrator cripple our agency in the local funding arena?

✔ Are other organizations doing what we do but doing it better? Why?

Funding goals

After you've done the assessment of funding needs, move on to articulating your goals. Goals should be global and futuristic. They describe where you want to be at the end of a funding period. From the Jefferson County example:

Goal 1: Secure general operating grants to assist the Jefferson County Regional Health Care Consortium in fulfilling its mission statement.

Goal 2: Secure seed money grants to host an emerging health care needs and community disease prevention education conference.

Goal 3: Secure grant monies to create an endowment to ensure the long-term financial stability of the Consortium.

Funding objectives

Your goals are not able to stand alone. They need to be buttressed by objectives. Objectives are like benchmarks or reference points. They're measurable steps that must be taken in order to achieve the goals. Every goal must have at least one objective. Here are objectives of the Jefferson County Health Care Consortium. Note how they relate to the goals:

Objective 1a: Raise $100,000 annually to support 100 percent of the general operating expenses for the Jefferson County Regional Health Care Consortium.

Objective 1b: Identify at least five local and/or regional funders that will each commit to funding 20 percent of the annual operating budget.

Objective 2a: Raise 100 percent of the funds needed to host the regional conference, at a minimum, every other year.

Objective 2b: Increase awareness of the Consortium's need to convene health care service providers by 50 percent or more among state agencies and elected officials.

Objective 3a: Increase community-wide awareness of the Consortium's long-term financial needs by 100 percent.

Objective 3b: Raise $20,000 for the endowment fund annually.

Action plan

Funding Activity	Support Percentages	Person(s) Responsible
General operating	Foundation: 100% (years 1 to 3) and 50% (years 4 to 5)	Grant writer
	State: 25% (years 4 to 5)	
	United Way 25% (years 4 to 5)	
Seed money for conference	Federal: 50% (renewable annually)	Grant writer, with congressional support
	Foundation: 25%	Grant writer
	Corporate: 25%	Grant writer and board members
Endowment	Foundation 100% (years 1 to 2)	Grant writer and board members
	Individual: 100% (after the first 2 years)	Contracted endowment development specialist and board members

Monitoring and evaluation of funding objectives

The Executive Committee of the Jefferson County Regional Health Care Consortium will be responsible for convening quarterly to review the funding plan's objectives. Staff and/or volunteers will prepare written reports on the funding activities for review by the committee. An evaluation report will be prepared for the full board of directors and shared with staff, volunteers, and the funders.

Improving Your Odds of Getting a Grant Award

Moving from one funding source to many funding sources is a logical step in grant seeking. Preparing one grant application or proposal, mailing it to one funding source, and waiting an infinity for the outcome is like taking the slow road to China. The best way to sustain a high funding success rate is to identify multiple funding sources for your project and submit your grant application to *all of them.*

Is doing so allowable? Of course. It's standard practice, as long as you let all of the funders know that you plan to approach other sources. Providing a simple, one-page attachment labeled "Funding Sources Receiving This Request" is the most ethnical way to inform all funders. I provide an example for you in Chapter 6.

In the sections that follow, I show you what you need to know to find a broad range of funding sources.

Following the steps to sure funding

Suppose you've been asked to write a grant for a regional community health care consortium. Members of the consortium represent the county public health department, a regional major medical center, a community wellness clinic, the local medical association, and a regional health care planning agency. This group would like to plan and host a conference on emerging health care needs and community disease prevention education.

Your group has been meeting for several months to brainstorm where the money will come from for a $40,000, three-day conference to be held nine months from today. Grant monies are needed to secure conference space in a local hotel; to print and mail invitations, program brochures, and conference handout packets; to pay honorariums to keynote and session speakers (health care professionals invited from other areas of your state and from a national level); and to pay for the opening banquet and the closing luncheon.

The clock is ticking. What's your plan? To diversify your funding sources, follow these steps.

Step 1: Conduct a federal funding search

Searching the *Federal Register,* you find an announcement under the U.S. Department of Health and Human Services (HHS) for the Center for Disease

Control. The deadline is about 30 days away, so after reading the announcement and downloading the grant application kit with forms, you are off and running on your first potential funding source for your public health conference. (See Chapter 2 for information on using the Register.)

You're slightly disappointed when you realize that this grant opportunity won't fund your entire conference; and because it's federal, it's highly competitive. Being wise, you decide to apply for $20,000 at the federal level but look for foundation and corporate monies for the full $40,000.

Step 2: Conduct a funding search of your state government's resources

Let me supply an actual state and county. The Consortium is located in Birmingham, Jefferson County, Alabama. The Internet search turns up the list of state agencies and you locate the Alabama Department of Public Health at www.alapubhealth.org/index.htm.

Much to your disappointment, the state Web site contains nothing that seems helpful. Making a call to your state senator's office, you find that most of the monies that come into the Department of Public Health are used for department-sponsored programs. At this point, calling the department to see if they would like to sponsor your conference is a good idea. Although you may not receive grant monies, you may receive planning support and technical assistance.

Step 3: Conduct a foundation and corporate funding search

Visiting your local library to use FC-Search (a registered product of The Foundation Center) or using your own Internet search resources can help you identify local, regional, and national funding sources for possible conference support.

To learn more about FC-Search, visit the Foundation Center's Web site at www.fdncenter.org.

You identify 12 funding sources in Alabama — nine in Birmingham and three elsewhere in the state. You also identify three corporations that have operating locations in or near Birmingham. In total, you have 15 possible sources.

Step 4: Follow the funder's guidelines

Reviewing their initial approach preferences, you find what each funder wants to receive in order to consider your request. Developing a work plan and plotting this information, as shown in Table 4-2, is a good idea.

Table 4-2	Keeping Track of Multiple Grant Proposals		
Funder	**Initial Approach/ Copies**	**Deadline**	**Average Range of Funding**
1	Letter/1	None	Up to $10,000
2	Letter/1	Quarterly	Up to $50,000
3	Proposal/1	None	Up to $50,000
4	Letter/1	May and October	Up to $50,000
5	Letter/1	None	Up to $10,000
6	Letter/1	None	Up to $100,000
7	Letter/1	April and October	Up to $50,000
8	Letter/1	Quarterly	Up to $140,000
9	Letter/1	October 31	Up to $45,000
10	Letter/1	None	Up to $10,000
11	Letter or Proposal/12	September 21	Up to $30,000
12	Letter or Proposal/6	April and October	Up to $100,000
13	Letter/1	None	Up to $5,000
14	Letter/1	None	Up to $100,000
15	Letter/1	Varies	Up to $150,000

Meeting the request for a letter of inquiry

Many foundation and corporate funding sources state in their published guidelines that they prefer the *initial approach* (your first contact with the funder) to be a letter rather than a full proposal. Asking for a letter allows them to make sure that what you're requesting is in their area of interest and range of funding award. Often, the published guidelines in funding directories (Internet or print copy) are not the funder's most current area of interest.

Starting out with a letter can save you time and effort. Although rejections are still rejections, you would rather be rejected after you write a letter than have your rejection come in response to a full-length application. And you may be asked to submit a full proposal by over 50 percent of the funders you approach with a letter.

At the top of the letter (refer to Figure 4-1), make sure to type *Letter of Inquiry*. The suggested length is two to three pages.

Letter of Inquiry

December 1, 2000

Ms. Mary Jones, Director
ABC Foundation
1234 Riverdale Avenue
Birmingham, Alabama 35298

Dear Ms. Jones:

Introduce your agency in the first paragraph.

I am writing you on behalf of the Jefferson County Regional Health Care Consortium. Our organization was formed in 1998 for the purpose of improving health care services in our region. Members of the Consortium include the county public health department, a regional major medical center (university affiliated), a community wellness clinic, the local medical association, and a regional health care planning agency. Our service area covers 19 communities and represents 657,422 residents (1999 Census estimate). A fact sheet on our organization is attached.

Get to the point on what you plan to do.

Our Consortium is planning to do an independent health care needs assessment for Jefferson County. However, prior to conducting the survey, we feel that a regional health care conference is needed. Such a conference would convene health care service providers from all areas and practices to discuss emerging health care needs of the residents in Jefferson County and community disease prevention education.
Goal: Share resources, express concerns and combine efforts that positively impact health care statistical indicators for Jefferson County residents.
Objective: Convene 90 percent or more of health care services providers to develop a plan to address emerging health care needs of the service population.
Timeline: The conference is scheduled for August 13 - 15, 2001. It will be held in Birmingham at the Convention Center.
Benefits: Reduce duplicative efforts, improve communications between providers, increase awareness of the Consortium's role, increase collaborative efforts and improve the overall level of community disease prevention efforts in Jefferson County.

Earlier in our planning phase, we thought grant monies would be needed to secure conference space in a local hotel/resort. However, much to our surprise, the Alabama Department of Public Health and the City of Birmingham have agreed to provide space, free-of-charge, at the Convention Center. We still need grant funds to pay for printing and postage for invitations, program brochures, and conference handout

It's okay to do a little begging here. You really need foundation and corporate support.

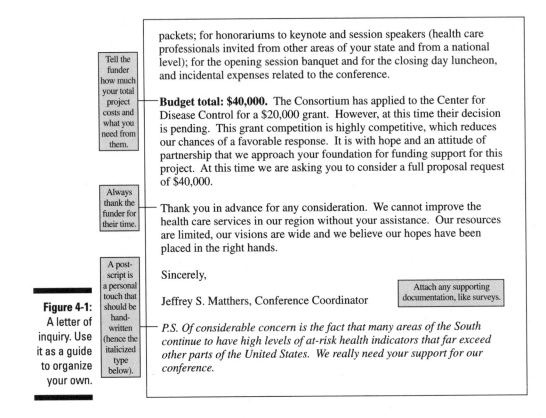

packets; for honorariums to keynote and session speakers (health care professionals invited from other areas of your state and from a national level); for the opening session banquet and for the closing day luncheon, and incidental expenses related to the conference.

Budget total: $40,000. The Consortium has applied to the Center for Disease Control for a $20,000 grant. However, at this time their decision is pending. This grant competition is highly competitive, which reduces our chances of a favorable response. It is with hope and an attitude of partnership that we approach your foundation for funding support for this project. At this time we are asking you to consider a full proposal request of $40,000.

Thank you in advance for any consideration. We cannot improve the health care services in our region without your assistance. Our resources are limited, our visions are wide and we believe our hopes have been placed in the right hands.

Sincerely,

Jeffrey S. Matthers, Conference Coordinator

P.S. Of considerable concern is the fact that many areas of the South continue to have high levels of at-risk health indicators that far exceed other parts of the United States. We really need your support for our conference.

Tell the funder how much your total project costs and what you need from them.

Always thank the funder for their time.

A post-script is a personal touch that should be hand-written (hence the italicized type below).

Attach any supporting documentation, like surveys.

Figure 4-1: A letter of inquiry. Use it as a guide to organize your own.

Handling Good Fortune

What if you receive more monies than you originally planned for? Is that bad or good? Good, because now you can expand your conference plans, and maybe even get permission from the funders to expend some of their money on the development of a long-range strategic plan.

Receiving more grant funds than you originally sought is a great compliment. You should have no guilt. Some of your envious peers in the grant seeking and grant writing field may point a few fingers and say that you've taken money away from other nonprofits that really need it by accepting more than you need. Don't listen to them.

Just as the early bird gets the worm, the best grant application or proposal gets the funding. The only guilt that you should ever have about grant writing is when you don't try hard enough to identify a sufficient number of funding sources for your project.

Of course, when you find out that you're getting grants funded all over the place for your project, you must dutifully notify each funder of your success and indicate how you would like to allocate the additional grant monies. Be courteous, be honest, and be open about where you have applied and how much you have received.

Chapter 5

Harvesting Critical Information on Foundations and Corporations

In This Chapter

▶ Zeroing in on great Web sites

▶ Collecting information and developing funding source files

▶ Targeting the best funding source for your project

▶ Taking a closer look at a funder's financial capacity

*Y*ou have to be really lucky to find a grant competition that you stand a good chance of winning.

But being lucky isn't really about luck at all. It's about becoming a sleuth, combing over minute details, and finding funding treasures where others see no hope. You can become the luckiest grant writer around if you work hard enough.

It's time to put on your high-focus visionary glasses and get ready for the fun part of grant writing — grant seeking. Ready, set, let's go!

Knowing the Secrets of Successful Grant Seeking

Do your homework before you ask a foundation or corporation for its money. Simply mailing a proposal without doing research is asking for a big-time rejection letter — and a waste of your time. Here are some things you can do to set yourself apart from the field:

- ✔ Use the public library and the Internet to look for Web sites of foundations and corporations.

- ✔ Subscribe to funding newsletters that contain articles about what types of grants various foundations and corporations fund and provide information on applying for them. Just a few of the many online newsletters that help you keep up with foundation and corporate giving are the *Philanthropy News Digest, Philanthropy News Network,* and *NonProfit Times.*

- ✔ Plan on setting aside at least four hours (for an electronic search) to eight hours (for a manual search) to identify all potential foundation and corporate funders.

- ✔ Request grant application guidelines, an annual report (which contains financial information on the funder and usually has a section on previous grants funded), and any other print literature that will help you tailor your grant application to the funder's current interest area.

- ✔ Follow all the directions provided by the funding source on how to apply for grants.

And, of course, there are some things to avoid. Don't

- ✔ Rely on outdated funding publications (older than one year) for current contact information.

- ✔ Buy anything that you can get for free at the public library or on the Internet.

- ✔ Call the funding source with a dozen questions — *self-destruction,* I believe it's called.

- ✔ Write a grant application or proposal and mail it without having done extensive research first. (I've already warned you about this, but it bears repeating.)

- ✔ Broadcast your funding sources to colleagues working for other nonprofits. Learn to treasure (in other words, keep quiet about) your findings, lest others apply before you. Remember that only a very small portion of the funding source's monies will be awarded in one geographic area. If your buddy's group gets the cash, you won't. The exception: funding sources that are local and only distribute funds in a specific city, town, county, or state.

Clicking in the Right Places

There are a zillion Web sites to screen. Then there are books and more books. So I want to give you my best hits on the Internet along with a list of some really great publications that carry news on the funders you want to know about. Using these resources is a must and saves you a lot of time.

Web sites worth visiting (just a sampling)

The Internet is your best friend in writing a grant. It's convenient. It's free. Even if you don't own a computer, you can probably browse the Web at the library, at a friend's, at the office of the organization you're seeking funding for, or maybe even on your lunch hour at work, if you have a day job that doesn't involve the nonprofit for which you're procuring funds. Here are my picks for best sites:

✔ www.fdncenter.org: This Web site carries extensive links to foundation grantmaker sites. You can click on entry after entry to link to private foundations, corporate grantmakers, and community foundations. When you read something about a potential funding source in a newspaper or magazine, you can hurry over to this site and look for a link to harvest additional information.

✔ www.aoa.dhhs.gov/jpost/gr-foundations.html: Many branches of the federal government have Web sites that contain links to foundations that fund in the same area as they do. A great site to visit is the U.S. Department of Human Services Partner Gateway Web site. This site has great links. (See Chapter 3 for more on visiting federal agencies on the Web.)

✔ www.hoovers.com: The Hoover's Online site has a link to companies and industries that helps you find corporate addresses and contacts when a corporation does not have a foundation or corporate giving program listed in any of the published funding directories.

How can you use this information? You read a newspaper article on a new business planning to relocate to your community. Using Hoover's Online, you can do your homework on the new company. Look for the address of its headquarters and the contact person(s) for corporate or community affairs. If no one is listed, then address your request to the chief financial officer or the vice president of marketing.

Hoover's is a subscription-based service; only skeletal information is available for free. The basic information on a corporation is free. If you want a detailed profile of the corporation, such as financials or the locations of all corporate facilities, then you have to pay an annual subscription fee. Also, if you want to create a mailing database of a group of corporate contacts on the Hoover's site, you need to pay a fee.

Some companies on the Hoover's site have a link to their corporate social responsibility Web page. Once there, you can find information on how the company provides financial support to communities where it has a *presence* (defined as the headquarters or an operating location). This support is in the form of grant awards or product donations.

✔ www.fundsnetservices.com/2000/directory.asp: The Fundsnet Services site is a great little treasure trove of foundation and corporate links. When I found this site, I couldn't believe how well-organized it is or how much time it can save a grant seeker.

✔ www.fundersonline.org: Funders Online is an initiative of the European Foundation Centre (EFC) that promotes foundations and corporate funders in the New Europe. If you have some projects that are international, this Web site will give you some new leads for untapped dollars.

✔ www.ncup.org/links/nonprof.htm: The National Center for Urban Partnership has so many valuable funding source information links that it's like finding a resource oasis in the information superhighway desert.

✔ philanthropy.com: *The Chronicle of Philanthropy* is the newspaper of the nonprofit world. It's published every other week and can be accessed online. Although this is a subscription-based resource, some portions of the Web site are viewable free of charge.

Looking at selected print resources

The Foundation Center has an extensive online catalog of funding publications. I have subscribed to every one of their funding books over the past decade or so. I could have gone to a local foundation collection site, but I wanted desktop convenience. I also tend to burn the midnight oil — when most libraries are closed. Print funding resources published by the Foundation Center are on the Web at www.fdncenter.org. Some great directories that you may find yourself using daily are

✔ *The Foundation Directory* contains grantmaker information on over 10,000 foundations in the United States. Two additional books are available for purchase in this collection, *Part 2* and the *Supplement.* When you use all three, you have information on over 18,000 foundations.

✔ *The Foundation 1000* profiles the top 1,000 major foundations in the United States.

✔ The *National Directory of Corporate Giving* profiles more than 3,000 corporations that have grantmaking programs in the United States.

✔ *The Foundation Grants Index* profiles over 97,000 grants that have been awarded in the United States.

The Foundation Center also publishes national guides to funding in specific program areas such as arts and culture, community development, education, environment, health, information technology, international and foreign programs, libraries, religion, social services, and women and girls.

The Taft Group publishes print directories as well as CD-ROMs. When I did rely on print directories, my library was half Foundation Center publications and half Taft Group publications. Unfortunately, most public libraries carry very few resources from the grant-information publishing line of the Taft Group. However, Taft does have an online newsletter that is full of funding source information. The Web site address is www.taftgroup.com. Using information from both Taft and the Foundation Center provides you with a mix of the best and the best.

The Funding $ourcebook offers the latest research on grants for telecommunications, multimedia, curricula development, teacher training for private and public schools, higher education, museums, libraries, arts and culture organizations, health and social service agencies, and grassroots community organizations. The Web site address is www.technogrants.com.

Scanning the Most Important Information Fields

The first step after you locate information on a foundation or corporate funding source is to quickly scan its profile to determine whether you have a *perfect* match. A perfect match means that your program or project fits their funding priorities 100 percent. Remember that you can't persuade a funder to change its award guidelines or funding priorities; you're the one who has to do the changing to fit the funder's funding criteria. If you cannot change your program or project, then this particular funding source is not for you — keep looking for a better match.

Every print publication listing funding sources presents the information on the funder in a generalized format referred to as a *profile*. When you look at each funder's profile, you can scan some specific information fields to determine if reading any farther on this particular funding source is worth your time.

✔ **Limitations:** The limitations field is where you should look first. It describes the geographic area that grant awards are limited to and the types of grant applicants or project areas the funding source will not fund. Does any wording in this section eliminate your program or project? If so, move on to the next funder's profile. If no, then move on to the other critical information fields.

Be certain to read this entry first. Your organization may be eliminated before it can even get to the starting gate.

REMEMBER

✔ **Purpose and Activities:** Every foundation and corporate giver has a purpose statement. You can find it at the beginning of the funding profile. Does the funding source's purpose statement reflect your organization's values? Do any of the activities that the funder prefers to fund encompass activities that your organization is or will be undertaking? If not, read no further. Move on to another funder's information profile. If you can identify with this funder's purpose, then move on to the next information field.

✔ **Fields of Interest:** Does the program area that you are seeking grant funds for fit into any of the funding source's fields of interest? Keep in mind that sometimes the language you use to describe your program may not be the language the funder is using to list their fields of interest. Think in broad terms and generic categories.

For example, you need grant funding for a program that will tutor and mentor at-risk elementary-aged youth after school and on the weekend. You probably won't find any of the following terms in the funder's fields of interest entry: tutoring, mentoring, at-risk, after school. However, you will find these descriptors under most funders: education (K–12), elementary education, public education, private education, youth programs and services. See the difference? If you find any terms in the field of interest section that seem like a match to your program or project area, then move on to the next information field.

✔ **Types of Support:** What types of activities is this funder willing to pay for? If you are trying to erect a new building and the funder only lists *general operating support, conferences,* and *seed money* under types of support, then this may not be the funding source you want to approach for a grant to erect a building.

Even if this funder isn't willing to support the type of activity that you're currently seeking funds for, save its information if you think the funder may be willing to support some other aspect of your organization.

✔ **Previous Grants or Grantees:** Have any previous grants been funded in your state? Have any previous grants been for projects similar to yours or in your project area?

✔ **Amounts of Grants Previously Funded:** Does your guestimated project budget fit into the range of prior grant awards?

Don't be discouraged the first time you start reading funders' profiles. Qualifying or disqualifying a funding source may take up to ten minutes. The more you scan funding profiles, the quicker this process will be.

Taking the Next Step — Prioritizing the Funders

Now that you've e-mailed, written, or called each one of the funding sources that surfaced in your funding search and you've requested their annual reports (if they're foundations or corporations) and grant application guidelines, you're ready to take the next step.

Organize your potential sources by application due-dates. This is a critical first step, because some funders only have once-yearly competitions. You could be a few weeks or many months away from their annual date for grant submissions. After all of this hard work, you don't want to miss an opportunity to get a grant funded because you submit it late. Develop a good filing system. Use a separate folder for each funder. You should have massive amounts of information at this point, so keeping it in order is crucial. Sorting it by due-date helps you anticipate how much work you'll have in any given month.

Your first writing priority is for those funders that have due-dates in 60 days or less. Get busy!

After you've organized the potential sources by due-date, look for the funders who will accept generic, NNG (National Network of Grantmakers), or regional common grant format applications anytime during the year. These grants are normally fairly easy to write.

The National Network of Grantmakers (a large group of local, regional, and national foundations) created a standard grant application format. The format is great — it organizes all the information that the funder needs to know into clearly outlined sections that guide your writing.

The last funders that you should turn your attention to are those that have their own application forms. You may have to scan the form into a computer and enter the requested information or type in the requested information (slowly, with correction fluid nearby). I prefer scanning the forms onto a computer; it's just plain easier and allows for editing and the reuse of application forms in future grant submissions.

When you've finished the application for a specific funder, keep everything for that funder in a folder. When you first make contact with a funding source (via phone, fax, e-mail, or letter of inquiry), ask to be included in its mailing list. Doing so normally means that you'll get annual reports, grantmaking guidelines, research, and other information that keeps you up-to-date on each funder. Add this information to the folder.

How much money are they giving?

You can find out how much money a foundation or corporate giving entity is awarding in grants each year. It just takes a little digging around.

Form 990 is the information return that nonprofit organizations file annually with the Internal Revenue Service. Foundations are required to file this form when they have revenue of more than $25,000. This information is available for anyone to view on the Internet.

Look at these forms to see who was given grant monies and for what purpose. Look in the section labeled "Grants and Contributions Paid the Year or Approved for Future Payment."

I use this form to get the latest scoop on the types and sizes of grant awards made by a particular funder. It also helps me to supplement any intuitive feelings I have about asking for a large (over $200,000) grant from any one funding source. I scan the 990 Grants and Contributions page to see what percentage of grants recently awarded are over $200,000. If 25 percent or more of the grants awarded are over $200,000, I feel comfortable asking for a large grant.

Organize, organize, and organize! Always know what's due and where all the relevant information is. Be able to put your finger on what you need right away.

Even the best laid plans of mice and men (and women) go astray. But sloppily laid plans? Poorly laid plans? These plans are *bound* to go astray. Be as organized as possible to maximize your chances.

Make sure to update your funding plan once you've selected the funding sources that you're applying to. (Chapter 4 shows you how to create a funding plan to organize your grant seeking efforts.)

Chapter 6

Talking the Talk of Grant Writing

- -

In This Chapter

▶ Learning to speak "Grantlish"

▶ Supplying the right information

▶ Understanding what each section of a grant requires

- -

Writing effective grant applications and proposals takes time, patience, and an understanding of the terminology. Before you jump right into writing the request, be sure that you know the correct terms to use. Your goal is to write with clarity and directness — important attributes in winning more points from the grant reviewer. Knowing the language of grants assists you in writing clearly and directly.

On the other hand, using incorrect language, especially for the type of support you're seeking, can lead to confusion, delays in decisions, and possibly rejection!

Understanding "Grantlish" — Your Second Language

This section is meant to give a huge boost to the newcomer to grant writing. If you're new to writing grants, carefully studying the language of grant writing can propel you out of the starting gate. Remember that winning grants is all about knowing how to complete and submit your grant application effectively, competitively, and *correctly*.

Speaking of your qualifications

The funding source will have questions about your legal authority to apply for a grant award. Although the wording may vary slightly from one application to another, the cover documents and narratives of grant proposals and applications all ask for the same basic information. Understanding what's being asked for and knowing how to reply in the right language is critical.

Legal name of organization applying

You need to type in your organization's legal name, the one that appears on your IRS 501(c)(3) letter of nonprofit determination. If your organization does not have such a letter, like a city, township, village, or county unit of government (which are all considered nonprofit entities), then the legal name is the incorporated name. Cities, townships, villages, and county units of government are all considered nonprofit entities, but they aren't charitable organizations that fall under the IRS 501(c)(3) classification.

Don't hesitate to call the funding source for assistance if you have any questions.

Type of applicant

You will find the type of applicant category on federal and state grant applications. Select the appropriate category. The list usually includes these choices: state, county, municipal, township, interstate, intermunicipal, special district, independent school district, public college or university, Indian Tribe, individual, private, profit-making organization, and other (specify).

The majority of grant opportunities are earmarked for nonprofit organizations. If you're a for-profit, call first to see if you're eligible; if not, look for an eligible partner to act as the grant applicant and fiscal agent (the one that is accountable for the grant monies).

Tax-exempt status

You find this information requirement on a standardized grant request format for foundations and corporations. It usually appears on a cover form. Contributions to nonprofit organizations that have tax-exempt status are deductible for federal income tax purposes.

Year founded

You need to supply the year that your organization incorporated or was created.

Current operating budget

You need to supply the organization's operating budget total for the current fiscal year.

When it comes to money, supply information that portrays the truth and nothing but the truth!

Employer identification number

You need to provide the taxpayer identification number assigned by the Internal Revenue Service to your organization. It begins with two digits, followed by a dash and seven additional digits. It's also called a _reporting number_.

Organization's fiscal year

You need to indicate the 12-month timeframe that your organization considers its operating year. The period is defined by the organization's bylaws and can correspond with the calendar year or some other period, such as June 1 to July 31. The federal government's fiscal year begins October 1 and ends September 30. The fiscal year does not change from year to year. Financial statements usually are compiled and reported on a fiscal year basis.

House and Senate districts

You need to supply the federal congressional districts, both House and Senate, in which your organization is located. If you don't know what districts you're in (most people don't), call the public library — the reference librarian is able to determine your districts by your address. Why do federal grant applications ask for this information? First, because the information assists federal agencies in distributing awards with some geographic balance; second, because when your grant has been recommended for funding, your senator and representative in Washington, D.C., are notified — usually before you are!

Knowing who represents you in Washington and at your state capitol is critical. You always need friends in high places.

Contact person information

You need to provide the primary contact name for grant negotiations, questions, and written correspondence. When an application requires this information, the funding source wants to know who is in charge administratively and who will be the day-to-day contact person for answering possible questions that a funder may have.

Not all executive directors run programs on a daily basis or have the right answers about information in the grant application. Make your contact person an individual who helped write the grant and who's quick enough on her feet to answer tough technical questions from the funder, especially by phone.

Address

You need to supply the current mailing address for the applicant organization. Always use a street address on all proposals and grant applications. Never use a post office box as your only address. The use of just a post office box makes it appear that your organization isn't a permanent one. This is especially true if your organization is a new 501(c)(3) organization without a funding track record. Don't look shaky and temporary!

You absolutely must have an e-mail address. These days, an organization without an e-mail address looks pretty shabby. So if you *still* don't have one, enroll at once with one of the free e-mail sites, such as: Juno, Yahoo!, or Hotmail. Surf and search until you find the free e-mail service that fits your communication needs.

E-mail is the preferred way of communicating with the funder after you have sent in your grant application.

Telephone/fax/e-mail information

Remember to include the area code for your telephone and fax numbers. Also, double-check your typed entries; transposing numbers is all too easy — and then you wonder why no one has called! Funders won't track your organization down if there are other grant seekers who have provided the correct information.

Filling in the blanks with style

Filling in all of the information fields on a grant application form or cover sheet is critical! Leaving any field blank makes you look nonresponsive, and this alone could turn off a funder's interest in reading any further into your application.

Creating a project name

List your project name on the cover letter, the cover form, and any other documentation. People have names. Pets have names. Projects for which you are seeking grant funding must have names.

Don't be too cute with your name. Also, don't select a name with an acronym that's offensive. For example, the Children's Reading and Understanding Drama (CRUD) Program has a disgusting acronym. Would you really want to refer to your special program for little people as CRUD throughout the proposal or grant application? As a grant reviewer, I certainly would be turned off by CRUD!

Everything, everyone, every project needs class and character. A project's name is a part of conveying its class and character.

Summarizing your organization's mission

Provide a summary of your mission statement. Keep it short and keep it simple. Foundations and corporations ask for a summary on the cover form of nationally and regionally formatted grant applications.

The operative word here is *summarizing*. Don't include your five-page mission statement.

Writing about the purpose of the grant request

Write a short statement about what the grant funds will be used for. This is about what the grant monies will do for whom and where, as well as what activities will occur and when. It is required on the grant application cover form for national and regional grant applications to foundations and corporations, as well as state and federal grant applications. Remember to get to the point!

Giving dates for the project

What you need to provide are the proposed starting and ending dates of the project. The dates are expressed in month and year. Do your homework! Before settling on dates, find out if the funding source only funds in one-year cycles or funds for multiple project years.

Stating the amount requested

List the amount you're asking for from this specific funding source. Conducting research on the funder's grant award range will help you look modest here. (Chapters 3 and 5 cover how to research a funding source.)

Including the total project cost

List the total cost of the proposed project. The number you enter here must match the total cost of the project in the budget narrative and on the budget forms. An error in math — totals that don't match — can cause your request to be rejected. At the federal level, if you're off by $1, you're going to be penalized by losing criteria review points.

Stating the geographic area served

List the location of your project: city (county), state. It should be typed this way: Chandler (Maricopa County), Arizona.

Always include your county and state. Some funding is designated by specific states and some funders even select individual counties within a state for funding projects.

Adding signatures

The chief executive officer of your organization (CEO, CFO, president) should sign cover letters, cover forms, and all other forms requiring a signature. All original signatures should be in blue ink. Some funding sources ask for multiple copies of proposals or grant applications. Blue ink makes it easier to distinguish the original from the copies.

Learning the lingo for the main event

In the body of the grant application/narrative, you'll see the following headings (listed in the order of appearance).

Executive summary or abstract

Give a brief overview of the proposal or grant application. Limit this section to one page if an executive summary is called for. An abstract is similar to an executive summary; however, it should be limited to 125 words or less (according to suggested professional writing standards).

Meeting the purpose of the authorizing statute/act

Authorizing statute sounds like a legal term, and it is — in this section, you show that you qualify for funds. Meeting the purpose is definitely a requirement for federal grant applications. The authorizing act is the legislation that allocates grant funds. Unless your project meets the intent of the authorizing act, don't bother applying for funding. There is *no* flexibility here.

Defining the parts of the narrative

In order to receive a grant award, you must write a concise story illustrating why funds are needed and how funds will be expended. The following sections make up the narrative. (Chapters 10 through 16 show you how to write a winning narrative.)

Introduction to/background of the organization

Write about your organization, when it was founded, its purpose, its mission, and its location.

History and major accomplishments

Write about who founded your organization, why, and major achievements since its founding. Remember to write only about events and accolades that are relevant to the project that you're asking grant funds for.

Current programs and activities

Write about the current initiatives that your organization is involved in. Name each program and write a sentence or two about the program's purpose and its clients, patients, volunteers, and so on. List the events, activities, and current happenings going on at your organization. Be brief; you can always attach brochures, flyers, newsletters or other *for your information* (FYI) materials.

Description/demographics of your constituency

Talk about the population that your organization provides services to. Include age range, gender, ethnicity, economic status, educational level, and other characteristic descriptors. It's important for the proposal or grant applicant reader/reviewer to understand whom you serve and what's special about your target population.

Description of community

Write about the make-up of your community. Describe the community by providing a combination of city/county information, such as geographic proximity (for example, 80 miles north of Detroit); total population; and population percentages for the largest age group, largest ethnic group, largest economic group, and largest educational level group. Include any additional information about your community that would be considered interesting (trivia) and grant getting!

Description of work with local groups

Write about other organizations in your community that you work with, plan events with, share end-users with, and have affiliations with. This sections looks great in a two-column table, with the local group names in one column and the type of work they do with your organization in the other column.

Proposed initiative

Write about what you plan to do with the grant monies. State it simply and directly in one or two sentences: "The purpose of this request is to . . . ." Got it?

Problem statement/statement of need

Write about the problem you will combat with grant funds. State the truth about your need, but use compelling words to relay the gloom, doom, drama, and trauma of your situation and why your organization needs grant funds.

Program design/plan of action

Write about what steps your organization will take to solve the problem or need. This section is about how you will proceed once grant funds have been awarded. Don't skimp on words here. This section is the heart of your proposal and is the place where you can persuade a reviewer that your organization can do what it proposes. But don't start talking about the problem or need again. Stay focused and don't revert to language you've already used in previous sections of the narrative.

Goals

Write, in direct terms, about where your organization and the target population of the grant will be at the end of grant funding. Goals aren't measurable. Goals are global, visionary statements that create moments of *awe* for the writer and the reader. Always, always have more than one goal. And for every goal, have one or more measurable objectives. Goals and objectives should be numbered like this: Goal 1, Objective 1a, Objective 1b; Goal 2, Objective 2a; and so on.

Goals and objectives are where many grant writers falter. Make sure you check out Chapter 13 for more information.

Measurable objectives

Write about the measurable steps (sometimes referred to as *benchmarks*) that must occur in order to reach the goals. Objectives must state who will benefit, how, when, and how much.

Activities/strategies

Write about how you will reach each objective in terms of actual activities, tasks, and strategies.

Timeline

Write about when each activity will begin and end. Do this in a table that makes it easy to see what activities will be undertaken and when.

Consider interspersing tables throughout your application. Besides conveying information quickly, they give the reader a break from reading straight text.

Impact on problem

Write about how what you are doing will reduce the problems discussed in the problem statement/statement of need.

Project significance

Write about the impact the project will have on the target population. This is a continuation of the previous section, but it talks about the impact from a global perspective.

Systematic change

Write about how the program you will develop with grant funding will make significant strides in changing our society for the better. Be grandiose. Think big.

Key personnel/staffing

Write about the staffing needed to carry out the program or project. First list those staff members who will be funded out of the grant budget. Then list those staff members who will contribute to the program/project, but will not be funded out of the grant. For each staff person, indicate (as a percentage or decimal) how their time will be allocated to the project and from which budgets their salaries will come.

Management plan/organizational structure/administration

Write about who will report to whom and where the built-in assurances of administrative and financial responsibility occur. A flowchart is a good way to depict the project management structure and who will be responsible for the various program components. Also write about how your organization appoints members of the board of directors, the length of their terms, and their involvement on the board and in the organization. Include staff in key positions in the program. Include their names, job titles, and other pertinent information.

Adequacy of resources

Write about financial, physical, and personnel resources available to the program/project. These are resources your organization already owns or has access to that can be used for program activities.

Equitable access/statement of diversity/nondiscriminatory policies for hiring new personnel

Write about how your program will guarantee access to underrepresented groups, including the physically challenged. Include your organization's nondiscrimination policy using standard Equal Employment Opportunity (EEO) language. If you have vacant positions to fill with the grant monies, you must show the funding source that your organization will hire personnel that reflect the community's demographics and the program participants' make-up.

Performance evaluation/evaluation/evaluation plan

Write about who will conduct the evaluation. The most popular type of evaluation is called a *stakeholders evaluation*. People who are impacted by the program — stakeholders — are a part of the evaluation team. In addition to end-users, stakeholders can be board members, local employers, and the general public.

Keep in mind that the frequent and unbiased feedback from members of the grant's target population is critical to an accurate program evaluation.

Also write about how you will prove that each measurable objective was achieved. State what evidence you'll have on file to prove that you hired project staff, conducted training, provided assistance, monitored retention, provided follow-up support, or did any of the activities you outlined in the proposal.

Dissemination

Write about who will receive a copy of the evaluation findings. Will you share your successes and failures with other organizations around the state or country that are attempting to provide effective programming for the same constituency that your organization serves? Will you attend regional and national conferences to present the do's and don'ts of your program? Will you create a how-to book for free distribution? Will you create a video for purchase or free distribution that covers your program from start to finish?

Dissemination materials are important for reporting to current funders and can sway future funding sources when you attach them to proposals and grant applications. These items are proof that you can successfully manage and run a grant-funded program.

Wrapping Up the Grant Request

Additional information about your organization follows the grant narrative in the form of attachments. Some of the things you probably will attach to your grant are described in the following list.

- **Budget summary/cost summary.** Be prepared to fill in the blanks on a standard worksheet with the project's budget. It lists line items and expense amounts. Note that in federal and state grant applications, the budget summary may appear *before* the narrative. Follow the grant guidelines/directions closely.

- **Budget detail/budget narrative/cost justification.** Write a detailed narrative on each proposed expense. Placement of this information could also be before the grant narrative.

- **Most recent financial statement.** This statement or letter, usually prepared by a certified public accountant, is your organization's current report of revenues and expenditures. It can be audited or unaudited; there should be an explanation of any findings of concern. New nonprofit organizations may have a very simple financial statement prepared by a bookkeeper or by the board treasurer. Both financial statements and letters are accepted by funding sources.

- **Proof of tax-exempt status.** This is a copy of your letter from the Internal Revenue Service that is dated the day your nonprofit status was recognized by a certifying agency. Just having a nonprofit recognition from your state is not enough to qualify for foundation and corporate grants, and in some cases may not be enough to qualify for a federal or state grant award. For these kinds of awards you will definitely need an IRS 501(c)(3) letter of nonprofit determination.

- **Board of directors with affiliations.** This attachment lists representatives of your organization's governing body (board of directors, city council members, village trustees, and so on) and their positions in the community. It also includes the title of their position on the board, as well as length of board term elected to and time remaining. Some funding sources will request the gender and ethnicity of your governing board members. Their request helps them determine if your board comprises fair and equitable representation of the community that your organization provides services in.

- ✔ **Letters of support.** Ask for these early in the writing process and include at least three letters of support with all proposals and grant applications. Who can you ask for letters of support? Constituents, partnering organizations, previous grant funders that have supported your organization, elected officials, local business owners, and others that have a vested interest in seeing your organization continue to provide services to its constituency.

If the funding source's guidelines indicate that no attachments will be accepted or that any additional material besides the grant application will be cause for nonreview, then omit letters of support.

- ✔ **Annual report.** Include an annual report (brochure, booklet, or newsletter) as an attachment to your proposals and grant applications. It doesn't matter whether the report is a professionally prepared booklet or an insert in an end-of-fiscal-year newsletter, as long as it provides an overview of your organization and service and financial statistics for your programs.

- ✔ **Recent print reviews.** Attach letter-size photocopies of project-related newspaper articles about your organization.

- ✔ **Other documentation.** Some funders will want to see one-page resumes of key program personnel. Others will want a complete and thoroughly detailed resume.

Part II
Understanding the Rules of the Grants Game

The 5th Wave   By Rich Tennant

"I appreciate you sharing your dreams and wishes for starting your own pool and spa business, but maybe I should explain more fully what we at the Make-A-Wish Foundation are all about."

In this part . . .

This part focuses on understanding the expectations of the people who read grant applications submitted to government funding agencies. The knowledge shared in this part shows you how to decide if a grant announcement really fits your organization, how to understand and interpret the weighting and scoring process for grants, and how to write using words that help to rack up high review points for all types of grant applications.

Chapter 7

Preparing for Review Criteria of Government (and Other) Grants

In This Chapter

▶ Understanding the importance of the authorizing act
▶ Prequalifying your organization as an eligible grant applicant
▶ Thinking along the same terms
▶ Collecting the background information

*T*he *review criteria* is the point-based rating system that a government agency or a foundation or corporate funder uses to decide whether your grant application cuts the mustard — whether it's good enough to receive funding support. Your grant application must score a certain number of points to get recommended for funding. The basics of review criteria apply to all types of grants: federal, state, foundation, and corporate. Because federal grants are the toughest, I use them as my example in this chapter.

All grant funders have published *guidelines* for the type of grant application that they expect grant seekers to submit. The guidelines generally shadow the funder's review criteria.

Paying attention to detail and adhering to the guidelines is as important as finding the right funding source and using compelling language. Once the foundation, corporate giving entity, or governmental unit issues the grant application guidelines, you must read and reread every sentence. Check for technical requirements, writing formats, and preapplication or full-application requirements.

Detailing a Federal Grant Announcement — the Early Steps

You've found an announcement in the *Federal Register,* and you think that you have a chance to win the grant. But you don't know where to start, or if it's really worth going for. In this section, I walk you through the essentials of determining if this is the right competition for you and point out some important "grantlish" (the art of talking about grants).

Daily *Federal Register* announcements can be retrieved online or viewed at any public library that serves as a depository of government documents (big city and university libraries, generally).

Deciding whether the timing is right

First, look for the *closing date.* The closing date is the date by which the funding agency must receive the grant application, or, in some cases, the date the grant application must be postmarked by. The announcement will tell you which.

If this is your first attempt at writing a government grant, look for a closing date that allows you at least 21 days for researching and writing. Having less than three weeks to write your first federal grant may be overwhelming, unless you can devote 100 percent of your work time to the grant. Normal writing time for a federal grant is 40 to 60 hours. Research can add up to another 20 hours. So give yourself ample time — even if you're a veteran grant writer.

Knowing whether this is the right grant competition for you

Grants are brought to life by laws, or *legislative authority.* All the rules and guidelines of a grant are developed based on the legislation enacted by Congress. You can find this language in the first part of the *Federal Register* announcement. It will be in the "Legislative Authority" section. If any language eliminates your organization from being an eligible applicant, look for another community-based organization that is eligible and consider being a collaborative partner. If you're seeking funding for a program that does not include any of the activities outlined as eligible for funding and you're not willing to change the program, then this is not the grant competition for you. Keep searching the *Federal Register* and look for a grant that is better suited to fund what you have your heart set on doing.

While you're scanning a grant announcement, look for the purpose statement. This is a statement about the intended purpose of the grant funding. When you start writing your program design, remember to incorporate key words and phrases from the purpose statement. During the grant review process, this will help readers clearly make a connection between the purpose of the act and your needs statement and program design — which should fit like a soft leather glove to the federal language.

Before you conclude that a particular grant makes a match with your needs, check out the eligibility paragraph. Make sure that your organization is eligible to apply for these federal funds.

Terms you need to know

All grant announcements in the *Federal Register* have two types of terms: general and program specific. General terms are words or phrases that appear in all grant announcements. Program-specific terms are phrases that are used in connection with a particular program. Some terms that you see:

- **Budget period:** The interval of time into which a multi-year period of assistance (the project period) is divided for budgetary and funding purposes.

- **Nonprofit organization:** Any organization (including a community development corporation) exempt from taxation under section 501(a) of the Internal Revenue Code of 1986 by reason of paragraph (3) or (4).

- **Project period:** The total time a project is approved for support, including any extensions.

- **Third party:** Any individual, organization, or business entity that is not the direct recipient of grant funds but will subcontract with the grantee to carry out specified activities in the plan of operation. For example, the Montana Wildebeest Protection Agency (MWPA) applies for a federal grant. They are the grant applicant, therefore the direct recipient of grant funds. However, in order to carry out the proposed project, the MWPA will subcontract with the local U.S. Forestry Division to provide animal tagging services. The U.S. Forestry Division is considered a third party by the funder.

- **Third party agreement:** A written agreement entered into by the grantee and an organization, individual, or business entity (including a wholly-owned subsidiary), by which the grantee makes an equity investment or a loan in support of grant purposes.

- **Third party in-kind contributions:** Noncash contributions provided by nonfederal third parties which may be in the form of real property, equipment, supplies, and other expendable property.

Every government program, both federal and state, has its own specific terms and definitions. These are published in the grant application guidelines.

The government provides its own definition of the terms found in the purpose section of the "Legislative Authority" and throughout the grant application guidelines to guide you in writing your grant application. Use the same terms as those published in the announcement. By using the government's terms and its definitions, you meet the basic requirement of the review criteria — you show that you understand the language the feds are using.

Calculating money and chances

Before you decide to apply for a federal grant, quickly cruise through the grant announcement and check out the number of grants that will be awarded and the size of an average grant award. The odds are right when the number of grants awarded is 10 or higher and the average award is $100,000 or more.

Gathering eggs for your grant basket

Some funding guidelines give favorable consideration to applications that can get cash or in-kind (noncash) contributions from other organizations — your agency's partners.

Two types of partners exist: *community* and *collaborative.* Community partners are usually nonprofit organizations or businesses that you work with on a regular basis to provide services to your constituency. Collaborative partners are local, state, or regional agencies that can bring their resources to the table to help your organization better deliver the services the grant is funding.

When looking for a partner, look for an agency that already serves all or part of your target population. If you're trying to secure funding for an adult literacy program, an environmental group may not be a good partner. An agency that focuses on retraining low-skilled, adult workers may be perfect, and offer an in-kind gift of classrooms, computers, books, or other services.

Don't limit yourself to just one partner — the more, the better.

Before you meet with a prospective partner, prepare a fact sheet on the grant program's purpose and goals. Fax or mail a copy to each agency you plan to invite onto your team. This way, even before you meet face-to-face, the other agency can start thinking of ideas and ways to collaborate with your organization.

At your first meeting, ask for one or both of the following:

- ✔ **Cash-match monies:** A commitment of actual cash in the form of a grant toward your proposed program's expenses.

- ✔ **In-kind contributions:** Donated personnel, office space, training space, transportation assistance, supplies, materials, printing services for classroom training use, and other needed items.

If you receive a commitment for cash or in-kind contributions before you even write your grant application, you've already chalked up points with reviewers. In the eyes of those who get to hand out the money, you will have a huge advantage over any grant-seeking organization without partners.

The existence of your benefactors must be documented in the form of written letters of commitment. Start collecting the required documentation before you start writing the grant application. Sometimes, even the best of community partners drag their feet and procrastinate. Ask for letters of commitment upfront, as soon as you decide to write the grant application. Make sure that the letters describe the value of what is being committed. Happy letters of support — with no real financial commitment — will not cut the mustard with the review board.

Some grant competitions call for written, signed agreements from any community partners and from the state job training agency. Meet early with your partners and with the designated state agency. Get all details of any written agreements decided on early in the planning process.

I've been around grant writing enough to know that time is always tight — no matter how far ahead of time you start writing the grant. Scrambling at the last second to get letters of commitment isn't a good way to spend that precious time when the grant is almost due. And if the letters don't come in on time? Goodbye, grant. Getting the letters early in the process is always a good idea.

Gathering Research for Your Request

The first step in gathering research is to carefully look at the grant application. Determine what the federal government is trying to accomplish by making the money available. Make note of any geographic restrictions. Notice any extensive language on the target population (the group the grant monies are designated to be used on).

Knowing the grant's intent or focus sets the direction for the type of research you must do in order to write a high-scoring competitive grant application. Using the public library and the Internet, you can get a jumpstart on your grant application by searching for existing model programs in the area of the grant competition. Remember, there's a ton of stuff out there, you just need to decide which programs look like the kind you want to propose in your grant application.

Start researching the target population's demographics in your state and region — those counties or parishes that make up your Metropolitan Statistical Area (MSA). Call state and local agencies that provide services to the targeted groups and ask for reports with demographics on this target population.

Identifying Other Players and Bringing Them in Early

Writing a federal grant requires making new friends in your community — not just community partners, but also community specialists, like evaluators. (I talk about the evaluation process in Chapter 15.) You can always score higher review points by using an outside evaluator.

Look around the community for retired college or university faculty. Often they've participated in the grant writing process and have even helped their development office design evaluations. Look for retired government personnel who have worked in an administrative capacity in a finance department. In some communities, there are evaluation consultants — people with years of experience just in the field of evaluation. Try calling your local community foundation. Often they use evaluation specialists to assist in evaluating their programs.

Going online to do a search on the Internet is also helpful, but you may not locate an evaluator close to home. If you use an evaluator who doesn't live in your city or town, that's okay — as long as he or she is familiar with the area.

Although foundation and corporate funding sources prefer a *stakeholders evaluation* (local end-users of your service or program form the evaluating team), the majority of government funders require a third-party evaluator. This is basically a person or organization that can operate in an objective mode and give you factual, nonemotional feedback on your grant-funded goals and objectives. Remember, look for the ideal evaluator — someone that has expertise in nonprofits like yours, and someone who has done this type of evaluation before and has a track record.

Making Sure You're Eligible

Most federal grant programs award extra review points if you're located in a federally designated area, such as an empowerment zone or an enterprise community. In some grant competitions, you can't even apply unless you're located in one of these special areas. So determine whether you're in an empowerment zone, enterprise community, or colonias area. Start collecting proof to support your federal community designation status early, and keep it in a file for future grant writing opportunities. You can find out whether your community has a special designation by contacting the mayor's office, the county economic development office, or by logging on to the U.S. Department of Housing and Urban Development's Web site.

Another important thing to keep in mind is that you propose a cost-effective program. The government defines *cost-effective* as when your cost to serve each program participant is less than the maximum allowed cost-per-participant. This number is calculated by dividing the number of persons your program will serve into the total amount of federal funds requested. The number must be at or under the maximum allowable federal amount.

Making Contact at the State Level

If you're in a state that requires notification to the *Single Point of Contact* (SPOC), meaning a designated state agency that you're required to notify in advance of your intent to apply for federal grant funds, then you should contact the agency as soon as you realize that you're going for the grant. Some SPOCs want only a letter with the name of the grant competition, the amount you're applying for, an *abstract* (an overview of your project), and the CFDA (Catalog of Federal and Domestic Assistance) number.

Each federal program is assigned a CFDA number. It's an important tracking number for all federal grant applications. Chapter 2 guides you through the CFDA funding search for federal grant funds. You can find updated listings of the SPOCs in the *Catalogue of Federal Domestic Assistance*.

States and U.S. territories that do not have Single Points of Contact are Alabama, Alaska, American Samoa, Colorado, Connecticut, Hawaii, Idaho, Kansas, Louisiana, Massachusetts, Minnesota, Montana, Nebraska, New Jersey, Ohio, Oklahoma, Oregon, Palau, Pennsylvania, South Dakota, Tennessee, Vermont, Virginia, and Washington. In these states, you do not need to notify anyone of your intention to apply for a grant.

Chapter 8

Writing to Meet the Review Criteria of Government Grants

- -

In This Chapter

▶ Understanding how your federal grant application is rated

▶ Following the guidelines to meet pre-review criteria

▶ Competitively responding to the review criteria

▶ Finding resources to aid you at all levels of grant writing

- -

Writing to meet the grant application's review criteria is as important as identifying the right funding source and preparing to meet the review criteria for government grants. A request for applications has already been published in the *Federal Register* (which can be read daily on the Web, through any government publication gateway) and you've completed the planning and research phase. Chapter 7 covers your preparations; this chapter details the writing process based on standard federal review criteria.

The basics of review criteria apply to all types of grant guidelines: federal, state, foundation, and corporate. Since the federal guidelines are the most rigid, I use them as my example. Remember: When you can write federal grants, you can write anything!

Passing the Pre-Review Process

Applications that pass the *pre-rating review* (or simply *pre-review*) are assessed and scored by reviewers. The pre-rating review includes checking to see if you've filled in all of the required forms and signed them. The pre-review process also checks your page length for the narrative (many federal and state grants have restrictions, such as being limited to 20 double-spaced pages). If you fail to follow directions, your application could get rejected for failing to pass the pre-review process.

Read and reread the formatting criteria. It can make or break your application.

This is an example of the type of criteria you see in a grant announcement. Checking to see that you follow the criteria is a part of the pre-review elimination process.

> A program narrative, not to exceed 25 pages (excluding forms, assurances, and appendices) must be submitted on 8½- by 11-inch paper, double spaced on one side of the paper in a standard 12-point font. The one-page project abstract must also be submitted on 8½- by 11-inch paper, double-spaced on one side of the paper in a standard 12-point font. These standards are necessary to maintain fair and uniform standards among all applicants. If the narrative does not conform to these standards, OJJDP (Office of Juvenile Justice and Delinquency Prevention) will deem the application ineligible for consideration.

Understanding the Peer Review Process

Once you've passed the pre-review, your application is given to a peer review panel. This panel usually includes three experts from around the country who work in the field that the grant competition is directed to. It's called *peer review* because you're accepted or rejected by your peers, not by a federal or state program officer. Each reviewer gives a numerical score to each application reviewed. These numerical scores are supported by explanatory statements on a formal rating form describing major strengths and weaknesses under each applicable criterion published in the *Federal Register* announcement. Scoring is based on a total of 100 points.

I can see you waving your hand, about to ask, "How many pages do I have to write?" As a general guide, plan to write one page for every five review points assigned to each narrative section.

Normally, your grant application needs to score 92 points or above to make the cut between being recommended for a grant award and being rejected based on low scores from the three reviewers.

You may be asking what happens when two of the grant reviewers rate you high (92 or above) and the third reviewer rates you below the cutoff score for an award. Well, once each reviewer independently scores your application, they get together (over the telephone or in person) and discuss and defend their score. The normal rule is that all three reviewers have to come within ten points of each other; often, after discussion, points change, sometimes in your favor and sometimes not.

Getting approved — but not funded

Being approved for funding is the easy part for some grant seekers. Actually getting the money once you've been approved, in some rare instances, is a feat in itself.

Sometimes the federal government publishes grant competitions in the *Federal Register* and calls for proposals — *before the funding has been approved by Congress.*

You've gone to all the trouble to put a federal grant application together; it moves into the review stage and actually scores well; but the letter you get says you were *approved* but *not funded.* You weren't funded because there aren't any funds! When this happens, call your elected officials in Washington and scream, holler, and jump up and down. It actually helps to have a congressional advocate on your side. Sometimes, the bill that will authorize the expenditure is still working its way through Congress. In other cases, you're straight out of luck.

The length of time from the moment you submit your grant application for funding consideration to the time you receive notification of funding could range from three months to six months, depending on the program and the number of grant applications it received.

Reading and Writing the Federal Way

Read the grant application's guidelines! Now, read them again. I usually read them three times. The first time to check for due-dates, number of awards, average size of grants, and eligible applicant (is my organization eligible to apply for this grant?). The second is to look at the technical requirements. By *technical requirements,* I mean whether the grant competition requires that you submit your grant application earlier than the due date to a state agency for pre-approval. This could mean moving up your writing timeline in order to get your application signed off on at the state level — before you can mail it to Washington, D.C. The third time, I read for narrative content requirements. I walk you through the narrative content requirements so that you can understand what I look for in content requirements. (These same steps apply to state grant applications.)

Addressing the program goal for funding

Your must address the goal of the federal funding in every section of the grant application. The federal program goal must also be your program's goal if you're going to write a winning grant application for this competition.

Using federal or state announcement language to your benefit

The objectives of the federal program are what you write about in your grant application narrative. For every objective in the grant announcement, you write narrative in the needs section or problem statement and in the project design section to meet each of the program's objectives.

The program objectives in the grant guidelines are like a big finger pointing in the direction that you need to write in order to win a grant award. The objectives shout to you, "Write me, write me."

Every narrative section has assigned review points. The point total is usually 100. Sometimes extra points are assigned for your location, your target population (whom the grant will benefit), or for cost effectiveness. When you calculate the number of pages required in each section required to meet the review criteria, a good rule that I use (and state elsewhere in this chapter) is to assign one writing page to every five review points.

Pushing the point for your needs

The first section in federal or state grant narratives is usually the problem to be addressed. Normally, this section is worth about 20 of the 100 points. Write about the problem in your community that the project you propose is going to address.

This is the time to not only write about your own research findings on the target population, but to bring in facts and figures from regional and national research. See Chapter 7 for more information on how to gather all the information you need before you start to write.

Write about every problem you can unearth. Don't talk in generalities here, use facts, statistics, quotes, and citations. Cite all of your sources and stay current; don't cite anything over five years old. Show that you know what you're talking about. To win all of the points allocated to this section, you write four pages about the following areas:

- The results of a community needs assessments. Build a large black hole of gloom and doom.
- The current lack of services or programs in your area.

You're not exaggerating, you're simply writing to meet the review criteria and you're addressing each point in the program's objectives. You will end up with one paragraph to describe each service that's lacking in your area.

Aiming for a strike with goals and objectives

The second section in most federal and state grant applications usually asks for goals and objectives. This section is often given the same review criteria ranking as the problem or needs statement: 20 points. Write goals and objectives that reflect those of the federal or state program's goals and objectives. Give the government agency reviewers back the same language they've seen in the application announcement and in the guidelines for grant review criteria.

Always write measurable objectives that state who will be impacted, where they will be impacted, at what rate (in a percent), and by when (timeframe). The timeframe language is optional in the objectives only when the grant application guidelines ask for a separate timeline section.

Project design — in words that look familiar

A federal or state grant application should contain a lot of words and phrases that you cull from the grant application guidelines. Plan on using these terms in almost every section of your grant narrative.

The third section in the narrative is usually about the project design, often called the plan of operation. It's usually weighted at 20 or 25 points in the review criteria. The project design must be sound and contain program elements directly linked to the achievement of project objectives. Therefore you write with the federal or state program's objectives language. This is the section in which you try to have a written conversation with the grant reviewers.

Evaluating your objectives

Most federal and state grant announcements mandate a separate section for the evaluation plan. If you find an application that doesn't have a section for the evaluation plan, you must be quick on the computer keys and close out the project design section with your evaluation plan.

Sound evaluation plans are essential to winning big review points. In writing about the evaluation of your project, you explain how you propose to answer the key questions about how effectively the project was implemented. The key questions are

✔ Whether the project activities, or *interventions,* achieved the expected outcomes, and why or why not (this is called a *process evaluation*)

✔ Whether and to what extent the project achieved its stated goals, and why or why not (this is called an *outcome evaluation*)

Together, the process and outcome evaluations should answer the question: "What did this program accomplish and why did it work — or not work?"

You also write about how you will document and report your project's activities and the project's effectiveness and the planned frequency of your reporting. I like to see an interim evaluation (every six months during the grant period) and a final evaluation (upon completion of the grant period) progress report.

If you brought in your third party evaluator in the planning stages for this project, she is now on board and is a member of the grant writing team. The evaluator can write this entire section. Plan on spending some of your agency's dollars to secure her ahead of time. Remember that you want all the points in this section, so don't be a miser.

Showing that you're capable

This fourth section in your grant narrative usually carries the same weight as the problem or needs statement. It's the project management and overall organizational capability section. Write about your capacity to successfully operate and support the federally funded grant project.

You cite the organization's capability and relevant experience in developing and operating programs that deal with problems similar to those addressed by the proposed project. You also cite the organization's experience in operating programs in cooperation with other community organizations. You identify agency executive leadership in this section and briefly describe their involvement in the proposed project and provide assurance of their commitment to its successful implementation.

Keep in mind that all key personnel (the persons responsible for the project's implementation) should have had extensive experience in programs like the one you're proposing. You will score more points if you can name actual staff instead of relying on the standard "yet-to-be hired" statement. **Note:** You need to have the third party evaluator identified upfront; be ready to include a full resume in your appendices, if requested.

If grant guidelines state to include complete information on each key person and the evaluator, then be prepared to reduce your resume content to one-half page per person. Give the most space to the project director and the evaluator. As a federal reviewer, these individuals' credentials are what I look at first in the key personnel section. Does the person in charge have the credentials, experience, and the administrative authority to effectively carry out the grant-funded program? Is the evaluator a third party independent person (or organization) and does she have experience in evaluating programs similar to the grant-funded program?

Include documentation that briefly summarizes similar projects undertaken by your organization and the extent to which your objectives were achieved. You also note and justify the priority that this project will have within your organization, including the facilities and resources that are available to carry out the project.

Even losing one or two points in this section can hurt you when the total score is tallied.

Connecting numbers to words

Your budget forms and detailed narrative must show the grant reviewer that your costs are reasonable, allowable, and are worth the activities that are proposed. This section is usually worth the remaining review criteria points.

In most federal grant competitions, you are asked to provide a detailed budget worksheet with the budget narrative for each year of the project period, including the basis for computation of all costs.

Add your budget and add it again. Make sure each expense is directly related to an activity that's necessary to reach the project's objectives. Introduce no new costs here that you have not written about throughout your narrative.

When you read the guidelines for preparing the budget, look closely for any language about construction costs. Most federal grants will not cover new construction, but will allow program-related renovations.

When in doubt, call the federal program officer and ask. The more you call, the better. These calls — even if they seem trivial — can establish a relationship that could be beneficial to your grant getting funded.

Close this final section with a quotation that reaches into the federal reviewer's heart and mind and leaves a lasting impression.

Getting Help from the Feds to Score Higher

Most federal agencies produce publications. These valuable resources can help you write all types of grant applications: federal, state, foundation, and corporate. These items can be obtained from each federal department's information clearinghouse. Check out the department's Web sites for a link labeled "Resources" or "Publications." You may encounter any of the following terms:

- ✔ **Bulletins:** Bulletins summarize recent findings from federal program initiatives. Bulletins, which may contain graphic elements such as tables, charts, graphs, and photographs, are designed for use as references.

- ✔ **Fact sheets:** Fact sheets are one- or two-page documents that highlight key points and sources of further information on federal programs and initiatives.

- ✔ **Journals:** Some federal departments publish journals highlighting innovative programs and publications on critical issues and trends.

- ✔ **Reports:** These publications contain comprehensive research and evaluation findings; provide detailed descriptions of innovative programs implemented at the national, state, and local levels, including case studies, field studies, and other strategies used for assessing program success and replication; or present statistical analysis, trends, or other data on selected topics. Some reports provide training curriculums and lesson plans.

- ✔ **Summaries:** These publications describe key research and evaluation findings that may be used to enhance future policies and practices and highlight funded programs implemented at the national, state, or local levels that may serve as models for other jurisdictions. Summaries are generally 30 to 90 pages in length and usually include appendices and lists of resources and additional readings.

I stock up on every print publication I can get my hands on. Grant writing is so easy when you have information at your fingertips.

Chapter 9

Words that Work and Win Grant Funds

In This Chapter

▶ Using the right terms

▶ Cruising with combinations of words

▶ Bringing your scenario to life

*Y*ou've come a long way, baby — now it's time to *write* the right way! Write each section of the application using direct language. Support your statements with facts. Convey who you are, why you deserve the funds, and what you'll do with the funds if you get them.

This chapter gives you the words that work to win grant funds. Some of these words are old standards; some are merely playful. But every word is selected to catch the attention of the grant reviewer — you know, that guy who decides if your grant will be recommended for funding.

Doing the "You" Stuff Right

The opening section of your request for funding is all about you. The focus is on the problem *you* want to solve, where *you* are located, what *you've* done as an organization, and what *you're* doing now. This section is a key ingredient of your winning grant recipe.

The examples that follow are excerpted from well-written content about the applicant — from real applications that won real funding. The names and places have been changed to protect the privacy of the winners, and I've added my comments to explain why these examples are so effective.

Winning example: Application from a religious organization

We've been **talking about it** for a long time, the newspapers have been **writing about it**, and now it's time to **actively do something about it.**

The bolded words are an example of the *groups of three* tactic. The words that stick in our minds forever usually come in groups of three. For example: baseball, apple pie, and Chevrolet; reading, writing, and arithmetic; and red, white, and blue. Research shows that groups of three are effective in getting your audience to remember an important point. In this case, the grant reviewer has been given a rhythm of words that will be imbedded in her mind. It works!

To continue the example I began above . . .

What is it? Discerning and **building on strengths** of the adolescent and young adult generation.

The bold strongly suggests that the organization isn't begging for grant monies with both hands out, but has some resources or strengths already in place to build on — a very good situation to be in. The grant reviewer is more likely to bestow review points on an organization that already has some assets — not just cobwebs — in its corner.

Who fits into this category? Young teens, ages 12 to 15: They are **unsure** of themselves, are **seeking** their identity, and are **looking** to their peers for answers.

The bold are three key terms calling out to the grant reviewer. This group of three whispers: "Needy, needy, needy."

They may have already experimented with a gateway drug **seeking a way to escape** the dilemmas of the early teen years.

The bold is a powerful term that you can use in your grant applications to describe any isolated class of people. It moves the grant reviewer to a new level of emotion. She's not just reading dry text with facts and statistics. Emotion is what's needed to generate higher review points and the beginning of the recommendation for funding.

They want to take risks, but **seek safety** on the path of self-exploration.

The bold is definitely an empathy-and-sympathy phrase. It gently implores. The phrase can evoke tears or memories from one's childhood. Either way, the grant reviewer begins to identify with the need for your program.

Winning example: Special training grant request

Problem statement: Problems and needs to be addressed

The setting of the problem is Adams County in southwest Mississippi. The county is a retail and service center in the heart of the pine forest region. Wesley Center, the county seat, is on Interstate 55 just 50 miles south of Jackson, 140 miles north of New Orleans, and 60 miles from Natchez. U.S. Highways 43 and 59 intersect in Adams County, and a mainline of the Illinois Central Gulf Railroad runs north-south through the county. The communities of Morency, Albert, Brooke, Chilton, Union Courage, Crinshaw, Henryville, Mattney, Summerton, and other small towns are in close proximity to Wesley Center and depend on the county seat for their retail needs as well as human and social service needs.

Painting a written picture of where the problem is located, geographically, is especially important to potential funders not located in or near your community.

History and major accomplishments

The United Action of Adams County is an efficient, financially sound IRS-designated 501(c)(3) nonprofit organization. Founded in 1960, our agency has always met each annual campaign goal with pride. The 1995/96 campaign goal of $148,000 has been met. Annually, over 100 volunteers work diligently to ensure that the funds are raised. The budget is disbursed to the 23 local agencies that we support.

All funding sources want to see volunteer involvement. It's a highly favorable grant writing tool of the past, present, and future.

Knowing the Important Steps to Remember When Talking about Yourself

I can offer you three steps and my personal guarantee that if you follow them with a *passion* you will dance a virtual *tango* of a personal story.

Step 1: Who and where

Tell them who you are and where you are — with passion and flavor. Are any of these examples *you?*

Gently nestled . . .

Snuggly tucked away . . .

Immersed and surrounded by . . .

A place in rural America that resembles Walton's mountain, but is more like a fury unleashed — a small town full of anger, crime, and indifference . . .

Located less than 50 miles from a major metropolitan area, yet so isolated from the resources needed to keep our community thriving and alive — economically and socially . . .

Organized to bring about a community-wide change . . .

Incorporated for the purpose of creating a metamorphic difference for humankind . . .

Don't think that these phrases are too flowery. When you're asking for money, pull out all the tricks. In this case, the tricks are those words that get your grants funded each and every time.

Step 2: The bad stuff

Present the problem as if your organization is holding the gloom, doom, trauma, and drama of the world in its hand and is extending that hand upward for grant support.

You can really bring in the bucks with deft use of words like those in the following list. Use them to make your sentences memorable to the grant reviewer as he learns about you.

Abandoned, abominable, abruptly, abscess, agonize, alleviate, asphyxiate, avoid, and awe.

Backslide, badly, bankrupt, barbaric, bare, barely, battery, because, become, beforehand, beleaguer, benign, blatant, borderline, and brim.

Cancel, capture, cast, categorical, cessation, cesspool, circumvent, citizenry, clear-cut, climax, closed-minded, colossal, commitment, commonplace, compulsion, consequence, contradictory, and corrupt.

Damage, dangerous, debilitate, decrease, deep-seated, difference, dire, disaster, disarray, dismay, dispel, doubt, downtrodden, and dwindle.

Earmark, ebb, economically, embrace, emit, enact, enable, entirety, entrust, environment, equivalent, erupt, essential, eventual, evoke, excessive, exhaust, and explode.

These are strong action words that also carry with them the definite flavor of emotion. Use them to create strong sentences that say, "We really need this funding."

Face, facilitate, fail, fared, fateful, fearful, firsthand, force, foremost, frequently, futile, and future (the lack of).

Gang, gauge, generate, genesis, glaring, glimpse, glimmer, global, glut, graphic, grapple, grim, and guilty.

Habitual, halfhearted, halfway, halt, harbor, hardened, harmful, hasten, headlong, heartbreaking, hesitant, hinder, holdover, and hurtful.

Identify, ideology, idle, ignorance, ill-adapted, illiterate, illusion, image, immediate, imminent, immune, impair, impasse, impatient, impede, imperative, impossible, ineffective, infest, intent, and issue.

Jaded, journey, judge, junction, just, justifiable, justify, and juvenile.

Keeper, kick, kindness, kindred, and knifelike.

Laborious, lacerated, lack, languish, lapse, leaving, lessen, lethargic, liable, lifelong, listless, longing, looming, losing, lower, and lull.

Strong words give you the winning edge every time. Grant reviewers see so many grants that you need to use strong language to make yours stick out.

Magnetic, magnitude, mainstay, major, malcontent, manifest, massive, material (noun), meaningless, measureless, methodical, midst, milieu, mimic, minimal, mirror, misbelieve, mitigate, mobile, monumental, motionless, and mythical.

Naive, narrow, nearly, necessary, needful, neglect, never, nip, nonfunctional, and numb.

Obligation, obscure, obstruction, occurrence, offensive, olden, once, only, opposed, opposite, outcast, outmoded, overage, and oversight.

Pacify, pain, pale, paralyze, past, penetrate, perplex, plunge, poor, potential, poverty, poverty-stricken, powerless, primitive, priority, probable, and proximity.

Qualify, quest, questionable, quit, and quota.

Radical, radius, random, rank, range, rash (adjective), realistic, recover, reflection, regardless, relate, relieve, remedial, remote, replace, require, resolve, restore, restrict, reverse, revive, ruin, rupture, and run-of-the-mill.

Just writing the way you normally talk doesn't work in creating a winning grant request. You need to start collecting new words like these for your treasure chest of terms.

Sabotage, sacred, saddened, salvage, scarce, secluded, senseless, separate, serious, severe, shock, shortcoming, shortsighted, significant, similarity, situation, sluggish, society, somber, spectrum, spiritless, standard, status, and stigma.

Taboo, tangible, temporary, tend, tenure, term, terrible, threadbare, threaten, throughout, thrust, totality, tough, towering, trace, track, transitional, transparent, turbulent, typical, and typify.

Ulterior, ultimate, unacceptable, unaware, unbending, uncalled, uncommon, uncontrollable, undergo, undo, unknowing, unnecessary, useless, usually, and utopia.

Vacant, valid, vandalize, variable, vast, very, viable, violent, vision (the lack of), volatile, and vortex.

Want, warn, wary, waste, weaken, weigh, whelm, whimsical, will-less, wiped out, withhold, without, woeful, worry, worthless, and wrong.

Yearn, yesteryear, yield, and youthhood.

Zero and zone.

Don't underestimate the power of the written word.

Step 3: Use a thesaurus

Don't be shy about using a thesaurus to bring your thoughts to life in a way that conveys *need*. Keep a thesaurus on your desk to help you select words that work when writing about your organization and the problems it's faced with.

Doing the Request Stuff Right

When you write the request section of your grant application, remember that it's about what you want to do with the grant monies. The request section includes a description of your program, goals, objectives, activities, and a timeline for implementation. It also talks about whom you serve, partnerships with other agencies in your community, and the change you're seeking to make. The request is the big event, so weigh every word. Make your sentences work together like magic. Here are excerpts from a winning grant application that requested funds for a health care facility.

> CAHC realizes that the grant amount needed is extremely large for one funding source alone; therefore we are submitting this proposal to multiple foundations and corporations that have demonstrated previous grant support for health care organizations.

All funders want you to spread the burden of your program's costs between several funding sources. No one funder wants to receive the only grant request. The grant reviewer needs to know that you understand the rules of grant seeking, and trying to spread the cost is one of them. If you do know the rules, that works favorably in the funder's decision making process.

> Goals for implementing **grant-funded changes** in the seven-county service area:

The bolded language implies to the grant reviewer that the grant monies will make a difference!

*Provide a **continuum of comprehensive and intensive** medical, nursing, and therapeutic services in a supportive and **cost-effective environment**.

All funders want you to design a cost-effective program. Cost-effectiveness means that their monies won't be wasted or poorly allocated. Also, learn to use big, bold, sweeping language when you write about your proposed program.

*Develop and maintain adequate **financial stability** to meet current and future needs of the CAHC **systemwide strategic improvement plan**.

The first bolded phrase is another "we have our act together" phrase that tips the scales in your favor — toward a funding recommendation. The second bolded phrase emits the message that your organization isn't just looking for some first aid, but wants to truly change its practices in and out and is looking ahead. Look out, here come more review points!

*Create programs to support day-to-day holistic living, wellness, and disease **prevention**.

Direct and to the point. Grant funds will make a difference. The grant reviewer will not overlook the bolded word.

*Develop formal and informal health education resources for **learners of all ages**.

The bolded are words for this millennium. They let the reader know that you're up-to-date and comfortable with the idea of lifelong learning. They're strong and powerful words that grant reviewers want to see and bestow points upon.

*Provide medical and nursing staff with staff development opportunities on an ongoing basis to keep them abreast of the changes in their respective fields and to renew their dedication to a high quality of care for CAHC's constituency.

This statement is packed with words (*abreast, changes, respective, renew, dedication, quality,* and *constituency*) that help your grant reviewer to envision the same successful project that you've got in your mind. A blank check may be coming your way!

In most of my writing, I use tables to capture key points and to also give the grant reviewer a break from reading straight narrative language. Refer to Figure 9-1 for an example. It's another excerpt from the health care example. It shows you how to word your objectives to capture the reader's attention — and win the grant.

Measurable Objective	One-Year Progress			
Quarterly Benchmarks	1	2	3	4
Expand capacity for surgical diagnostic procedures by 10 percent or more.	■	■	■	
Improve mental health treatment capabilities by 50 percent or more.	■	■	■	■
Replace 100 percent of the furnishings used by residents in the long-term care/nursing home unit.	■	■		
Upgrade 75 percent or more of the equipment at the Burnsville Family Practice Clinic.			■	■
Increase the hospital's self-sufficiency and constituency outreach capacity by 50 percent or more in the area of Environmental Services.				■
Improve Quality Services by 25 percent or more.	■	■	■	■
Replace 14 percent of the beds in acute care with new, more functional beds.	■			
Renew hope and support vigor among 100 percent of the nursing home's residents through new recreational therapy approaches.	■	■	■	■
Provide free community wellness screenings to 50 percent or more of low-income residents seeking Laboratory Services.	■	■	■	■
Increase staff morale by 75 percent or more with Staff Recharging conference and Employee Recognition Program.				■
Create Guide to Guest Services Directory for 100 percent of the patient rooms.			■	■
Expand the Community Health Education Program by 75 percent or more.	■	■	■	■

Figure 9-1: Showing when work occurs on each objective over a one-year period.

Focus on positive, measurable progressions for the attainment of the grant's objectives. Doing so tells the grant reviewer that every dollar requested will have a direct impact on the improvement of your program.

Here are some important points to remember when talking about your request:

- ✔ Describe your program with facts, statistics, emotion, and gusto by using power-packed words. Use words like: *overall, establish, cooperative, expanding, enhancing, existing, strategies,* and *achieve.* They point to taking action.

- ✔ Present your goals in visionary terms and your objectives in measurable terms. Use words like: *develop, deliver, establish, provide, increase, decrease, improve,* and *produce.* They point to meeting a level of performance.

- ✔ Don't beat around the bush about future funding. Use words and phrases like: *external, internal, local fundraising, creating future funding partners, inviting more external funding sources to the organization's table of partners,* and *seeking to identify more investors in our stakeholders.* These words don't just point, they rocket off of the page and say, "We're planning for the future of this organization and we're asking for your help."

Part III

Putting Together Your Grant Application

The 5th Wave   By Rich Tennant

"No, I don't think including a lock of your hair is the right way to personalize your cover letter."

In this part . . .

Y ou're ready to start assembling the information needed to put a grant application together. When is it appropriate to write a cover letter? What type of funder needs a cover form? Who really needs an abstract? Where does the table of contents go? How is the organization introduced to the funder? Why is the needs statement so important? What is the plan for using grant funds? Who will be responsible for carrying out the day-to-day activities for the grant-funded program? How is the project's budget developed and where does it go in the grant application? This part answers these driving questions and shows you how to lay out the grant cards, the order to put them in, and how to play a winning grant game.

Chapter 10

Fashioning the Little Essentials: Cover Letters, Abstracts, and Such

. . . .

In This Chapter

▶ Attending to the opening courtesies

▶ Forming the picture of your project

▶ Filling in the blanks on cover sheets

▶ Creating a menu of the ingredients

. . . .

*P*icture a table covered in crisp white linen, gleaming silverware arranged in military ranks left and right (let's see, do I start with the outside fork and work in or vice versa?) and the water glass and the bread plate and the leather-bound menu as big as the Sunday paper.

In a seven-course meal at a five-star restaurant, some important introductory matters always precede the presentation of the entrée. In this case, your delectable and critically acclaimed narrative is the entrée. At the restaurant, the introductory matters may include the wine presentation and sumptuous appetizers that whet the appetite. In a grant application, the introductory matters, like a table of contents and a cover letter, also must whet the appetite — of the grant reader.

You think I'm overstating the importance of these parts of a grant request? Only a little. The way you introduce your grant application or proposal is just as important as the narrative you create. Knowing when to add a cover letter or how to fill out foundation and federal cover forms correctly, when to use an abstract or executive summary, and where to place the table of contents will keep you feeling absolutely secure as you place your order — oops, I'm still in the restaurant — as you make your request for funds.

With so many types of grant applications, trying to determine what goes where can be confusing. I explain it all for you in this chapter. By order of appearance, the up-front stuff (items that come before the grant application narrative) should be the following. Note that not all of the pieces apply in every case:

> ✔ Cover letter (only on foundation and corporate requests)
>
> ✔ Common Grant Application form (only on foundation and corporate requests)
>
> ✔ Application for Federal Assistance (only on federal grant applications)
>
> ✔ Abstract (only on foundation and corporate requests for research projects)
>
> ✔ Executive summary (on federal grant applications, when requested in the guidelines, or on foundation grant applications when required by some regional grantmaking forums)
>
> ✔ Table of contents (only on federal and state grant applications)

Setting the Tone for Your Request with the Cover Letter

The cover letter should be reflective and from-the-heart, providing only a taste of what's to come in the grant request. The cover letter should *not* be simply a regurgitation of the abstract or executive summary. That's about as dumb as the hostess telling you about the lamb chops as she leads you to your seat — premature for sure.

When a funder opens your grant application or proposal package, the cover letter provides a first inkling of how well you understand the person you have addressed the letter to, the funder. Save the cover letter for last, after you've completed the entire grant application and when you're in a reflective mood.

Let the creative, right side of your brain kick in as you consider your great achievement (the finished grant application) and connect those feelings to the person who will help make your plans come true.

I use cover letters only on foundation and corporate requests, not on federal or state grant applications. Government funders want you to provide only the parts they ask for, and they rarely, if ever, ask for a cover letter. Foundations and corporations usually expect to see a cover letter. Figure 10-1 gives you a basic format, with my side notes for guidance.

Open with the contact person, title, funding source name, first address line, second address line, city, state, and zip. Remember to double check the address with an advance telephone call or e-mail to the funder.

Use the same date that the complete grant application will be sent to the funding source.

The Safe Place
2001 S. Hideaway Drive
Anywhere, USA 55555
(555-555-1212)

December 1, 2000

Make the first paragraph short and focused. The introductory statement should include your title and your organization's name and end with the action you request by the funding source.

Ms. Ellen Merryweather
Executive Director
Domestic Violence Prevention Foundation
2222 Many Oaks
Anywhere, USA 55555

Dear Ms. Merryweather,

As the Executive Director of The Safe Place, an emergency shelter for male victims of domestic violence, it is with urgency that I write to your foundation seeking seed funds for our same-gender group counseling program — the Male Moment.

Make the second paragraph a long three- to six-sentence statement explaining why your organization is targetting this funder for support.

Your foundation's mission statement, *Providing funding support for programs and services that demonstrate sensitivity and humaneness to the rights of all victims of domestic violence,* seems to have been written for our organization. The Safe Place is a unique type of domestic violence program that addresses the forgotten gender — males — who are undoubtedly included in your all-encompassing funding priorities. Our board of directors reviewed your annual report and grant-making guidelines and wholeheartedly felt that the Domestic Violence Prevention Foundation's ethical stance on the inclusion of both genders under the definition of *victim* would be a perfect fit to meet our needs.

Make the third and final paragraph a closing thought or reflection about what this funding partnership can mean for the future of your target audience.

Your partnership in funding the Male Moment is critically needed in order to expand our programming efforts in Anywhere. Abused males do not have to remain in a volatile situation. The Safe Place meets their need for shelter. Your grant award will ensure that their psychological needs are also met.

Use a standard closing, such as "Sincerely," or (my choice in this case) "With hope."

With hope,

Figure 10-1:
Showing the parts of a fully developed cover letter.

Sign your first name only; doing this invites an informal, long-term relationship. Type your full name, including middle initial.

Taylor (*signed in ink*)
Taylor I. M. Doingright

This indicates that there is a grant application in the same packet.

Enclosure

Use the letter in Figure 10-1 as a guide when you write your cover letter. Create compelling sentences that make the reader want to read more — just like a delicious appetizer at a restaurant makes you even more excited about the entrée. (Chapter 9 covers, in more detail, how to create exciting, vivid language.)

Creating the Common Grant Application Cover Form

The Common Grant Application (CGA) cover form comes from the National Network of Grantmakers (NNG) Web site at www.nng.org. The form follows the cover letter and provides an overview of organizational and project-related information. It is brief and to the point (take a look at Figure 10-2). Using this format to approach a foundation or corporate giving entity eliminates the need for an abstract or executive summary, unless the funding source specifically asks for one in their guidelines.

Not all foundations or corporate funders participate in the NNG; however, I have been using this form to approach any funding source that does not have its own application. The results have been terrific! It gives the right amount of critically needed information about you and your project. I've made some modifications to the form to accommodate mail merge fields and to make sure the right form is matched with the right cover letter.

The following information gives the funding source the straight and narrow information about your eligibility to apply for funds.

Note that most foundation and corporate funders only award one year of grant support at a time.

Seed money is defined as beginning monies to start a new program.

The word "summarize" is the key here. If you have a long mission statement, give the abbreviated version. Remember the entire grant application cover sheet must fit on one page.

Figure 10-2:
The Common Grant Application cover form.

Wait until you have written the grant application narrative. Then cut and paste the most effective sentences that summarize your project into this section.

GRANT APPLICATION COVER FORM

Submitted to: The Domestic Violence Prevention Foundation

Organization name: The Safe Place
Tax exempt status: 501(c)(3)   Year organization was founded: 1999
Date of application: December 1, 2000
Address: 2001 S. Hideaway Drive, Anywhere, USA 55555
Telephone number: (555) 555-1212   Fax number: (555) 555-1213
Director: Taylor I. M. Doingright
Contact person and title (if not director): Same as above

Grant request: $59,200   Period grant will cover: One year

The funding source wants to know how much money you're asking for before it even reads the full proposal. This grant request shows that you are only asking for a portion of the monies needed to implement your project. This is the first clue to the funder that you will look elsewhere for the balance of the monies needed.

Type of request: Seed money

Project title: The Male Moment
Total project budget: $76,900
Total organizational budget (current year): $236,000
Starting date of fiscal year: January 1

Summarize the organization's mission: The Safe Place is a safe haven for male victims of domestic violence in Anywhere (Hurtful County), USA. The Safe Place will open its doors and resources to adult males that are the target of physical violence from same gender or heterosexual partners. Unconditional acceptance and understanding for the victimized adult male is the sole focus of all services provided by The Safe Place.

Summary of project or grant request: The Male Moment is a new program that will offer group counseling to The Safe Place residents daily during their first 14 days in emergency status. Once our clients move into transitional group housing (another Safe Place program), they will continue to receive group counseling biweekly. Regardless of insurance and payment ability, no male will be turned away from The Safe Place.

There are no signatures on the NNG Common Grant Application Form. Instead, signatures appear on the cover letter.

Filling In Federal Cover Forms

All federal cover forms come with detailed instructions and are easy to quickly fill in. While the type of form varies from agency to agency, the standard form used is Form 424 — Application for Federal Assistance. Figure 10-3 shows you how to fill in this critical federal grant application cover form. If you'd like to see a blank form, flip to Chapter 3.

Figure 10-3: Form 424, the Application for Federal Assistance — filled in.

APPLICATION FOR FEDERAL ASSISTANCE

OMB Approval No. 0348-0043

2. DATE SUBMITTED 12/1/2000
Applicant Identifier

1. TYPE OF SUBMISSION:
Application
☐ Construction
☒ Non-Construction
Preapplication
☐ Construction
☐ Non-Construction

3. DATE RECEIVED BY STATE
State Application Identifier

4. DATE RECEIVED BY FEDERAL AGENCY
Federal Identifier

5. APPLICANT INFORMATION
Legal Name:
The Safe Place

Organizational Unit:
Anywhere Council of Churches

Address (give city, county, State, and zip code):
2001 S. Hideaway Drive (Hurtful), Anywhere, UR 55555

Name and telephone number of person to be contacted on matters involving this application (give area code)
Taylor I.M. Doingright (555) 555-1212

6. EMPLOYER IDENTIFICATION NUMBER (EIN):
5 5 - 5 5 5 5 5 5

7. TYPE OF APPLICANT: (enter appropriate letter in box) **N**

A. State
B. County
C. Municipal
D. Township
E. Interstate
F. Intermunicipal
G. Special District

H. Independent School Dist.
I. State Controlled Institution of Higher Learning
J. Private University
K. Indian Tribe
L. Individual
M. Profit Organization
N. Other (Specify) _501(c)(3) nonprofit_

8. TYPE OF APPLICATION:
☒ New   ☐ Continuation   ☐ Revision

If Revision, enter appropriate letter(s) in box(es) ☐ ☐

A. Increase Award   B. Decrease Award   C. Increase Duration
D. Decrease Duration   Other(specify):

9. NAME OF FEDERAL AGENCY:
U.S. Department of Housing and Urban Development

10. CATALOG OF FEDERAL DOMESTIC ASSISTANCE NUMBER: 0 0 - 0 0 0
TITLE: Transitional Housing

11. DESCRIPTIVE TITLE OF APPLICANT'S PROJECT:
His Place - A transitional housing program for male adults in need of safe communal quarters, psychosocial counseling, and societal re-entry.

12. AREAS AFFECTED BY PROJECT (Cities, Counties, States, etc.):
Anywhere (Hurtful County), UR

13. PROPOSED PROJECT
Start Date 10/1/2001   Ending Date 9/30/2002

14. CONGRESSIONAL DISTRICTS OF:
a. Applicant 99
b. Project 99

15. ESTIMATED FUNDING:

a. Federal	$	200,000
b. Applicant	$	50,000
c. State	$	.
d. Local	$	50,000
e. Other	$	.
f. Program Income	$	.
g. TOTAL	$	300,000

16. IS APPLICATION SUBJECT TO REVIEW BY STATE EXECUTIVE ORDER 12372 PROCESS?

a. YES. THIS PREAPPLICATION/APPLICATION WAS MADE AVAILABLE TO THE STATE EXECUTIVE ORDER 12372 PROCESS FOR REVIEW ON:
DATE 12/1/2000

b. No. ☐ PROGRAM IS NOT COVERED BY E. O. 12372
☐ OR PROGRAM HAS NOT BEEN SELECTED BY STATE FOR REVIEW

17. IS THE APPLICANT DELINQUENT ON ANY FEDERAL DEBT?
☐ Yes   If "Yes," attach an explanation.   ☒ No

18. TO THE BEST OF MY KNOWLEDGE AND BELIEF, ALL DATA IN THIS APPLICATION/PREAPPLICATION ARE TRUE AND CORRECT, THE DOCUMENT HAS BEEN DULY AUTHORIZED BY THE GOVERNING BODY OF THE APPLICANT AND THE APPLICANT WILL COMPLY WITH THE ATTACHED ASSURANCES IF THE ASSISTANCE IS AWARDED.

a. Type Name of Authorized Representative
Taylor I. M. Doingright
b. Title
Director
c. Telephone Number
(555) 555-1212

d. Signature of Authorized Representative
Taylor I.M. Doingright
e. Date Signed
12/1/2000

Previous Edition Usable
Authorized for Local Reproduction

Standard Form 424 (Rev. 7-97)
Prescribed by OMB Circular A-102

Writing the Abstract or Executive Summary

The abstract or executive summary is a brief, one-page overview of what the grant reviewer will find in the full grant application. Brevity is important, so this section is written (or assembled) after the grant application narrative has been entirely written. Keep in mind that all of this must fit on one page. You can create an abstract or executive summary by gleaning the most significant sentences from each key writing section in the grant narrative and doing a quick cut and paste (refer to Figure 10-4). You need to lift key sentences from the following areas and keep them in the same order in the abstract or executive summary that they are in the narrative:

- Proposed initiative
- Program design/plan of action
- Problem statement/statement of need
- Goals
- Measurable objectives
- Impact on problem

State the project's intent upfront.	**The Safe Place** **A Proposal to the U.S. Department of Housing and Urban Development** **Anywhere (Hurtful County), USA**
Tell what your organization does and where services are provided.	This project, intended for the Transitional Housing Supportive Services application area, represents a unique partnership between The Safe Place, the Hurtful County Human Services Agency, Regional Psychosocial Services, Inc. and the statewide Council of Churches network to create a comprehensive residential counseling and follow-up peer support group program for male victims of domestic violence in Hurtful County.
State how grant monies will be used and what these funds will do for the target population.	The Safe Place will use federal, local, and internal funds to develop the first comprehensive counseling support program intended for male victims in the United States at His Place. Group and one-on-one counseling venues will be implemented using mental health professionals and former residents who have transitioned successfully into more peaceful domestic relationships.
Sneak in a little gloom, doom, drama, and trauma (the problem/need).	Of this county's increasing numbers of adult males (28,000 based on police reports for one year) that are subjected to same gender and heterosexual incidences of domestic violence, 90 percent do not have any type of shelter or counseling program available to them. Being male and being a victim of domestic violence is something victims tend not to talk about and are rather ashamed of in our society.
Show how your proposed program will solve the problem.	His Place will demonstrate to the greater community of domestic violence service providers that male victims need to be recognized and receive supportive services in order to reduce household domestic violence incidents. His Place will be the site of the first pilot for male victim-directed psychosocial residential counseling. His Place will also be the first of its kind effectively delivering long-term follow-up mental, physical and social support services to male victims of domestic violence.
Squeeze in the funding period and the number of persons to be impacted.	Over the one year grant-funded period, 125 males will be impacted and a model counseling and supportive services program will have developed from a small-scale pilot into a fully replicable national model.

Figure 10-4:
The abstract or executive summary.

Where, Oh Where Is Everything?

Whether you include a table of contents depends on the grant application guidelines. Rigidly structured guidelines typically call for a table of contents, particularly if the narrative is long (more than ten pages) or if there are volumes of attachments or appendices.

The table of contents should not include the abstract or executive summary, since those parts almost always precede the table of contents. Exceptions to the rule are applications from state or federal agencies that stipulate a format placing the table of contents before the abstract or executive summary. Grant guidelines and writing formats vary from one agency to another and even within departments in an agency. Read the grant application guidelines and follow the same format listed in the reviewer's criteria. See Table 10-1 for an example.

Table 10-1   Federal Grant Application Table of Contents (Example)

The Safe Place

Table of Contents

Project Narrative Review Criteria Responses	Page(s)
Section 1 — Project Definition	1–3
Section 2 — Evaluation	3–4
Section 3 — Significance	4–5
Section 4 — Project Feasibility	5–6
Section 5 — Community Involvement	6–8
Section 6 — Reducing Disparities	8
Section 7 — Documentation and Dissemination	8
Appendices to the Project Narrative	
Appendix 1 — Psychosocial Counseling Research	9–14
Appendix 2 — Applicant Agency and Key Personnel Qualifications	15–26
Appendix 3 — Needs Assessment Results	27–31
Appendix 4 — Implementation Plan	32
Appendix 5 — Partnership Letters and Letters of Support	33–35
Other Required Forms and Documentation	
Standard Form 424A	N/A
Budget Narrative	424A-1 to 424A-10
Statement of Matching Funds	424A-11 to 424A-12
Negotiated Indirect Cost Rate Letter from the Anywhere Council of Churches	424A-13
Standard Form 424B — Assurances	N/A
Standard Form CD-511 — Certification	N/A

Note: Standard Form LLL, Disclosure of Lobbying Activities, is not applicable.

Note that

- Only the main sections of the grant application are listed.

- Appendices always are listed and numbered in a federal grant application.

- Federally mandated forms always are listed. This way the feds know you included them in the application. If one of these disappears during the review process, at least the grant reviewer can affirm that it was included in the original application.

Chapter 11

Putting the Spotlight on Your Organization

In This Chapter

▶ Introducing your organization to a funder

▶ Talking about where you've been and what you've done

▶ Sharing what you're doing now

▶ Presenting your constituency and describing your community

▶ Highlighting successful partnerships

*T*he opening narrative section of your grant application introduces your organization to the grant reviewer. When you write the opening words, keep in mind the way that people behave when they meet for the first time. The cordial thing to do is to engage in general chitchat about what you do for a living. Well, it's no different when you're introducing your organization on paper to the funding source — you have to cover the formalities of who, what, where, and how. (See Chapter 10 for what to put in the application prior to the narrative.)

In the first few sentences, share some basic information, like the year the organization was founded and the purpose of the organization today. Explain how the organization benefits the community in which it's located. Incorporate some demographics of the target population. Use colorful words to paint a graphic picture of your locale for the grant reader. Remember that this is the section that communicates who you are, where you are, and what you do as an organization.

A little trivia and a lot of facts create the kind of reader interest every successful grant writer hopes for with every project. The longer you can keep readers' attention, the better your chances are of getting recommended for a grant award.

When you're introducing your organization, be sure to divide the information into sections. Each step below is a subsection in the grant narrative under the *Organization Introduction* header:

- History and major accomplishments
- Current programs and activities
- Constituency demographics
- Work with local groups

I've included two full-length grant applications at the end of the book. Be sure to check them out before you write anything.

Explaining Your History and Accomplishments

Tell the grant reader, clearly and concisely, just enough information about your organization to pique her interest and keep her reading your narrative word-for-word. The suggested writing length for the history section is one-half page, single-spaced.

The grant reader wants to see:

- The year the organization was founded, by whom, and for what purpose.
- The location of the organization's headquarters and any other operating sites (name, city, county, state).
- The mission statement (use the abbreviated version).
- The organization's most important achievements that are related to the activities covered in the grant application.

If you're seeking, for example, grant funds for a new wing in a hospital, don't include nonrelated accomplishments — like the operating room nurses winning the 5K bed race on Founder's Day.

First, state the full legal name of your organization and its location (city, county, and state). Do your homework on why your organization is in existence. What group or individual founded it? Why, when, and for what purpose? If you don't know the answers to these questions, then ask a veteran employee or a long-time board member. Sometimes, the history of an organization is written up in its annual report or in an anniversary issue of its newsletter. Keep looking and asking until you strike gold. Complete this section by writing about important milestones in the organization's history.

Remember that you're just introducing yourself, and it's not polite to start right out talking about the money you need or the problems you have.

An organization's milestones may look something like this:

- ✔ Founded in 1976

- ✔ Opened first community youth center in 1978

- ✔ Celebrated International Youth Day with 20 other regional youth agencies in 1985

- ✔ Sponsored first Youth Exchange Month with sister city in Australia in 1990

- ✔ Received $500,000 grant to build new Eastside Youth Center in 1995

- ✔ Reached all-time high for number of youth served in a single year — 450 in 1999.

Even though your organization may have dozens of milestones, share only the top five or ten in the organization's history, using bulleted, abbreviated statements. This is the first section in the grant application. Write it in an *inviting* format, using a casual voice.

The example below shows how to write the section of the narrative about your history and accomplishments with language that works its way into the grant reader's heart and mind — which always help to push your grant request down the funding path.

> **History.** The Just Help Youth Center was founded in 1986 by Homer Stallworth, a local neighborhood activist and former juvenile offender. Homer's family moved to Smalltown (Mid County), Iowa when he was 12 years old. Deciding to rebel against his parents and new teachers, Homer began pulling pranks on classmates and vandalizing public property. After numerous offenses, a local judge sent Homer away to reform school before his 13th birthday. Unfortunately, Homer found out that the best way to get attention, even in reform school, was to act up and get in trouble. He stayed in reform school until the age of 18. Upon his release, he joined the Navy and, well, one might say that Homer learned how to straighten up and fly right. Mr. Stallworth eventually returned to Smalltown with ideas. For over 15 years, he has served as the president of the Just Help Youth Center. The Center's mission is to provide a safe haven where Smalltown youth channel their energy into recreational and educational programs that are designed to stimulate thought and create positive life change.

See how I (hopefully!) make the section inviting by weaving a story that brings a smile to a reader's heart. Try to write something so interesting that it gets the rest of your grant application read, rated, and recommended for funding.

In the next example, I list the Just Help Youth Center's accomplishments. Since I devote a dozen lines of type to the intriguing history, I have to get to the point in the accomplishments paragraph.

> The Just Help Youth Center is proud of the following achievements:
>
> *Historical academic achievements. From 1989 to 1999, 80 percent of the youth who participated in the after-school and weekend tutorial program received As and Bs in all of their classes.
>
> *Volunteer commitment. Since 1995, the Center has trained, employed, and honored over 100 volunteers annually. Most of the volunteers are school-to-work tutors; however, the midnight basketball program boasts 20 new volunteer coaches.

See how I take the mundane and make it interesting for the grant reader? This is not by accident. After years of experimenting with my writing style, this *hit them where their heart is* approach has pushed my funding success rate (the percentage of grants funded out of all of the grants I write on an annual basis) from 50 percent to 90–95 percent.

However, strong, emotional writing works best with foundation and corporate grant applications. Adopt a different writing style for government applications.

When you describe your organization's history in a government grant application, follow these tips to rack up the review points:

- ✔ Use a cut and dried writing style — only write what's asked for, no more, no less.

- ✔ Don't include trivia; stick with the cold, hard facts. Don't talk about anyone's feelings!

- ✔ Don't write in first person (I, Our, My). When you write the government, use Dear Sir–type language — formal and straightforward.

- ✔ Sterilize the writing content — don't use emotional terms.

For government grant applications, stick with factual, cold, and direct writing. For foundation and corporate grant applications, go for the creative, the bold, the intriguing, and the magnetic.

Describing Your Programs

Use this section to write about the day-to-day happenings at your organization. Describe the programs that you provide to your constituency (also called the *target population*) now, not what you plan to provide when your grant request is funded. If you work for a smaller organization, you probably have only one or two programs. Don't fear; this doesn't decrease your chances of winning a grant award. Grants are available for organizations of all sizes and shapes. Remember, it's all in the writing.

The grant reader wants you to

- Give the name of the program and state how long it has existed.
- Tell who it serves (youth, adults, women, the elderly, physically challenged individuals, or whomever).
- Describe how your target population benefits from the program.

If your organization has been around a long time and has more then five current programs to describe, only include the larger programs. Tell the reader that the full list of current programs can be found in the grant application's attachments. By doing so, you keep the section short and save writing space to use in the narrative sections that follow this one.

In the example below, I share with you a current programs section from a technical grant application that was written for a government agency. You can really see the difference in the writing style when you compare it with the Just Help Youth Center narrative earlier in this chapter.

> Currently, the National Virtual Manufacturing University (NVMU) is brokering, coordinating, and facilitating programs and courses in the following categories: auto service; business; computer software; electronics, engineering; failure mode and efforts analysis; health, safety, ergonomics; hydraulics/pneumatics; interpersonal skills; management; manufacturing processes/assembly; mathematics and statistics; project management; quality/continuous improvement, quality control/quality assurance, quality system requirements (QS9000); reading blueprints/gauges/routing; robotics/tool design/programmed control; statistical process control; and teamwork/team building.
>
> Current activities include planning for future course listings, interacting on a regular basis with planning teams, adding new industry-related partners to the NVMU membership, and planning for a school-to-work program that will provide educated, skilled workers for the top five highest paying jobs in the manufacturing industry.

Don't make the mistake of pulling the language for this section from a previously written grant (last year's failed attempt at getting a grant). Always use fresh, up-to-date programs and activities information. A grant reader is very intuitive and can pick up outdated, out-of-place information.

The suggested writing length for this section is one-half page, single-spaced. Don't write about what grant monies will do. Focus on what's already happening at your organization.

Let the complete examples at the end of the book be your guide. Don't even think about writing your grant application until you've pored over them!

Defining the Target Population

This is where you write about the people that you serve (normally). If you're serving organizations, write about the organizations. If you're writing a grant for an animal shelter, you would write about the animals.

Give just enough detail to aid the reader in understanding where your operating dollars end up — for use with the poor, the blind, the unemployed, high school dropouts, the homeless, or terminally-ill persons. Do your homework. Pull old evaluation reports from previously funded grants and review reports given to your board members.

The grant reader wants to see:

- ✔ Characteristics of your service population (age range, gender, ethnicity, education level, and income level).

- ✔ Numbers served by each program (make a table that covers the past five years).

- ✔ Changes in the service population that may relate to why you are asking for grant funds.

- ✔ Words and numbers to illustrate that you understand the population and their needs.

When you write this section, use bold font to make words describing your target population stand out for the grant reader.

If you work for the YoHoHo Animal Shelter, then talk about the **percentage of strays** the shelter harbors; the percent brought in by their owners; the **percentage sick or injured**; the **percentage destroyed**; the **percentage adopted** into the community, and more. You can do this successfully with descriptive narrative that tells the reader, in detail, about those that you serve.

Use a pie chart or bar graph to make this section stand out. Write some non-statistical narrative language, but cap it off with one or two fact-telling black-and-white charts. Avoid using color graphics when you're begging for grant monies.

In the example below, I introduce a fire department to the grant reader. I want the reader to understand the importance of the funding request, so I insert a purpose statement (how the grant funds will be used) at the opening of this section. You can see that I use a lot of bold font to make phrases stick in the mind of the grant reviewer. This request was for turnout gear and breathing apparatus. Look at how I use numbers to suggest the wide impact that the grant will have.

> The Ross Fire Department will use grant funds to purchase critically needed, highly protective **turnout gear (bunker pants and coats) and air masks**, referred to as SCBAs (self-contained breathing apparatus).
>
> Each response to a fire brings unbearable heat, constant danger, and intense pressure. When lives of our service population are hanging in the balance — including those of firefighters — rescue and survival gear is not a luxury, but imperative.
>
> Who will benefit from the new turnout gear and SCBAs? In Thatcher County, over **5,000** residents will benefit; in Sexton County, over **10,000** residents will benefit. Seventy percent of the target population is **elderly**. Our region has become a retirement destination for many down river manufacturing workers who are seeking open farmland and pristine views of Pennsylvania's country-side. The majority of these **residents are on a fixed income**.

You write extensively to describe your target population, whether you're approaching a foundation or corporate funder or a government funder. This information is important. It tells funders that you're serving a constituency that falls within their funding parameters.

Note: I no longer include ethnic statistics in my grant applications or proposals, unless the funding specifically asks for it. This is a sensitive topic, and I'd recommend you follow my lead.

Writing about Your Work with Local Groups

In this section, write about your partnerships in the community. Who are the organizations that you team with to provide your programs? What organizations have asked you to write letters of support for their grant applications? What groups have historically supported you in your efforts to keep the doors open? Chapter 7 gives you more information about establishing community partners to give your grant application the competitive edge.

Partners are like friends: You get to know them inside and out and you compliment each other in the delivery of like or unlike services. For example, you operate a group home for mentally and physically challenged adults. You depend on the Get 'Em There Transportation Service to take your clients to and from medical appointments. When you get ready to write your grant application, you can list this agency, along with others, in this section of the narrative. You list the full name of the partner and its role in relation to your organization.

I like to present this information in a two- or three-column table.

The grant reader is looking for:

- ✔ Collaborative efforts with multiple community partners to maximize the use of grant funds through the coordination of services to the target population
- ✔ Partners that commit cash to reduce the amount of grant funding needed
- ✔ Partners that contribute personnel, space, equipment, supplies, and other valuable items to reduce the amount of grant funding needed

Your grant guidelines may call for your community partnership information at the beginning of the narrative, before the history and accomplishments. However, the partnerships could just as easily be asked for after the problem statement or as an attachment. Remember to read your grant application directions carefully before you start writing. The great thing about modern technology is that little thing called *cut and paste*. You can move anything anyplace once it's written.

In the following example, I briefly introduce a grant applicant's partners and their role in helping the organization coordinate its services.

The Rural Pioneer Foundation works closely with the Easter Seals Society, Mary Lane Homes, and the Signature Foundation. These organizations rent the camp for their own camping sessions for the disabled. It also works closely with the Volunteer Center to obtain camp volunteers.

For the past ten years, the Dallas Community Club has donated $5,000 to the Rural Pioneer Foundation's grant monies annually. Until about eight years ago, the Foundation received grant monies from the Murray Kavanaugh Memorial Club in the amount of $20,000 annually; however, its fundraising projects have dried up and we no longer receive funds from it. During 1997, our organization received a $5,000 grant from a fundraising group in Brownsville and $8,456 from other community clubs.

You can present this same information in a small table. Graphics and tables throughout your narrative give the grant reader a break from reading straight text. Remember that grant readers may have to read dozens of grant requests each week. You can give them a much-needed respite from sentences and start to win them over by using a table effectively. See Table 11-1 for an example.

Table 11-1	Community Partners
Local Supporters	**Role**
Easter Seal Society, Mary Lane Homes, and the Signature Foundation	Provide seasonal revenue and camper referral services
Volunteer Center	Provides camp personnel
Service organizations	Provide monetary donations from local fundraisers to support the camp

See how lean and clean this looks in a table? If you have a long list of supporters, especially those that have given your organization grants, then list each one separately and the amount of funding received. You can use one-half to a whole page to present your partners.

Chapter 12

Conveying Your Need for Grant Funds

In This Chapter

▶ Helping the reader understand the nature of the problem

▶ Using graphics to drive the point home

▶ Turning on the tears

▶ Knowing when this section is complete

*T*his is it! The moment you've been waiting for — show time! The weeks, maybe even months, of research and planning are coming to a head in the most emotive section of your grant application. If you don't feel like getting out a blank check after you write this section, no one else will either. So pay close attention, and remember to write with *power* and *directness*.

Telling and Selling — Making It Compelling

The needs statement, also referred to as the *problem statement,* tells the grant reviewer that you know what you are talking about. And it emits gloom, doom, drama, and trauma. You must get the point across in the most effective, attention-drawing, memorable way that you can. How do you do that? By writing and rewriting this section until you start to feel a tad bit sad yourself.

This section should be truthful, but it should also resemble a well-written soap opera. Whoever reads this grant application must make a decision to fund it or not fund it based on the written information you give them. When you write about your organization's needs or problems, the information is presented clearly with compelling statistics and carefully-chosen terms that convey a genuine need. (Chapter 9 shows you great words that will make this section magnetizing to the grant reader.)

Explaining the problem that grant funds will solve

Write about the specific problem that your organization is faced with. Tell the reader the nature of the problem at the local level, the number of persons or organizations impacted by the problem, and what others have tried to do thus far to solve it, including your own organization. Do your homework on the Internet — search out the same types of problems in other communities and look for their solutions to solving the problem.

The grant reader expects to see answers to the following questions:

- ✔ How and when did you identify the problem?

- ✔ Do you have a thorough understanding of the problem at the local, regional, and national level?

- ✔ Do you cite recent statistics and research conducted by your organization and others that support the problem statement? Is this information current?

- ✔ Are you seeking funds for a problem that can be solved in one year — the length of most grant awards?

Use the Internet to search for the most recent relevant information about your identified need and about your target population. Try doing a general search. For example, if your organization works with welfare recipients who are seeking job-skills training and gainful employment, then enter the phrase "employment issues for welfare recipients." In this case, you could find a lot of relevant information at your own state employment and training office Web site and on the U.S. Department of Labor's Web site.

The more information you have on the topic, the easier it is to write a winning statement of need. You won't be grasping for straws or generalizing; instead, you'll be able to give the grant reader some true, hard, grant-getting facts that include citations for data sources and names of noteworthy researchers.

Integrating charts and tables into your narrative

Use a graphic like Figure 12-1 to drive a point home about your target population and to give the grant reader a break from reading text. Reading a lot of sentences can get dull!

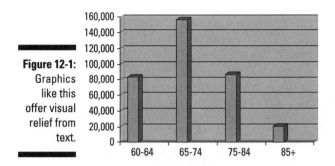

Figure 12-1:
Graphics
like this
offer visual
relief from
text.

Use more than one type of table if you have a lot of demographics on your target population. Try a mixture of bar graphs, pie charts, and tables. Figure 12-2 demonstrates the visual impact of an ordinary pie chart.

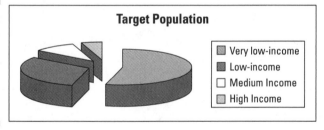

Figure 12-2:
Pie
charts add
"color" —
even in
black and
white.

Using a color printer to produce your grant applications has both pros and cons. The con side is that you'll look like you have state-of-the-art word processing and printing equipment and that you aren't so needy after all. The pro side is that grant reviewers read hundreds of pages of requests every day. Using color draws attention to your request and makes it memorable.

Don't go to extraordinary means to produce color charts. If you don't have a color printer, then just work with what you have. Your words will work just as well with black-and-white graphics as they will with color. If you really don't have much to work with (no computer, for example), your first grant proposal can seek funding for the tools needed for effective grant writing!

Table 12-1 shows you how to use routine census information to build a table that leaps off of the page. A newspaper headline table title provokes thoughts of a critical need for grant funding in the mind of the grant reader. How do I know? I review and rate grants and make recommendations for funding to government agencies.

Table 12-1	Trouble in Williams County, Alabama	
Economic Indicators	*Williams County*	*Alabama*
Free/reduced price lunches (a major indicator of families living in poverty)	44.7%	30.5%
Families receiving AFDC	30.6%	14.7%
Families receiving food stamps	33.1%	17.4%
High school dropout rate	24.9%	7.0%

Charts and tables make the grant reader linger longer on a page. The longer someone reflects upon your particular problem, the better your chances are for receiving funding.

Don't mix apples with oranges in a table. In Table 12-1, I show the grant reader the problems in the community and compare them with the same types of problems at the state level. However, I don't use any economic indicators that show progress or suggest that anything good is happening in the community. Don't mix the good with the bad when it comes to statistical profiles of a community or a target population.

Some tips on using charts and tables:

- ✔ If you have more than three numbers that describe the target population, tell it in a table.

- ✔ If you talk about age ranges, income by groups, and numerical breakdowns of target population indicators, tell it in a bar graph or pie chart.

- ✔ If your project is not located in a major urban area, show where you are by using a map. The map can be a graphic insert or a watermark (in the background).

Knowing When You've Written the Right Stuff

Determining when you've finished writing the problem statement can be difficult. After you've written five to ten grant applications, you develop an intuition as to when it's time to wrap up a section and move on to the next one. But in the beginning, knowing whether you've written enough to convince a grant reader that you truly have a need that can only be solved with grant funding is difficult.

EDGE

How to win the Nobel prize for grant writing

If you haven't read Chapter 9, flip backwards and peruse that chapter's hints on writing effectively. Chapter 9 tells you how to make the cake. The tips in this sidebar are the icing.

Capture a grant reader's attention by telling her how the monies can make a difference. You don't want to write about the program design until you're in the section that's all about the program — but including how the funding will be used is okay in the needs section as well, as long as you don't go into details.

Elevate your grant writing by using bold type and italics to make a word or phrase stand out. Don't hide key words or phrases in ordinary type text. I call attention to important text with bold black font or bold red font. Stimulating the reader by playing with the look of the text results in a speedy funding decision.

Another great technique for making your sentences leap off the page is to use bulleted lists to organize bits of critical information. They call attention to each set of details and give your narrative an appealing visual.

Bulleted lists are used throughout this book. Here's an example of how one could appear in a grant application:

✔ The local unemployment rate is three times higher than that of the state.

✔ The hospital's annual occupancy rate is averaging 49 percent of the total beds available for new admissions.

Another tip: Write each paragraph so that it builds on the preceding paragraph. Make your ideas connect and flow. Each new paragraph is a step toward the final paragraph that asks for funding support to solve the problem. Each new paragraph adds excitement and urgency.

I love to use words that work, like *suffer greatly, market share decline* (grantlish used to explain that multiple service providers are all trying to provide the same service to the target population; some agencies are getting all the clients, while others are experiencing a market share decline), *noticeable shortage, insufficient feeder pools* (grantlish used when there are not enough job training applicants in a geographic area), *going unfilled,* and *meeting the demands.* Are you getting the picture of need? This type of writing works well in government or private sector grant narratives.

You can also crank up the tears and your chances for funding by using extreme adjectives like *worthless, tiny, outdated, inadequate,* and *underserved.*

Grant readers also want to see large population impact numbers that show how far you can stretch their grant dollars, thus making a difference for many, not just a few.

When I first started writing grant applications, I let the page limits on the narrative determine when I needed to stop writing — but this is not a good method. If a funding source limits the entire narrative section to five pages, or even twenty pages, can you ever really write enough convincing language to sell your project?

At the end of the needs section, what you've written should be *compelling* to the grant reader. If you can make it compelling, you're on the way to a funded grant!

In the example below, I include a little history in order to set the tone for why grant funding is needed. I don't have enough numbers to use a table, so I let the numbers in the narrative remain in normal text. Six-digit numbers catch the reader's attention without any extra effort. An impressive amount of monies were raised in the example. The language shows widespread community support for the original structure — the one that is too small now. It also shows the funding source that local resources have already been tapped and that it's time to look for grant support.

> The need for the Hazardous Materials Training Center (HMTC) was identified in 1989. Private industry and the State of Oregon joined together in a partnership toward the development of the HMTC where emergency responders could train for hazardous materials incidents. In 1990, approximately $500,000 was collected to construct the HMTC building, located on a four-acre site right next to the Oregon State Police Training Academy. Development of the center was timely. Some 500,000 shipments of hazardous materials were being made daily across the United States. These shipments totaled 1.5 billion tons between 1988 and 1998. During that time, there were, on average, 6,175 incidents per year involving a release of hazardous materials; the incidents resulted in approximately 250 injuries to first responders and citizens.

Writing about the continuing saga of this agency is important because it is requesting grant funds for capital infrastructure (to build a building) — the most difficult type of grant funds to obtain. The next example shows you how to write a second paragraph in the needs statement that builds on the first, opening paragraph.

> Training performed at the HMTC would help reduce the risk of incidents, as well as contamination to the public and the environment after an incident occurred — not only in Oregon, but nationwide. A steering committee was formed from government, industry, and the fire service to develop the training curriculum, acquire funding and equipment, ensure course availability to both public and private entities, and to maintain the objective to train public and private hazardous materials response teams. Since 1992, the Center has grown at an overwhelming rate. Thousands of students have come from across the United States to enroll in courses. New programs are added on a regular basis. Available training curriculum has expanded dramatically, from **32** courses servicing **864** students in 1992, to over **600** programs and nearly **25,000** students in 1999.

I like to see numbers jump off the page. Bold type font helps to give action to significant numbers like those in the example above. These numbers say that there were just too many demands on a training facility that was built for a much smaller populace. The next example builds the case for a new facility.

> **Today, the Center is out of space!** Oregon has over 67,000 dedicated personnel in fire service, law enforcement, and emergency medical services, providing protection to nine million citizens. Direct training is provided to more than 4,000 individuals each year through the Center, with another 20,000 trained through the field delivery system. **The demand for training has exceeded the Center's physical capacity.**

When you hammer a point home, hit the nail even harder by putting in more dire need language. Strong language really helps build the picture for need!

If you have a summary of a needs survey or letters from organizations that are on a waiting list for your services, attach these documents. Always reference attachments in the narrative. I attach lengthy support documents that a grant reader may want to look at to verify the actual need for grant funding.

When you can answer yes to the following questions, you're ready to move to the next section in your grant application:

- ✔ Did you use recent research by others on the issue?
- ✔ Did you include relevant statistical indicators?
- ✔ Did you give the grant reader enough information to understand the problem? (Assume that she has no prior knowledge of the problem.)
- ✔ Did you use maps and words to bring the grant reader into your community?
- ✔ Did you present recent findings of your own surveys and constituent feedback?
- ✔ Did you stay focused and write only about the need — staying clear of the solution until the next narrative section?
- ✔ Did you use words that have the ability to create compassion and urgency in the grant reader's mind and heart?

You know you've written a convincing needs statement when you get out your hanky to dab away a few tears after you've reread it!

Chapter 13

Demonstrating How Grant Funds Will Be Used: The Plan of Action

In This Chapter

▶ Writing a purpose statement

▶ Creating a vision through the goals

▶ Perfecting the objectives

▶ Plotting the activities

▶ Developing a plan

*1*n this chapter, I show you how to lay out your plans for solving the problem. This is the main event. Time to talk the talk and walk the walk. You're ready to write about your vision — what positive changes you could bring about, if only you had some money! This is my favorite section because it's uplifting. It focuses on the future. Use the word *will,* not *would.* Be optimistic while you write this section.

Describing Your Vision to the Funder

This section in the grant application narrative is referred to by funding sources as the *program design,* the *plan of action,* or the *workplan.* A plan of operation and a program design are the same thing. I show you the unique aspects of a workplan later in this chapter. No matter what it's called, the section that details your plan links the program's goals with the funder's money, explaining how the money can accomplish the goals.

The section should include:

✔ **Goals:** Where you want to be when the grant funds are used up

✔ **Objectives:** Measurable benchmarks, often in steps that lead up to the goals

✔ **Activities and strategies:** How you plan to meet your objectives

✔ **A timeline:** To explain when the objectives are going to be met

Most importantly, you must explain how your target population will benefit from the program!

Expressing Your Organization's Purpose

The first sentence or paragraph of the purpose statement tells the grant reader why you're asking for grant monies. Two types of purpose statements are used: *indirect* and *direct*. An indirect purpose statement does not include the dollar amount that you're seeking from the funding source. The example language below shows you how to write an indirect purpose statement.

> The purpose of this request is to seek grant funding to plan four new exhibits at the Intergalactic Zoo and to acquire the exotic animals needed to complete the zoo's expansion plan.

A direct purpose statement includes the amount of the requested grant award. Remember that even when you mention a dollar amount, the purpose statement should not exceed one sentence. This example shows you how to write a direct purpose statement.

> The Intergalactic Zoo Foundation is requesting a $150,000 grant to plan four new exhibits at the zoo and to acquire the exotic animals that are needed to complete our expansion plan.

The purpose statement should be a one-sentence, direct, concise explanation of what the funds are sought for.

Writing Goals and Objectives

Always provide objectives for each goal and for each year for which you are requesting funds for an activity. The ability to show that grant monies will be spent prudently and wisely is determined by the measurability of each objective that accompanies the related goal.

I don't have a magic number for goals and objectives. However, when I do work with a nonprofit organization to develop the goals section of the grant application, I can't stress enough that the goals are based on its vision of where it wants the program or target population to be when the grant period is over.

If the grant reviewer can't look at the goals and objectives and figure out from them what the entire program is about, then you've failed to write a sufficient number of clearly stated goals.

Writing great goals

If you're new to grant writing, you may sometimes mistake goals for objectives, or vice versa. To keep these two terms straight, think of *goal* first and remember that it is, according to *Webster's New World College Dictionary,* the "end that one strives to attain." The key word to keep in mind is *end.* A goal is where you are when you're done. Grant application narratives must have goals to show the funder that you have a vision for solving the problem.

Okay, what about *objective?* An objective is, simply, a major milestone or checkpoint on your route to a goal. It's a place where you can say (and report to a funder, if necessary), "We've come this far, and we have this far remaining before we reach the goal." Objectives have to be attainable and serve to keep goals realistic. And that, in one small acorn, is the sum total difference between goals and objectives. But if you still don't get the difference, take a peek at Chapter 6.

Write clear, concise, one-sentence goal statements. The goals can apply to where you picture either your organization or your target population at the end of the grant period. But don't include any measurements or timelines in the goal statement.

In the examples below, you see a number of sample goal statements. These statements should give you an idea of how to express your goals.

Goal statement for senior caregiver project:

Senior Referral Services will meet the need of Universal County's elderly population by linking them with individuals who have experience and/or training in home health care, housekeeping, and companion services.

Goal statements for an infrastructure project:

Goal 1: Once expanded, the Hazardous Materials Training Center will be able to meet the training and certification needs of fire fighting and law enforcement personnel from throughout the northwest United States.

Goal 2: To continue to be a role model for successful private/public collaboration in other states.

Goal statement for a public library project:

This project will improve library and information services to under-served cities and townships, targeting services to children, ages 13 to 17, from families with incomes below the poverty line.

Goal statements for a postsecondary education project:

Goal 1: The FREEDOM PROJECT will demonstrate successful partnerships with federal, state, and local agencies and organizations to provide English Literacy/Civics Education and related support services to newly arriving immigrants with low-skill levels in Big Ben County, Texas.

Goal 2: The FREEDOM PROJECT will develop effective technology-integrated curricula and draw upon existing assessment tools to address emerging areas in English Literacy/Civics Education from a cross-cultural perspective for non-English speaking and limited English–speaking immigrant students, including those with learning disabilities.

Goal 3: The FREEDOM PROJECT will become an effective practice model for English Literacy/Civics Education curriculum for new immigrants.

I can check the goal statements above by asking myself the following questions:

✔ Did I use one sentence?

✔ Is the sentence clear and concise?

✔ Does the grant reader know who the target population is?

✔ Did I deliberately *not* include measurements and timelines?

Yes, yes, yes, and yes.

Writing super objectives

Successful grant writing requires understanding the two types of objectives and when to use them. *Process objectives* and *outcome objectives* exist. Use them both to rack up points and win big dollars. ***Note:*** Objectives can also be referred to as *milestones* or *benchmarks*.

Objectives are normally something you can measure at a certain point in time. You normally write objectives in quantitative terms that enable you to determine if you're making progress in your program plans. Taking a look at your progress is called *monitoring*. Determining how much progress you have made is called *evaluating*. Chapter 14 talks about monitoring and evaluation.

Some program designs have more than one objective for each goal. Just make sure that you number and alphabetize them to eliminate confusion for the reviewer — for example, 1a, 1b, 1c, and so on.

Process objectives

You can tell you've written a process objective if you started with words such as: *to provide, to develop,* or *to establish*. Another indicator that you've written a process objective is that it's not quantifiably measurable. A process objective is quite abstract in its wording.

Unless your grant application guidelines specifically ask for process objectives, don't write them. Why? They don't describe the end results or outcomes for your target population. But, if you're writing a federal grant application, the plan of operation or program design section often asks for both types of objectives, process and outcome.

The next examples (and remember that these are taken from actual proposals) show you process objectives. Note that each describes the process to reach the end result, rather than focusing the grant reader on the end result itself. Process objectives are rather lengthy because they have to explain a process.

> **Process objective 1a:** To **establish** an advisory committee inviting representatives from each of the following entities: Port Authority of Texas and Oldtown, U.S. Department of Immigration and Naturalization Service, Big Ben County Legal Services, Frederick Public Library, Middleton Public Library, the Housing Authority of the City of Frederick, City of Frederick Mayor's Office, and the Workforce Investment Board.

> **Process objective 1b:** To **provide** the project with one full-time Webmaster/Instructional Designer to create multilingual (Spanish, Portuguese, Polish, Haitian Creole, Gujarati, and Russian) basic information software programs for the kiosks and instructional programs in the first quarter.

> **Process objective 1c:** To **develop** a directory for participants that lists all educational institutions, immigration services, legal services, public agencies, social services, medical and mental health care, housing, transportation, and libraries.

Outcome objectives

How do you recognize an outcome objective? Look for words such as *to increase* or *to decrease* that imply some sort of measurable change. If you see words like *to provide,* you may be looking at a process objective — unless the words are followed by something quantifiable, like *to provide 80 hours of staff support.*

Always provide objectives for each goal and for each year for which you are requesting funds for an activity.

Grants for staffing are not easy to get, but some funding sources in every state do support general operating expenses — including salaries and fringe benefits. In the next example, I show you how to write measurable objectives for a grant request intended to fund full-time personnel.

Measurable objectives for the senior caregiver project:

Outcome objective 1a: Dedicate 80 percent of founder's time to directing the program staff and recruiting new caregivers and careseekers.

Outcome objective 1b: Dedicate 100 percent of the office manager's time to implementing the program expansion activities.

Outcome objective 1c: Dedicate 100 percent of the administrative assistant's time to managing the day-to-day paperwork, creating the client services database, and compiling the monthly accounting reports.

Bricks-and-mortar grants are not as plentiful as other types of grants, but a few funders in each state will look favorably at capital infrastructure grant requests. In the examples just ahead, grant funds are requested to add 3,500 square feet onto an existing state training facility.

Outcome objective 1a: Expand the 2001 course offerings and available classes by 50 percent or more over the previous year's capacity.

Outcome objective 2a: Collect 100 percent of the $248,000 needed to start construction from the private sector, including previous contributors to the Center, as well as new partners.

Suppose a public library must demonstrate that it will increase its equity of information access for underserved school students if it wins a grant. The next example is apt:

Outcome objective: The First Reasoning Public Library will increase equity of information access by 30 percent or more by providing new technologies and related items to underserved children (ages 13 to 17 and from families with incomes below the poverty line) from the City of First Reasoning and four surrounding communities.

See how I use the *1, 2, 3 writing style* for objectives? One, what type of progress will occur? (An increase in the equity of information access.) Two, who will be impacted by the progress? (Underserved children.) Three, how will they be impacted? (Through new technologies and related items.)

Making the connection between goals and objectives

Each goal is stated and is followed by the objectives for that goal. In the following example, you can see how to coordinate outcome objectives and process objectives with the goals in developing a program design.

Goal 1: Create a safe harbor in downtown Wickie-Up for the community's homeless by offering them emergency shelter and food.

This goal's measurable objectives are:

Outcome objective 1a: Reduce the number of homeless persons sleeping in public places by 50 percent or more.

Outcome objective 1b: Decrease public panhandling by the homeless in the central business district by 25 percent or more.

The other goals and objectives:

Goal 2: Improve the downtown business owners' understanding of homeless persons.

Outcome objective 2a: Reduce incidences of business owners calling the local police department to arrest homeless persons for loitering by 25 percent or more.

Outcome objective 2b: Increase the number of businesses that accept the universal meal coupon for a free, boxed, take-out dinner at the back kitchen entry by 30 percent or more.

Goal 3: Educate homeless persons on remedies to their situation.

Process objective 3a: Establish a toll-free 24-hour homeless hotline staffed with volunteers trained in helping others to access community resources.

Process objective 3b: Provide homeless persons coming to the new downtown shelter and soup kitchen with a local post office box located in the shelter so that they can apply for entitlement benefits using a stable mailing address.

Process objective 3c: Develop a case management file for each homeless client that outlines their needs, referrals made, results of referrals, income situation, ability to work, and overall psychosocial condition.

In the preceding example, I used the 1, 2, 3 writing style for objectives. One, what type of progress will occur? (An increase or decrease.) Two, who will be impacted by the progress? (Identify the target population.) Three, how will they be impacted? (Name the services or programs.)

Remember to look to the future, when your grant funds will be gone. What do you want your program to have accomplished?

Describing Your Strategies

If your goal is to create a safe harbor in the downtown area for the community's homeless by offering them emergency shelter and food, what steps do you need to take to make this happen? The steps that need to occur comprise your *implementation strategy.*

Before you actually try to write the narrative to this section in the grant application, sit down and brainstorm all of the steps in chronological order that need to occur in order to reach this goal and meet the targets set in the objectives.

The following examples show you effective language for the implementation strategies section.

Project Implementation Strategies

*Schedule board of directors meeting to notify board members of grant award(s) and have them vote on a resolution to accept the grant funds.

*Meet with community partners (city, county, local human and social service agencies, homeless coalition, and other service providers) to notify them of the receipt of grant funds and to begin scheduling service planning meetings.

*Have board review contractors' bids and select the winning bid. Notify contractor and schedule meeting to go over administrative concerns/suggestions.

*Meet with municipal planning committees one more time with the approved plans and work with contractor to get all permits needed to start the project on time.

*Hire homeless outreach specialist. The agency will select someone who has been homeless and is now employed in a social service position locally.

*Work with outreach specialist to develop an effective plan for getting the word out to the homeless and to area businesses (the number one group concerned about downtown vagrancy).

*Begin recruiting volunteers for the soup kitchen.

*Develop a staffing plan for the shelter and begin advertising for positions.

*Plan grand opening date and festivities.

*Start visiting downtown business owners to develop an open line of communication on the needs of the homeless and how the shelter can help meet those needs.

*Develop a coupon for homeless persons that downtown restaurants will honor for hot meals, to go, on certain days each week. The purpose of the coupons is to supplement the shelter's own ability to serve meals on high-demand days or after the shelter's regular, once-daily, congregate meal service.

*Create a holistic case management approach to treat the basic social and psychological needs of a homeless person.

*Work with the U.S. Postal Service to establish a mail system at the shelter so that homeless persons can use the shelter as their temporary address to receive mail, including Social Security and other entitlement payment checks.

*Develop an ongoing stakeholders evaluation process to monitor the project's progress toward its objectives.

When you're writing your strategy for implementation, include every detail. Why? To assure the funding source that you know what it takes to have a successful program.

Good performance outcomes are responsive to the project's activities, which in turn are the actions that must occur to achieve the project's objectives. Performance outcomes also add substance to your project design or plan of operation. In addition, they are a critical component in the project's work-plan, which I explain at the end of this chapter.

Making a Timeline That Tells the Story Accurately

A timeline tells the grant reader when activities will begin and end during the grant's funding period (which is usually a 12-month period). Table 13-1 shows how.

Table 13-1	Homeless Impact Project			
Activity	**1st Quarter**	**2nd Quarter**	**3rd Quarter**	**4th Quarter**
Resolution	X			
Post-award planning meeting	X			
Select contractor	X			
Obtain permits and begin renovation	X			
Renovation period	X	X		
Hire outreach specialist	X			
Recruit volunteers		X		
Interview and hire shelter staff			X	X
Grand opening				X
Homeless prevention education				X and ongoing
Community tolerance efforts		X	X	X and ongoing
Monitoring and evaluation activities	X	X	X	X

If you're requesting a grant for more than one year, you need to develop a timeline chart for each year.

The timeline table tells the grant reader that the funds needed to renovate the donated building will be expended in the first two quarters. The grant monies needed to pay for the evaluation process are needed immediately and will be expended throughout the grant period. It also shows the funder that the grant monies needed to hire personnel are minimal at start-up, but increase in the third quarter and continue through the end of the grant period.

When you develop a project timeline, keep in mind that the grant reader wants to see answers to the following questions:

- ✔ Does the project's purpose connect to an area the funding source wants to fund?

- ✔ Are the goals realistic based on the amount of money requested in the budget section and the length of time you indicate you'll need to implement the project?

- ✔ Can you reach your targets (outlined in the objectives) in the indicated timeframe?

- ✔ Are the objectives quantifiable? Did you use percents to show increases or decreases for the target population?

- ✔ Did you include all of the activities and steps necessary to implement the project in the timeline?

Making an Impact Statement

An *impact statement* is a paragraph or two at the end of your action plan that illustrates the impact your program will have on your local community, the region, and even the world.

These are some questions to help you brainstorm while writing the impact statement:

- ✔ How is the project significant or unique?

- ✔ How is the project forging new ground while addressing social issues in the community?

- ✔ How will the project generate systemic change within my organization — and for other organizations doing what we do for the same population in other communities? (Look for broad impact — beyond the local community.)

Take a look at this example of an impact statement:

> There are no similar existing projects that replicate the services of the Hazardous Materials Training Center in the United States. The Emergency Management Division administration will continue to share information with other states, similar departmental entities, and all other private and public emergency management personnel. Trained and informed crisis response personnel result in the saving of lives, fewer critical injuries, and the preservation of the United States' environment. The lessons learned in reaching our goals and objectives will be shared with other regions across the country seeking to build and staff their own hazardous materials training facility.

When the funding source asks for an impact statement, it wants to determine:

- ✔ Can our money make a difference beyond the local community?
- ✔ Can this project help us fulfill our own mission statement?
- ✔ Is this project replicable in other communities?

Formatting the Workplan

At the beginning of this chapter, I write that funding sources use several different names for the way you present the vision for how grant funds will be used by your organization. Once you've requested and received the grant application guidelines from a funding source, you know immediately what type of narrative format is required for this section of your grant application. Most often, you see this section referred to as a *workplan* by units of government at the federal or state level.

These are the characteristics that distinguish a workplan from a plan of operation:

- ✔ It typically does not ask for goals, only objectives.
- ✔ Each objective and the information written about it are kept together in subsections or graphic tables.
- ✔ It calls for procedures/activities, performance outcomes, responsible person(s), and a timeline for each objective.

You can organize your workplan quite simply by laying it out like this (don't forget to fill in the blanks!):

**Objective:** _____

**Procedures/Activities**   _**Performance Outcomes**_   _**Timelines**_   _**Responsible Persons**_

Create one of these simple charts for each of the objectives. So if you have written five objectives, you create five annual workplans. Here is the key to the terms:

Procedures/activities: You insert the implementation strategies.

Performance outcomes: You write about the resulting action of your activity.

Timelines: You insert the start and stop months for the project's activities.

Responsible persons: You insert the job titles or committee names of those who will be responsible for carrying out the project's activities.

A workplan is a roadmap for the grant reader. It shows her, in detail, every step that will occur in the proposed project or program. The more information you can give the grant reader, the better your chances are of receiving the full amount of grant monies that you request.

When you look back over this chapter, don't be overwhelmed at the extensive writing requirements of a plan of operation. Write narrative responses in the order that the information is requested in the grant application guidelines. Think about one subsection at a time. First, visualize how you see the funded project working. Ask yourself what needs to be in place in order for the project to be successful. As ideas start jumping into your head (at least this is how visualizing is supposed to work!), begin writing down what you're thinking. Begin to pull out the purpose statement, goals, objectives, implementation strategies/activities, performance outcomes, timelines, persons responsible, and the impact statement _from your brainstorming_. The more you practice this process, the quicker the information flows into your mind. Practice makes perfect!

Chapter 14

Profiling Personnel, Resources, and Equity

. . . .

In This Chapter

▶ Knowing whom to put on first base

▶ Showing accountability

▶ Making the fair treatment statement

▶ Looking like you have something tangible

. . . .

Showing your prospective funders that you've selected all of the right people for the right jobs in your proposed project is not as easy as you may think. Sometimes, when you get to this point in the grant narrative, you're so glad to be nearing the end that you slip and slide with the selection of the project's key personnel.

Another area where many grant writers fall short is in not being able to convincingly show that they have a *management plan,* meaning that they can clearly describe the reporting lines and accountability.

A solid grant application must also show that there are plans for addressing equitable access to the project's participants throughout the management of the grant.

This chapter gives you the ins and outs on writing these key narrative sections. You can easily go astray here. But just follow my advice and you'll find the clear path through the middle of this thorny part of the application narrative. And keep in mind that I've included examples of winning grant applications at the end of the book!

Making the Right Choices for Project Personnel

When you put together your grant narrative, either based on specific grant guidelines or using the National Network of Grantmakers (NNG) Common Grant Application, you are required to write about your project's key personnel. (Scope out Chapter 1 for more information on the NNG.)

If the funder's limitations don't preclude hiring or contracting personnel, then you can actually ask for the cost of key personnel for your proposed project. Whenever you ask for salaries and fringe benefits or contracted services in the project budget, you must include narrative to answer the following questions:

- ✔ Who will manage the project?
- ✔ Who will direct the project?
- ✔ Who will carry out the day-to-day activities in the implementation plan?

As a federal grant reader, I can tell you that the rest of your grant narrative can be perfect, but if your project personnel don't qualify, you can easily lose up to 10 points — a fatal loss. On a point scale of 100, projects scoring 92 points or higher are recommended for grant awards. Even 90 points just won't cut it. Making the right choices for project personnel results in winning a big grant award. Making the wrong choices . . . .

Starting the personnel selection process

Before I show you how to develop this part of the grant application narrative, I want to give you a brief overview of the project I draw my examples from.

Purpose of proposed YouthBuild project: To annually provide 20 economically disadvantaged young adults in the Lanesville School District and Marystown Community Schools (a neighboring school district) with opportunities to obtain their education, gain building trades employment skills, and come together with Habitat For Humanity (HFH) volunteers. The young adults will learn while expanding their social and academic horizons in a meaningful on-site Habitat work experience. They will serve their local community while, ultimately, learning self-sufficiency.

These are the rules for selecting project personnel:

✔ Identify a *project administrator*. The administrator is the individual who provides management oversight. This person should be able to allocate up to five hours per week of their work time to making sure the project meets its grant-funded conditions. The project administrator, along with the project director, usually attends meetings with the project's community partners. (Chapter 11 covers establishing partnerships with other organizations in your community.)

✔ Identify the personnel needed to carry out the project on a day-to-day basis. This usually means selecting a *project director*. The project director is responsible for the program's implementation. This individual reports directly to the project administrator. Identify a project director that has relevant and extensive experience in the same area as the project.

This is not the time to do a favor for your out-of-work, unqualified buddy!

Given the scope of the proposed YouthBuild Project, using a school superintendent or other administrator for the project director won't work. A project director should have day-to-day duties for the direct implementation of the project's activities. I recommend that the project have two codirectors. One employed by one of the school districts mentioned, and one employed by HFH, the partnering organization. The next example shows how I present the codirectors to the federal grant reader.

> **Key personnel.** Joe Bologusi, an alternative education teacher at Lanesville, will be one of the project's codirectors. He has been with the district since 1987. For 19 years before joining the district, he taught in both private and public school classrooms and gained extensive administrative experience. He holds a Bachelor of Science in education from Williams State University and has an 18-hour continuing certificate.
>
> Mr. Bologusi will devote 50 percent of his time to the project. His salary, fringe benefits, and travel expenses will be an in-kind contribution by the Lanesville School District. His paper credentials do not reveal his high level of commitment to at-risk students and ongoing drive to assist adult learners in achieving lifelong goals.

Following my lead in the preceding example, write about present employment first and include the year employment began. If prior experience is not relevant to this specific grant application, then just write a summary sentence. Always include the most recent educational attainment.

The grant reader (the person employed by the funding source to review, rate, and make recommendations for funding or not funding the grant request) is looking for written narrative in the key personnel section that answers the following questions:

- What are the project administrator's qualifications?
- What are the project director's qualifications?
- Who are the project personnel that will carry out the day-to-day activities?
- Do the project's personnel have extensive experience in the project's focus area?
- What percentage of their time will be charged to the project?
- Is the time allocated for each person sufficient to carry out the activities described in the plan of operation or program design?
- Will their time be paid for with grant monies or through an in-kind contribution?
- What is their *line of accountability* (meaning whom they report to)?

The grant reader is looking for answers to some hard and fast questions that are critical to the success of your project. Even if you are not asking for grant funds to cover personnel, still do a brief paragraph on the key personnel and include the resume of the project director in the attachments.

Including the percentage of each person's time that will be devoted to the project is important. In the case of Mr. Bologusi, he is already employed by the school district, so his salary, fringe benefits and project-related travel are already budgeted. You don't need to request funds to compensate Mr. Bologusi under this grant.

When you can provide personnel at no cost to the grant, you look *great* in the eyes of the grant reader and score more points.

Here's an example of how to introduce key personnel with an emphasis on their education:

> Allan Smith, executive director of HFH, will assist Mr. Bologusi in directing the YouthBuild Program. He joined the staff in November 1994 and has a master's degree in education from Williams State University, where he has completed 90 percent of his doctoral studies in educational administration. Mr. Smith has 32 years of experience in education.

Because this is a school-based program, I introduce Mr. Smith's educational qualifications first. Then I write about his qualifications to act as the project's codirector.

If a program calls for combining two disciplines, you may need to find codirectors. This program includes both education and construction, so it has a codirector with educational experience and a codirector with construction experience. Of course, finding one person to be the director who has experience in both fields is great, but don't hesitate to use codirectors if appropriate.

> Mr. Smith's construction experience began in 1990 and continued through 1994 when he worked as director of operations for Marystown Community Schools in implementing construction and renovations funded by a bond issue. Since his tenure at HFH, he has been responsible for fundraising, public relations, and working closely with contractors and union-trades people and volunteers. Thus far, HFH has completed one house since the start-up of the Moore County chapter in January 1994. Mr. Smith will work closely with the Lanesville School District to plan and implement the YouthBuild Program. HFH will select a minimum of five new housing construction sites for YouthBuild coordination.

This person cannot work for free. Mr. Smith is already volunteering his time for HFH, so in the next example, I show you how to include language in the narrative that says to the grant reader, "We need money to fund personnel."

> Virtually 100 percent of Mr. Smith's time will be allocated to the YouthBuild Program. A stipend is being requested for his role in the grant-funded activities.

After you finish writing the key personnel section of the grant narrative, go back and read what you've written. When your grant application reaches the funding source, the grant reader looks for narrative language in this section that answers the following questions:

- ✔ Who will direct the program?

- ✔ Do their qualifications make them qualified to manage this particular program?

- ✔ Is it clear what personnel will be charged to the grant's budget?

- ✔ Does a clear line of accountability exist? (More information on the line of accountability is in the following section.)

Integrating the management plan into key personnel

In the case of the YouthBuild Project, I haven't included the line of account-ability in the above narrative. How can this be fixed? By adding the following paragraph and possibly an organizational chart like Figure 14-1.

> **Management plan.** The Lanesville School District is the grant applicant and will act as the fiscal agent for the management of grant funds. HFH is the participating agency. No memorandum of agreement is necessary.

A *memorandum of agreement* is a written document that outlines the roles of other organizations participating in your program or project's implementation.

> The project's lead administrator, Dr. Lois Garbo, is director of adult and community education. Both codirectors for the YouthBuild Program will report to Dr. Garbo, who reports to the district superintendent, who is responsible for carrying out the administrative duties under the direction of the district's board of education. The business manager for the district has over 20 years of experience managing grant-funded programs. A brief overview of Dr. Garbo's qualifications and the function of the business department is attached. The district's administrative organizational chart follows this section.

Check out how, in the preceding example, I write a brief but effective paragraph to show that the school district has a line of accountability. Sometimes, by this point in the grant application, you don't have a lot of pages left to devote to the remaining narrative sections. This paragraph shows a quick and concise way of summing up the chain of command.

When you bring community partners in as a part of your program design, government funding agencies usually require that formal written and signed memorandums of agreement be attached to the grant application. Because the Lanesville School District is the grant applicant and the grant guidelines state the only eligible applicants are *LEAs (Local Education Agencies)*, another term for a public school district, no partnership agreement is needed from the nonprofit community-based partner, which in this case is HFH.

When something is not applicable or not necessary, but the grant guidelines call for it, make a simple statement to indicate why something will not be attached or discussed further. *But attach all lengthy credentials, unless the grant application guidelines limit the number of pages that can be attached.*

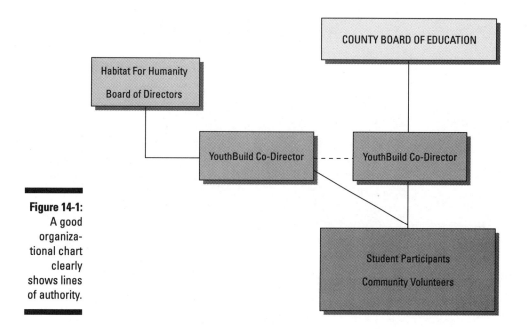

The key personnel section in the example that follows is written differently than the preceding example, in which the funding was for program implementation and was not weighted down with high personnel costs. This request that follows needs grant funds for *all* of the project personnel, including the project administrator. Even though the project administrator is employed by a public television station, this project is a private venture with the station agreeing to act as the grant applicant.

Purpose of proposed project. To produce a 19-part television series and companion telecourse about Canadian ecosystems.

Key personnel involved in carrying out the project's production plans

PROJECT ADMINISTRATOR

Glenn Symington — General manager of KLTC-TV, Channel 3, since 1973 and has privately owned Wilderness Productions, an international film company, since 1980. He has experience in conducting major capital campaigns, managing the infrastructure aspects of the station, and obtaining federal funding for broadcast improvement and viewership expansion. Mr. Symington graduated from the

University of Alberta and has completed advanced coursework at the University of Toronto. He has received numerous broadcasting awards. He will devote 1.0 FTE to the project and is included in the grant budget.

FTE means *full-time equivalent,* which can be between 30 and 40 hours per week.

PRODUCTION TEAM

Mark Calender — Founder of Mark Calender Productions, Ltd. He is the most recognizable and authoritative spokesperson for Canada's wildlife. He will work on the project at 0.75 FTE and be paid with grant funds.

Maria Genovosi — As the leading authority on Canadian wildlife, Ms. Genovosi has been an active wildlife enthusiast, naturalist, and educator since childhood. Most recently, she has returned from an expedition in South Africa. She is a graduate of Bennington University at Stratford. She will work on the project at 0.5 FTE and be paid with grant funds.

A full list of the production team is attached along with curriculum vitae for all grant-funded project personnel.

In foundation and corporate grant applications, I prefer to attach full resumes or curriculum vitae, rather than use up grant narrative to go on and on about the qualifications of personnel.

When you write a grant request that is seeking monies to compensate project or program personnel, you have to justify your request. You do so by explaining each key person's role in the projects implementation, indicating the amount of time each person will devote to the project, and stating how their participation will be paid for, either with grant monies or an in-kind contribution.

In the example that follows, I show you how to write about a *statement of fiscal agency responsibility.* It is a written statement by the chief financial officer (CFO) of the applicant organization attesting to the fact the agency will accept the responsibility of accepting the grant award, managing the grant award, and preparing and submitting financial and evaluation reports. It is done on the applicant agency's letterhead, signed by the CFO, and attached to the application.

Management plan

KLTC-TV is owned and operated by the University of Alberta. The station has its own board of trustees who provide administrative direction to the general manager, Mr. Symington. Both production team members will be charged to contracted services and will report to Mr. Symington. This project is a personal endeavor of Mr. Symington's for-profit company, Wilderness Productions.

The University of Alberta and the station's board of trustees have agreed to act as the grant applicant and fiscal agent for this most worthy project. A statement of fiscal agent responsibility has been prepared by the University's financial manager and is attached.

The preceding example presents a unique relationship that is allowable when an individual or a for-profit organization is seeking grant monies that are only available to nonprofit organizations.

So you've probably picked up on the fact that state and federal grants play by different rules than corporate or foundation grants. Be absolutely sure to carefully read the guidelines for each individual grant that you apply for, but here's one more difference to keep in mind: If you're writing to foundations and corporations, the funders don't usually ask for a separate narrative section on the management plan. You include it in the section for key personnel. However, state and federal funders usually ask for a qualification of key personnel section and a management plan. These sections are to be written separately and labeled clearly.

Always include a project organizational chart in the attachments. In federal grants, including a flow chart within the narrative of the grant application to show the chain of accountability is wise.

In Figure 14-2, I show you a flow chart for the public television project.

Check out, in Figure 14-2, how I combine key personnel responsibilities, project activity, and viewer feedback into one highly effective graphic. A flow chart gives the grant reader a clear picture of how the program will be implemented — and it shows accountability. But a flow chart takes up at least one page of the grant application narrative. If the grant application's guidelines limit the number of pages that you can write in the narrative, then a flow chart may have to be your entire management plan section, with no other narrative.

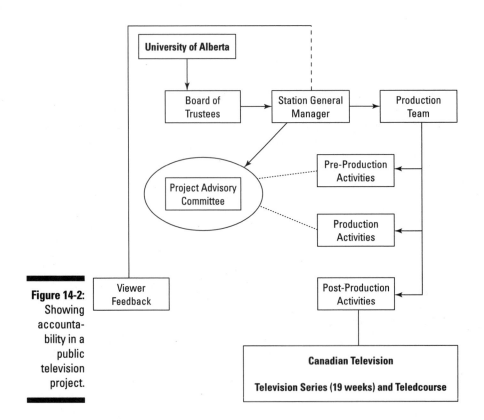

Figure 14-2:
Showing
accounta-
bility in a
public
television
project.

Identifying Resources That Will Be Available to the Project

In a federal or state grant, you have to address something usually called *adequacy of resources*. The next example is from a grant request to the National Aeronautics and Space Administration. (You may also be asked to address this issue in only the budget section.)

Adequacy of Resources

The Office of Intergalactic Research (OIR) has introduced a series of innovative projects that have proven highly successful — they're both fun and educational. It's built up an extensive range of educational space activities over the past few years, many of which have involved the construction of equipment; OIR now has considerable resources to draw upon. The science media has recognized the innovative nature of the projects on several occasions. The projects have received valuable national and local press and TV and radio coverage, both in the popular and in specialist technical/educational media.

You can see in the preceding example that OIR's contribution to this request is equipment related to educational space activities.

Here is another example of this very small but critical section — showing what the grant applicant is bringing to the table. The organization asking for grant funds has something of value already that will complement any incoming grant funds. This example is from a request for funds to hire additional law enforcement personnel. It was funded for $300,000.

> The Antioch Township Police Department already owns the patrol cars that the three new full-time officers will be driving. The cars are valued at $20,000 each. The value of the vehicles, office space, communications equipment, and other department resources is approximately $100,000. A federal grant award from the U.S. Department of Justice for $300,000, over a three-year period, will be matched annually by the Police Department's own internal resources that equal one-third or more of the grant request.

Your resources don't have to be written down as rows and rows of line items, at least not in this section. But it's a different story when you show your matching funds or in-kind contribution in the *budget* section.

Showing Equity in Your Personnel and Participant Selection

Equity is created when you manage a program in such a way that no one is excluded. All the individuals hired with grant funds and all the members of the target population (those people the grant funds will help) must be guaranteed a place in your project. Federal and state funders mandate a section on equity. Foundations and corporations usually don't have anything on equity in their guidelines, but it doesn't hurt to include a paragraph.

The next example is from a federal grant application to the U.S. Department of Education. It received all of the allocated review criteria points from the grant readers.

> Rio Bravo Community College has proposed to serve a multiethnic high-needs population of newly arriving immigrants into Big Ben County. The following barriers, under federal and state statutes, will not impede equitable access to or participation in the **FREEDOM PROJECT:** *gender, race, national origin, color, disability, or*

age. These or any other barriers (to be monitored in all project components) will not prevent students, teachers, volunteers, support staff, or others from access to or participation in this federally funded project. No immigrant seeking services will be denied access. Any superficial barriers imposed by any project staff will be cause for disciplinary action.

All project materials will be created in multiple languages, staff will be multilingual, and cultural beliefs will be honored. The monies awarded in the grant for the **FREEDOM PROJECT** will remove language, economic, and social barriers for an underclass of incoming immigrants.

Here's a quick and easy overview for writing the equity section without stress.

✔ **Ask HR for help.** Some grant application guidelines require that you actually cite the federal and state legislation that your organization adheres to in its hiring practices. The acts that you need to cite can be obtained from your Human Resources department.

✔ **Address equitable access for everyone.** The equity statement should include personnel (including the selection of volunteers for the project) and project participants.

✔ **Make a statement.** Writing that discrimination will not be tolerated is important.

In the statement of equity, the grant reader is looking for several key pieces of information:

✔ Does the grant applicant have team members capable of performing the activities outlined in the project design?

✔ Is this grant applicant worthy of a grant award? Can they be counted on to do what they have proposed?

✔ Does the grant applicant embrace a sense of fairness?

✔ Is the grant applicant willing to commit resources to the proposed project or program?

The personnel, resources, and equity section of the grant application narrative can range from one page to several pages for the entire section. Developing narrative language that meets the funding source's requirements in its grant application guidelines is important. Even though many funders accept a standardized grant application format like the NNG, some foundations and government agencies have their own specialized formats.

Read the grant guidelines carefully before you start writing this section.

Chapter 15

Writing the Evaluation Plan Section of the Narrative

. . . .

In This Chapter

▶ Understanding the language of evaluation

▶ Finding proven evaluation designs

▶ Taking the internal stakeholders' approach

▶ Using an outside evaluator

▶ Developing good measurements

▶ Telling the world about your model project

. . . .

*W*hen I first started writing grants (back in prehistoric times), I was comfortable with all of the sections of the grant application narrative except for the evaluation plan. I would read and reread the proposal's project design or plan of operation, examining the goals and objectives. I was searching for a way to prove that after the grant funds were used, the objectives had really been met. Eventually, I grew more comfortable with writing the evaluation plan. I'm glad that I can help you write great evaluation plans — and spare you the effort that I had to put into it!

This chapter gives you the information you need either to write a strong evaluation plan yourself or use a third-party evaluator to develop the evaluation plan section of the narrative.

Getting Comfortable with Evaluation Terms

I define an *evaluation* as what lets you and everyone else know that you kept your promises — in other words, that you met the objectives that you wrote about in the grant application.

The most important part of grant writing is the initial step of deciding what grants to pursue. But evaluating your project, once it's been funded, comes a close second. The evaluation plan section of the grant narrative explains to the potential funder how you plan to evaluate the success of your project. The evaluation plan includes

- A review of your program's objectives and how you will know if they've been met

- What type of information you plan to collect to use in the evaluation

- How often the information will be collected

- Who will collect the information

- Who will analyze the information and report the results

Before you can write an evaluation plan, you need to have a basic understanding of the terms that are commonly used.

Data is the information that's gathered, using evaluation tools, about your project. You collect data in order to find out if you're slowly but surely achieving the objectives that you describe in the project design section of your grant narrative.

Data analysis occurs when you examine the information that you collect with the measurement tools to determine what it means. If the data produces information that is not relevant to determining the progress of your project, then you need to go back to square one and design new data collection tools. Think about where the problem may lie: Maybe your survey didn't ask the right questions or perhaps it was administered in a setting that was not conducive to getting true responses. (Did your teacher ever hand out a questionnaire at the end of the year to see how you liked his class — and then walk up and down the aisles while you filled it out to see what you wrote? *That's* a setting not conducive to getting a true response.) When you hand out a data collection tool for participants to fill in, leave the room. Don't mess with the findings on your project. The truth is what you're hoping to discover; the truth will help you redesign the objectives and develop new ways to conduct a more effective program.

Evaluation standards are acceptable ways to measure various components of your project. The American National Standards Institute approved the four nationally used standards in 1994. A great resource to use to read about these standards and understand how they fit into your overall evaluation plan is *The Program Evaluation Standards* book (Sage Publications).

- **Utility standards** are how you plan to evaluate the information needs of the project's participants or end-users.

- **Feasibility standards** are how you plan to ensure that your evaluation procedures will be realistic, prudent, diplomatic, and frugal.

✔ **Propriety standards** are how you plan to show that your evaluation will be conducted legally, ethically, and with due regard for the welfare of those involved in the evaluation, as well as the welfare of those affected by its results.

✔ **Accuracy standards** are how you plan to show that your evaluation will reveal and convey technically adequate information about your project.

The entire evaluation process should incorporate these standards if the findings are to be accepted as valid by others in your field and the funders.

The **evaluator** or **evaluation team** is the individual or group of persons you select to determine if your project succeeded or failed.

You should not evaluate your own project. It's okay for you to be a part of the evaluation team if you decide to conduct an internal evaluation, but refrain from coaching or coercing other team members (your coworkers, board members, volunteers, community members, or project participants). Everyone on the evaluation team needs to be able to talk openly about her perceptions of the data findings. Focus on being impartial.

Even if you have failed miserably in your project (for example, the objectives said that 90 percent of the participants would be placed in gainful employment but only 10 percent were placed), you and your stakeholders, including the funders, want to know what went wrong and how it can be fixed. Sometimes in this *failed* scenario, your funding source will actually give you a second grant to fix the problem, which equates to another chance to succeed. But you'll only get the second chance if your evaluation team is objective and accurate.

Formative evaluations occur when you sit down with the project's stakeholders (community members, participants, and staff) and develop a list of questions that the funders may ask about your project in determining if their monies were well placed and used. The questions should provide answers about the quality of your project and if it can be improved. Looking at aspects of the project design — goals, objectives, and activities — stakeholders generate questions about how the project can become more effective or efficient. The formative process is ongoing from the time you receive grant funding until the completion of the grant timeframe. In light of this ongoing process, set a frequency for when the data will be collected to answer the questions you have posed.

If you can't make improvements to your project, a formative evaluation may not be the right approach to measure the success of your project; instead, focus on using a summative evaluation.

Internal evaluations occur when you decide not to hire an outsider to conduct your evaluation, but choose instead to use the stakeholders approach to creating an internal evaluation team.

Measurement tools or **evaluation tools** are what you use to collect the data or information that will show if your project reached its objectives. Information can be collected using surveys, pre- and post-questionnaires or tests, or oral interviews.

Objectives are measurable, progressive steps taken to achieve the project's goals. (Chapter 13 shows you how to write measurable objectives.)

The **summative evaluation** (often called an **outcome evaluation**) occurs near or at the end of the period you were funded for. The summative evaluation should produce extensive narrative to answer the following questions: What did you accomplish? How many participants were impacted and in what way? What overall difference did your project make? Is this project worth funding again?

Qualitative is the approach you take when you want to understand the impact of your project on the participants. A qualitative approach may mean that you develop questions and collect data to measure the success of the project or program that you implemented with grant funds. Your findings must focus on looking closely at your program from an operational stand-point and determining its overall impact on the target population (the end recipients of the grant-funded services or activities).

Quantitative is the approach that you take to measure your project's effects using a *design group* and a *comparison group*. For example, if you compare your participants' outcomes with a group of individuals sharing the same participant characteristics that have not had the benefit of a project like yours.

I like to combine both qualitative and quantitative approaches in order to examine data from a multi-dimensional viewpoint.

Stakeholders: The stakeholders in your project are those individuals or enti-ties that stand to lose something if your project falls short of its objectives and stand to gain if the project achieves it proposed objectives.

Third party Evaluator: This is an outside individual or company that designs and conducts your project's evaluation. You must remember to include an expense line in your project's budget to compensate the third party evaluator for their services. The standard amount to set aside for evaluation is 15 per-cent of your total project budget.

Finding Evaluation Plan Ideas Online

You must use frameworks and tools that are already developed and widely accepted when you write the evaluation plan. The Bureau of Justice

Assistance (BJA), a division of the U.S. Department of Justice, maintains a Web site that I find helpful. I return to www.ojp.usdoj.gov/BJA time and time again. It has a sample evaluation plan outline that was developed for the U.S. Department of Housing and Urban Renewal in 1997 by KRA Corporation. You can go online to see the entire example. I have changed or eliminated some of the terms to create a more general explanation of the evaluation process.

I've included many Web site addresses throughout this book. Using the Web to search for information that will help you write and win grants is a terrific idea. The one drawback is that Web site addresses seem to change almost daily. If any of the addresses I give you in this book don't connect to a Web page, go to a search engine and search for the relevant content.

Sample Evaluation Plan Outline

What are you going to evaluate? The initial program model — assumptions about target population, interventions, short-term outcomes, intermediate outcomes, and final outcomes; outcome objectives, stated in general and then measurable terms.

Are implementation objectives being attained? If not, why not (that is, what barriers or problems have been encountered)? What kinds of procedures facilitated implementation?

Are outcome objectives being attained? If not, why not (that is, what barriers or problems have been encountered)? What kinds of procedures facilitated attainment of outcomes?

Do outcomes vary as a function of program features? Which aspects of the program contributed the most to achieving expected outcomes?

Do outcomes vary as a function of characteristics of the participants or staff?

When will data collection begin and end?

Procedures for managing and monitoring the evaluation

Procedures for training staff to collect evaluation-related information.

Procedures for conducting quality-control checks of the information collection process.

Time lines for collecting, analyzing, and reporting information, including procedures for providing evaluation related feedback to housing managers and staff.

You can also link to other evaluation resources on the BJA Web site, including the following areas:

- Choosing an evaluation design
- Selecting, adapting, and developing data collection procedures
- Completing evaluation data collection procedures
- Data analysis

Other Web sites that I find very helpful are

- oerl.sri.com/plans/planscrit.html: Online Evaluation Resource Library
- www.sagepub.co.uk (Sage Publications): Even if your project isn't international, this site based in the United Kingdom is great!

Choosing to Conduct an Internal Evaluation

When you plan to conduct an internal evaluation — meaning that you won't be hiring an outsider to assist with or conduct the evaluation on your project — the best option is to propose a *stakeholders evaluation* in the evaluation plan section of your grant narrative. The easiest way to identify who the stakeholders are is to ask yourself the following question: Who has a vested interest in our project and will be impacted if we are successful or unsuccessful once the project is funded?

The outcome of the project definitely matters to your board of directors, if the organization has one. The outcome of the project matters to the staff assigned to work on the project. It matters the most to the participants that you recruit for your project. These are some of the folks you should consider inviting onto the evaluation team.

For example, say your organization proposes to implement a recycling program in your community. Each and every citizen who attended your public meeting to provide their input on the need for a recycling program is a candidate for the evaluation team. The owner of a local business who counts on reducing her trash pick-ups by recycling much of her waste may be a good candidate, as well as anyone who works for the project in any capacity. Be creative and try to combine people who have different perspectives — I always try to include a younger person, such as a college student, on my evaluation teams. The number of people who form the stakeholders evaluation team doesn't matter.

Do you have one or two board members who have wanted to work more hands-on with your organization? Having them be on the evaluation team is an ideal way to divert their energy from (possibly) micromanaging your executive director or staff to really helping shape the outcome of a grant-funded program — a program that could well be the most important part of your organization.

You're not looking for groupthink here, you want independent-minded people who can contribute to developing a strong evaluation plan once the project is funded.

The W. K. Kellogg Foundation has published a handbook describing how to go about an evaluation. You can view or download it at `www.wkkf.org/Publications/evalhdbk`. Among other tips, it contains great advice on how to choose the members of your stakeholders evaluation team.

Choosing an Outside Evaluator

If you decide to bring in an outsider to conduct your evaluation, that person is referred to as a *third party evaluator* in the grant narrative. Look in your own community first and talk to other organizations that provide programs similar to yours. Ask who or what they've used. Often, their evaluator was a university research department, a college faculty member, or a retired government employee with expertise in the project area. You may have to look outside your home area for an evaluator.

These Web sites can help you find a third party evaluator:

- ✔ `www.wmich.edu/evalctr`: The Evaluation Center at Western Michigan University
- ✔ `www.grantprofessionals.org`: American Association of Grant Professionals

What to look for in an external evaluator

You must choose an individual or organization that has experience in developing evaluation plans, creating monitoring guidelines that track the progress of a project's objectives, and conducting both simple and complex evaluations in the project's focus area.

What to ask a prospective evaluator

During your telephone conversation or meeting with the prospective evaluator, have a list of questions to ask. Write down the answers. You may have to decide from among several possible evaluators, and having the answers on paper will help you review and make your decision.

Suggested questions include

- What methodology will you use to understand the day-to-day operations of my project?

- How much time will the work take and what is the cost?

- How many on-site days can you provide in order to meet with project personnel and talk to participants? How much will it cost?

- Are you willing to give me a written description of your services and the cost of service if my organization cannot afford your services for the duration of the project?

- Are you willing to meet with my board of directors to provide progress reports on the evaluation?

- At what points will you give me written evaluation reports?

Brainstorm with your staff and come up with even more questions. Selecting an evaluator is a very important part of your project and to underbudget or fall short in writing this part of the narrative can result in not getting funded.

Once you find an evaluator, see if that organization or person can help you write the evaluation plan for the grant narrative. Of course, you may have to pay a fee for the evaluator's time. The money is well spent if you're going after a multi-million dollar, multi-year grant and the competition is heavy. If fewer than ten grants will be awarded nationwide in a major grant competition, that's what I'd call *heavy*.

Writing a Stakeholders Evaluation Plan

The fewer goals and objectives you create for your project, the easier it is to develop the evaluation plan. Here's a sample from a grant funded by the Michigan Department of Education. The evaluation team in this example is the technology action committee at the school district. As you can see, the plan is brief but effective.

Performance Evaluation. Ongoing summative evaluation of how technologies will be integrated into the school curriculum: Pre- and post-training written self-assessment, student assessment, and administrative assessment of each elementary teacher. The Charleston Public Schools (CPS) strategic technology action committee will develop assessment forms. Integration benchmarks will be every 90 days. Results of assessments will be compiled by building principals and reviewed with teachers.

<u>Ongoing summative evaluation of how technologies will improve student learning:</u> MEAP and MEAP HST scores in math and reading will be monitored districtwide. The base year will be the 1997 MEAP results. It is important to CPS that its students are Satisfactory and Proficient in greater percentages so it will meet the challenge of attaining the National Education Goals by the year 2000.

Evaluation results carry more credibility when you can cite standards from recognized initiatives such as the National Education Goals.

The next example was written for a local historical association's building fund project.

How the project's success will be determined:

Goal: To preserve the history of Montcalm County and to continue the commitment that has been made to the community by completing the restoration of the glider and to create the Military Museum.

A qualitative evaluation will be conducted to demonstrate the achievement of the following objectives:

Objective 1a: To break ground for the Fighting Falcon Military Museum when 100 percent of the grant funds are secured.

Measurement: Keep track of all donated monies and notify all funders of groundbreaking ceremony date.

Objective 1b: To meet 90 percent or more of the Museum's construction timeframes and stay within the projected cost.

Measurement: Monitor and report benchmarks achieved based on the contractor's work plan and make oral and written reports to the board of directors and funders.

When you ask for building funds, evaluation terms are developed to reflect proof of receiving full funding (after all, if you only receive half of what you request, you can't build half a building and let it sit!) and timely construction completion.

To continue the Military Museum example:

Who will be involved in evaluating this work?

The evaluators will be the stakeholders, which include all members of the Flat River Historical Society board and The Fighting Falcon Military Museum board, as well as members of the community, children in the schools, and tourists to the area. An evaluation form will be available at the museum's entrance for all visitors to complete.

How will the evaluation results be used?

Evaluation results will be available to all funding sources and will be used to ensure the continued success of The Fighting Falcon Military Museum, by providing input for making improvements to exhibits, enhancing educational materials, and maintaining the restored glider.

Writing a Third-Party Evaluation Plan

The next example shows you how to write about a third-party evaluator. Be brief in the narrative, but include the evaluator's full credentials in the attachments and note that these items are attached.

The evaluation will be done by Stone Mountain Research Associates (SRA) Inc., of Stone Mountain, Georgia. SRA has conducted research and evaluation studies of numerous projects since 1984. They are familiar with creating databases, developing surveys and authentic assessment tests, collecting data, designing evaluations, and conducting ethnographic studies. The staff at SRA is comprised of Sally Allen-Myers, Ph.D., Ginnie Golden, M.S., and Louise Taylor, M.B.A. SRA's evaluation credentials are attached. A portion of the grant budget will be allocated for the contracted evaluation activities completed by SRA for the Stone Mountain Charter School. A combined qualitative and quantitative approach will be used to determine the overall success of the project.

See how I word the measurements to show how the data will be collected? Objectives and measurements also can be presented in a table, like this:

Objective	Summative Measurements
Decrease the number of students scoring below average on the Stanford test by 10 percent annually in all areas of Language Arts. Rewrite and align 100 percent of Language Arts curriculum and raise course content standards throughout the high school.	Pre- and post-test scores on the Stanford Nine and on state standardized tests to be monitored annually
Increase students' time-on-task for each subject area, curriculum-wide (encompassing all academic areas), by a minimum of 40 additional hours each semester.	Documentation in each student's portfolio. Monitoring of students' grade point averages at the end of each semester
Enroll 75 percent or more of the District's students in flextime tutorial programs and/or the Summer Learning Academy for a minimum of 100 hours of additional Language Arts coursework. Math will be included for those students in need of additional time-on-task in this curricular area.	Documentation on student's attendance rate. Monitoring of student's core curriculum competency achievements as demonstrated by a letter grade of C or higher. Results of yet-to-be developed annual (prior to state assessment time) authentic assessments for each Language Arts component testing area

I like to use a lot of tables to give the grant reviewer a rest from reading paragraph after paragraph of narrative.

Getting the Word Out When Your Project Is a Model for Others

Disseminate means to scatter or spread widely. It's an important word for grant writers because your funding sources want you to share the findings or outcomes of your project with others in your field. Literally hundreds of nonprofits, spread across the country, are struggling to plan and develop programs or services like the one that you just successfully completed. Funding sources want you to compile your project's findings into a report, a video, a training tape, or a workbook, and send them out so that others can learn from your mistakes and successes. Another easy way to disseminate your evaluation findings is to prepare a presentation and get on the agenda at local, regional, and national conferences where agencies interested in your research will have members in attendance.

You don't need to write a major paragraph on dissemination in your application narrative, just a few sentences to show that you know how to do it and that you intend to do it. Here's a sample from one of my funded grants:

> Dissemination is an integral part of this proposal since the long-term goal is to reach a national audience of minority students in technical programs. Listed below are specific dissemination strategies for the CATCH Program.
>
> *Information regarding processes and program outcomes at each stage of the program will be disseminated to all interested institutions through reports and the Internet.
>
> *Templates and course content for various program modules will be disseminated over the Web site as they are developed. Institutions will be invited to participate in testing and reviewing these modules.
>
> *Many career counseling units will be available as presentation slides over the Internet for interested institutions. Also, presentations of international scholars and business leaders will be disseminated through videoconferencing or presentation slides.
>
> *Information about the program will be disseminated regionally through the New Mexico Consortium's *Latino TV* television show.
>
> *A CD-ROM documenting the experiences of participants and the impact, if any, of this program on their academic and professional success will be produced and made available on a cost-recovery basis. The CD-ROM will also profile minorities in nontraditional careers.
>
> *Dissemination of lessons learned and program success will be made through academic and professional presentations and journal articles.

You can request monies in the project budget to pay for dissemination costs.

Chapter 16

Presenting the Budget

- -

In This Chapter

▶ Understanding budget terms

▶ Turning thoughts into line items

▶ Finding matching funds

▶ Calculating costs beyond one project year

▶ Getting another agency to act as your fiscal sponsor

▶ Adopting an ethical approach to grant seeking

- -

Developing the budget section of your grant application shouldn't be like throwing a dart while blindfolded. The budget is linked by an umbilical cord to the project's objectives. In order to achieve the objectives, a series of activities must occur. The line items in your budget are the dollar cost of the activities. This chapter walks you through the budget preparation process. It also tells you what the funder's expectations are when it comes to your budget section.

Walking through the Terms

Most of the terms associated with the budget section are basically everyday terms — no big deal. But thoroughly understanding what's behind each term will move you from the "I'm not so sure" bench to the "I know how to do this" bench, ready to go out for the last inning in the grants game. And when you run onto the field, don't forget enthusiasm!

Allocation and budget summary

Allocation is the amount you assign to each line item, and *budget summary* is the skeletal outline of how the project's total cost is allocated to line items. Table 16-1 shows you how that works if, for example, you're requesting funding for a staff position.

Table 16-1	Project Budget Summary
Line Item	*Cost*
Personnel	$50,000
Fringe Benefits	$18,500
Total Project Budget	$68,500

Budget detail

Funders want to know what their dollars will be going toward. Hence, budget detail. But the budget detail section is not the place to spring surprises on the funder. Anything that shows up should have already been discussed in the project design section of the application. The following example uses the same request to fund a staff position that I use in Table 16-1.

Personnel: The Zenias Agency will hire one full-time (1.0 FTE) project manager at $50,000 annually to provide daily oversight of the program implementation phase for the Vineyard Project. A job description is attached. This position will be for 12 months.

Fringe Benefits: This line is calculated at 37 percent of total salaries and wages for a total of $18,500. Grant funds will enable the Zenias Agency to offer full benefits to the project manager. Current employee benefits include health insurance, life insurance, short- and long-term disability insurance, dental and vision insurance. The agency is also requesting grant funds to pay the employer-related expenses that will be incurred by the hiring of one new full-time employee. These expenses include the FICA match, workers' compensation, and unemployment insurance. These three employer-related expenses have been included in the 37 percent calculation. A more detailed breakdown of each benefit's actual percent is available from the business manager upon request.

The budget detail narrative section usually follows the budget summary. Researching the funding source's preference for developing this section of your grant application is important. Some funders only want the budget summary, while others require summary and detail.

Personnel

The personnel line is where you include any project staff that will be paid from the grant funds. If your organization is planning to assign existing staff to the grant-funded project, but not charge the staff to the grant, you need to create an in-kind column to show the funder how you plan to support the costs of the project's personnel. See Table 16-2 for an example.

Table 16-2		Project Budget Summary	
Line Item	*In-Kind*	*Requested*	*Total Line Item*
Personnel	$25,000	$25,000	$50,000

Travel

If you plan to reimburse project personnel for local travel, traditionally referred to as *mileage reimbursement,* include this expense in the travel line item. Also, if you plan to send project personnel to out-of-town training or conferences during the course of the project, then you need to ask for out-of-town travel expenses. Your travel explanation in the budget detail needs to include the number of trips planned, number of persons for each trip, conference name, location, purpose, and cost. Don't forget to include the cost for transportation to the events, lodging, meals, and ground travel.

One more pointer: You will come across the term *per diem.* It means the cost per day that your organization allows each employee to spend on meals and incidentals during their travel. Federal grant applications may have per diem limits, like $35 per day. Keep in mind that having a set amount for the per diem allowed could backfire when you or an employee travels to an area with a higher cost of living than the norm, like Alaska, the East coast, or the West coast.

Here's an example of a budget detail for Travel.

> Travel: Grant funding will reimburse Community Learning Network project staff for their on-site visits to the RBCC campus at Yorkville, the Housing Authority of the City of Yorkville site, and the Yorkville Public Library. Project staff includes the Project Administrator, Information Technology Director, the Trainer for Information Technology, and the Project Director. Each of these staff members will be conducting on-site visits to oversee the installation of equipment and the implementation of the project, to meet with project partners, and to train on-site facilitators

who will assist the students in the ITV programs for adult literacy and occupational training courses. Local travel is based on $0.32 per mile, per car, tolls and gasoline reimbursements. Total travel costs are calculated at $85 per month for 24 months. No federal funds are requested.

Federal Funds: $0   Matching Funds: $2,040   Total: $2,040

When you are writing a grant application that requires matching funds, always show three separate columns in your budget narrative. The first for the amount of federal funds requested. The second for the amount of funds you have to match the federal funds. The third column is the total of the two monies: federal + matching funds.

Be conservative, yet accurate, in calculating travel expenses. No funder wants to see their money pay for junkets or extended vacations. Don't look for conferences in exotic places, or you'll raise a red flag that could get your proposal tossed out during the review stages.

Equipment

This is where you ask for grant monies to purchase a major piece of equipment, like a computer or copy machine, usually costing $1,000 or more and having a useful life (the length of time the equipment is expected to be in service) of two years or longer. Some funding sources consider capital equipment an *unallowable cost,* meaning they don't fund it. Do your homework before asking for grant monies to cover this line item. Sometimes, you're better off asking a local office supply company to donate a big-ticket piece of equipment, rather than bogging down the grant budget by adding it to your line items.

Here's an example of the budget detail for Equipment:

Equipment: A vendor will be competitively selected to provide high-end multimedia desktop computers for participants at the Community Learning Network sites. The computers will provide access to courseware and the Internet and will function as the backbone of RBCC's Community Learning Network program for students and adult learners. Participants will be able to access computers for personal study on site without the need to travel to campus.

Federal Funds: $60,000   Matching Funds: $0   Total: $60,000

Think about leasing your capital equipment. Leasing is sometimes allowed by the funder when purchasing the item outright isn't. Also, at the end of the lease, you have the option to purchase the item. (Of course, you'll need to find the funds to do so.)

Supplies

Expendable materials and supplies needed in the daily implementation of the project go on the supplies line. I also include office supplies in this item in foundation and corporate grant applications. However, in federal and state grant applications, office supplies usually are included in the indirect costs.

Contractual

The contractual line is where you include the money to hire anyone for the project who is not a member of the staff (whose expenses are listed under personnel). For example, the organization may plan to hire an accounting firm to handle the fiscal reporting side of the grant's management or an evaluation specialist.

In some smaller nonprofit organizations, personnel hired with grant funds are considered contracted services — the term of employment is conditional on continued grant funding. The pro side of doing this is that it eliminates having departing project personnel file for unemployment compensation. The con side is that some really qualified and available individuals may want more of a commitment and may not remain with your project for the duration of the grant period. Also, the constant change of personnel can be a problem when it comes to the evaluation process. (Chapter 15 covers evaluation responsibilities.)

Construction

When you write a grant that's exclusively seeking funds for construction, you don't need to bother with a budget summary and a budget detail narrative. Just insert the bid. The *bid* is the written document submitted to you by the construction company that lists all the costs involved in the project. Shortcuts are nice!

Other

Where you put the expenses for printing, subscribing to publications, telephone and facsimile costs, and any other project expenses that do not fit in any other category. Think of *other* the same as you would *miscellaneous*.

Here's an example of budget detail for Other.

Other: This line item includes the following costs calculated for three-year period:

*Development, duplication, and distribution of training materials for teachers at 50 sites annually @ $50,000 per year × 3.

*Stipends/participation incentives of $1,000 for the first teacher in each new school site that agrees to become the honorary mentor for 50 teachers × 3 years.

*Postage, telephone, facsimile, and other project office expenses @ $5,000 per year × 3.

*Legal, accounting, and grants management @ $10,000 per year × 3.

Direct costs

All of the line items I've introduced so far are considered *direct* costs, that is, expenses for services and products that you need for the project and are not otherwise available at your organization. This term and the line item for it are used only in those state and federal grants where you actually see *direct costs* and *indirect costs* in the application guidelines and on the preprinted budget forms.

Indirect costs

Indirect costs — often called *overhead* — cover services and products like the telephone bill, rent payments, maintenance costs, and insurance premiums that are essential for your overall organization and consumed in some small degree by the project. The indirect cost line is another one of those *for state or federal grant applications only* terms. Indirect costs are usually calculated as a percentage of total direct costs. Your agency may already have an approved indirect cost rate from a state or federal agency and it may be on file in the business manager's office. Indirect costs can range from as little as 5 percent for a charter school to as much as 60 percent for a major university.

I've actually written federal grant applications with 60 percent indirect cost rates built in. This means that if the application is funded and the direct costs total $1 million, another $600,000 will be tacked on for indirect costs. (Your taxes at work!)

I have more information for you on indirect costs. If you apply for a federal grant and your organization has an indirect cost rate of 20 percent, you can choose not to ask for the entire 20 percent from the feds. Instead, because you want to look good and capable of managing a grant, you can ask for 10 percent from the feds and make up the other 10 percent as an in-kind contribution.

Look at this great example of an indirect costs narrative:

> The Rio Bravo Community College applies an indirect cost rate of 8% to all direct cost categories. A copy of the college's indirect cost rate with the U.S. Department of Education is attached to the Budget Narrative. Indirect charges are calculated for the total federal funds requested ($472,590) minus the contractual requested ($42,962), which equals $429,628 × 8%, or $34,370.
>
> *Federal Funds: $20,000
>
> *Matching Funds: $14,370
>
> *Total Indirect Costs: $34,370

In-kind

The in-kind line is where you list the financial contributions that your organization will make available to the grant-funded project, meaning that you're not asking for monies from the funder for these items. Some federal and state funding competitions require an in-kind match. This match can range from 20 percent to 50 percent.

Two kinds of in-kind exist: hard matching funds and soft matching funds. *Hard match* is an actual cash match from your own general operating monies, or even from other grants that may be awarded at the same time this grants funding cycle will begin. (I define *soft match* later in this chapter.)

Linking Dollars to Activities

In this section, I show you how to develop the budget from the project design section, using an example I also use in Chapter 13.

Goal:

To link, through referrals, individuals with experience and/or training in home health care, housekeeping, companion services, and adult day care with Universal County's elderly population in need of such services.

Activities:

The director will manage all referrals, ensure quality control, recruit caregivers, interview and screen candidates, conduct background checks, market to careseekers and caregivers (individuals and agencies), and conduct community relations (network with other service providers and identify future grant and fundraising opportunities).

The office manager will assist the director in all aspects of her job. She will also cosupervise the administrative assistant.

The administrative assistant will assist with referrals, file management, quality control, billing, application review, and community relations.

You know you have a problem if the line items in the budget don't match up with the project's activities. Making this cross-check is also a good way to determine whether you've left something out of the budget and vice versa. See Table 16-3 for an example of a project budget.

Table 16-3	Project Budget for RSC General Operating Costs
Line Item	*Cost*
Staffing	
Director (full-time @ $30,000 per year)	$30,000
Office Manager (full-time @ $19,000 per year)	$19,000
Administrative Assistant (full-time @ $15,000 per year)	$15,000

Line Item	Cost
Other Operational Expenses	
Liability and Contents Insurance	$600
Office Supplies	$1,200
Postage	$2,700
Rent	$7,200
Legal and Accounting Fees	$7,000
Dues and Subscriptions	$500
Printing	$1,200
Telephone (additional line for fax and monthly charges)	$1,800
Equipment upgrade (computer and software, printer, fax machine, flatbed scanner)	$5,000
Total Operational Costs	**$91,200**

This budget summary comes from one of my grants. It provided sufficient detail to the funding sources that received this request — several grants were awarded based on this budget summary and the rest of the proposal's narrative.

Scouring Up Matching Funds

When a grant application requires matching funds, it means that every dollar requested from the funding source must be matched with a specified percent of your own monies. The grant guidelines will tell you if the match is 20, 50, or 100 percent of the grant request.

Eventually, every grant writer comes across the challenge of finding the matching funds required to meet the conditions of a grant's guidelines. Push your fear aside and rev up your engine, because finding matching funds is about to become a lot easier. First of all, read the grant application instructions regarding matching funds. Ask yourself how this funder defines matching funds. Can the match be an in-kind contribution, also referred to as *soft cash*, or are you required to identify actual cash for the match? Actual cash is referred to as a *hard match*.

In my travels across the country, I'm amazed at the feedback I get about how hard it is for grant applicants to come up with the required match amount in order to qualify for some state and federal grants. I've put together the following information to assist you in finding those much sought-after matching funds.

Hard cash match sources

Here are some of the places you can look to see if you have cash available for a hard cash match.

- ✔ General fund.
- ✔ Specialized allocation.
- ✔ Other state or federal grant funds. (But check with the funding agency to which you're applying to make sure that these types of matching funds are allowable.)
- ✔ Private sector grants for portions of the project.

Soft cash match sources

Here are some great ideas for identifying sources of soft matching funds or in-kind contributions:

- ✔ Personnel who will provide direct or indirect services for the grant-funded activities, but who will not be charged to the grant's budget expenditures as a line-item request to the funding. So, on a prorated basis, administrative, clerical support, contracted, and facilities personnel (custodial should be included) positions can all apply as soft cash match line items.
- ✔ Fringe benefits for the above personnel (prorated based on the actual amount of time to be contributed to grant-funded activities).
- ✔ Travel expenses (grant-related for key or ancillary personnel that will not be requested from the funding source).
- ✔ Equipment (existing or to be purchased that will not be requested from the funding source).
- ✔ Supplies (on hand from existing inventory or newly purchased that will not be requested from the funding source).
- ✔ Contractual (contracted consultants that will lend their expertise and time to the project, once funded, but whose expenses may not be eligible for grant funding).
- ✔ Construction (any aspect of infrastructure work that will be donated by trade professionals or volunteers).

✔ Other, such as utilities and telephone expenses related to implementing the project, but not an allowable line item in the grant request; printing and copying; postage; evaluation expenses not included in contractual or supplies; and any other costs that will be incurred by your community that have not been requested from the funder.

✔ Indirect charges (range from 5 percent to 66 percent of the budget subtotal and are allowable *only* in federal grant applications). Indirect charges can be a line-item request in the grant budget; however, if you're struggling to identify matching funds, then use indirect charges as a matching contribution to be absorbed by your community.

Projecting Multi-Year Costs

When you're planning to construct a building or purchase specific items of equipment, you can usually get bids from engineers or vendors that are very close to the actual cost of the construction or equipment if you win the grant and make the expenditure. However, when you're seeking funding for personnel or line items with prices that fluctuate, take care to account for inflation. *In a multi-year request, your line items should increase by at least five percent per year.*

Table 16-4 is a request to a foundation for two years' worth of funding. Note that the Total column is the sum of in-kind funds and requested funds. Remember that your justification for each line item should appear in the budget narrative and be linked to the activities in the project design.

Table 16-4	Grant Application — Budget Summary				
Line-Item Expenses	**Year 1**	**Year 2**	**In-Kind**	**Requested**	**Total**
Salaries	$125,000	$131,250	$200,000	$56,250	$256,250
Fringe Benefits	$37,500	$39,375	$60,000	$16,875	$76,875
Contractual	$18,000	$18,900	$0	$36,900	$36,900
Travel	$4,000	$4,200	$0	$8,200	$8,200
Equipment	$14,000	$0	$7,000	$7,000	$14,000
Supplies	$3,500	$3,675	$0	$7,175	$7,175
Other	$22,000	$23,100	$17,000	$28,100	$45,100

(continued)

Table 16-4 *(continued)*					
Line-Item Expenses	Year 1	Year 2	In-Kind	Requested	Total
Project Subtotal	$224,000	$220,500	$284,000	$160,500	$444,500
Evaluation and Dissemination (15% of project total)	$33,600	$33,075	$0	$66,675	$66,675
Project Total	$257,600	$253,575	$284,000	$227,175	$511,175

The W. K. Kellogg Foundation Web site offers some really great guidelines on how to break down your budget request for multi-year proposals submitted to them for funding. Take a look at www.wkkf.org/HowToApply/finandefi.htm.

The Ontario Trillium Foundation Web site provides a great example of a multi-year budget. It shows how to incorporate the monies you are requesting from other funding sources into its budget summary. Take a look at www.trilliumfoundation.org/english/sample_budget_2.html.

Using a Fiscal Sponsor

A *fiscal sponsor* is an organization that has a 501(c)(3) nonprofit status awarded by the Internal Revenue Service. Usually, a fiscal sponsor is a veteran agency with a long and successful track record in winning and managing grants.

The role of the fiscal sponsor is to act as an umbrella organization for newer nonprofit organizations that do not have a track record in winning and managing grant awards. Your new organization is the grant applicant, but the established agency is the fiscal sponsor. It acts as the fiduciary agent for your grant monies. This means it's responsible for depositing the monies in a separate account and for creating procedures for your organization to access the grant monies. Sometimes, a fiscal sponsor wants you to add a line item in the budget for accounting services or grants management. This practice is acceptable to the funding sources. Just make sure to select a fiscal sponsor that you are on good terms with and have open lines of communication with. Otherwise, your grant monies could be slow in trickling down.

Having a written agreement is a good way to prevent any misunderstandings on how the money will be used and accessed.

Why would you use a fiscal sponsor instead of applying directly for grant funds yourself? Because some foundations and corporate givers don't award grant monies to a nonprofit organization that has not completed the IRS *advanced ruling period.* Be patient while I explain that jargon:

When your organization applies for nonprofit status, you may be granted an advanced ruling period of 60 months. During your first five years as a nonprofit charitable organization, the IRS allows you to operate as a public charity rather than as a private foundation.

A public charity means the majority of your operating monies come from public support — grants. A private foundation is just the opposite; the majority of its operating monies come from private support — contributions from individuals.

Ninety days prior to the end of the 60 months, you must file IRS Form 8734 (Support Schedule for Advance Ruling Period). If you fail to submit this form, your organization could automatically be reclassified as a private foundation and you would be required to file Form 990PF. (See Chapter 5 for more on the 990.)

Points to ponder:

- Who is responsible if you mismanage the money? The fiscal sponsor.
- Who is responsible if the fiscal sponsor mismanages the money? The fiscal sponsor.
- Who gets audited for financial expenditures? The funding source can audit the fiscal sponsor. The fiscal sponsor can audit your organization.
- What types of funding sources are likely to perform an audit? Federal and state agencies.

Crunching the Numbers Ethically

Developing thorough and accurate project budgets for the funders involves more than just putting numbers down in a line and adding them together. Completing a project budget can be an individual effort or a team effort. Either way, many factors affect the bottom line — how much you ask for in grant funding. Asking for too much is not looked upon favorably by any funding source. Giving money back that's left over at the end of the grant period is a straight road to *grant suicide — meaning you may not be able to go back to that funder, ever!* No one wants money back.

When a grant is awarded, it's awarded in good faith and based on your budget request and the funding source's grantmaking capacity. So fine-tuning your budget request to reflect the actual cost of your program needs is your first goal in developing the budget section of your application narrative. The second goal is getting it funded in full.

Using conservative and accurate cost figures

You're not sure what kind of budget numbers to put down? How much you'll have to pay a program director? How much you'll have to spend on a copy machine? I've got an easy solution: Use your telephone. You could call the United Way in your area to see what the salary ranges are for program directors, program coordinators, clerical support, accounting clerks, and other staff positions. Call vendors for specification sheets on equipment.

The Internet has a wealth of information on nonprofit organizations, including salary surveys.

Network with other organizations in your community to see if there are any purchasing cooperatives (in which multiple agencies place orders for like items in bulk, thus receiving a bulk purchase discount). All the members of the cooperative reduce their overall operating costs.

Don't plug in any numbers on your budget summary unless you have a backup file with supporting documentation. What if, after mailing the grant application, you get a call from a funder asking about a line item's cost? Rather than making something up off the top of your head, look in your backup file and talk about real costs.

Perhaps the funder thought that $15,000 was too much for a copy machine for your program. After you explain that the copier will be used to produce all agency reports and turn out a monthly newsletter for 7,000 readers in your community (you could mention that the newsletter will carry a funding appeal every month), and that having a copier in-house will save you $20,000 annually in typesetting fees and outside printing, don't worry; you'll get the $15,000 that you asked for!

Yes, funders do call to get more information on a line item. Be prepared!

Including all possible program income

If you anticipate having any program income at all, it must be listed at the end of your budget summary table and subtracted from the total project costs, which results in a lesser amount needed in grant funds. See Table 16-5.

Table 16-5	Abbreviated Project Budget Summary Showing Program Income	
Total Operational Costs	$91,200	
Projected Program Income (membership fees)	$24,000	
Grant Funds Requested	**$67,200**	

Examples of possible program income are

- ✔ Membership fees (shown in the example).

- ✔ Ticket sales for planned events. (You work in a performing arts organization. There are three plays at the local community theater, and patrons will purchase tickets to see your troupe perform.)

- ✔ Special events revenue (for example, you plan a fundraising event to get additional program monies for field trips, equipment, or other items or activities in the project's design).

- ✔ Interest (for example, you earn interest on an endowment fund that you are allowed to use annually to assist with program costs).

- ✔ Tuition (for example, you receive payment or reimbursement from a state agency for training welfare-to-work participants and your grant request was for monies to counsel and provide intensive follow-up coaching to new job entrants from the welfare-to-work pool).

Not showing this income is unethical. Just think about the dozens, hundreds, or thousands of proposals a foundation or corporate giving entity receives daily, weekly, and monthly. Ninety percent of the time, the funding source must send out letters to grant seekers regretfully stating that there are simply not enough funds available to fund all of the requests received. If you choose to omit the fact that you expect program income and greedily ask for the whole ball of wax, you are taking, in the example, $24,000 out of the funder's annual grantmaking budget. Your $24,000 excess could have funded another grant, perhaps for a struggling start-up agency with no other resources.

From an ethical standpoint, asking for grant funds means taking an oath with yourself to never ask for more than you actually need.

Part IV

Reaching the Finish Line with Your Grant Application

The 5th Wave   By Rich Tennant

"The short answer to your request for a grant is, 'No'. The long answer is, 'No, and get out of my office'."

In this part . . .

*E*very presentation has a finale, and a grant application is no different. In this part, you see the importance of putting the finishing touches on the grant application — and the great convenience of electronic submission. Once the grant application is in the mail (regular or electronic), you need to attend to some housekeeping issues. This part walks you through each of the follow-up tasks that better organize your grants life. I hold your hand through the final outcome — what you need to do if you win and what you need to do if you lose. Knowing how to play the grants *rewrite* game is necessary if you really want to win the big grants.

Chapter 17

Counting Down to Deadline: What to Check before Launch

. . . .

In This Chapter

▶ Checking yourself one more time

▶ Attaching the right documents

▶ Using paper that talks to the funder

▶ Mailing in your application the right way

. . . .

*A*fter you put together the body of the grant application or proposal, you must attend to some finishing touches before you mail your gem to the funding source. Be sure to take a tally of the attachments that you referenced throughout each of the narrative sections. Carefully choose the type of paper you print the application on. Even pay attention to how you bind or clip together the pages of the application. This chapter shows you what to do just before you mail in your application. For more on writing the application, see Chapters 11 through 16.

Using a Checklist for Assurance

Before you start putting the attachments together for your grant application, go back to the beginning of the application narrative and look at the order of your information. Making a checklist to double-check yourself is the best way to verify that you have included all of the information required in the application narrative. Look for any narrative references to the attachments. While you are celebrating the end of the narrative writing process, you can easily forget the minute details that, if missing, can lead to a rejection notice. In other words, you can lose a lot of money because of a *small* mistake.

The final check-off

Make sure that each part listed here is finished, well done, and in place.

❑ A cover letter, typed on the organization's letterhead and signed by the president of the board or the executive director.

❑ All prenarrative forms in place, with empty fields merged.

For the National Network of Grantmakers (NNG) Common Grant Application format, I use mail merge to insert the funding source's name after *Submitted to* and the amount of monies I am asking for after *Grant request.* (Chapter 1 includes an overview of the Common Grant Application format.)

❑ The abstract — did you write a brief overview of your request to fulfill the abstract requirement (if you wrote a request for research funds from a foundation or corporation)? Remember to keep the abstract at 125 words, or less, and on a separate page.

❑ The executive summary — did you write a brief overview of the contents? The executive summary is the same as the abstract, only with a different title. It's used in federal grant applications; also, some regional grantmaking forums have designed applications that call for an executive summary.

❑ The table of contents — federal and state grant applications call for a table of contents.

Introduction to your organization

Did you write about the organization's

❑ History?

❑ Major accomplishments?

❑ Current programs and activities?

❑ Demographics for its target population?

❑ Cooperation with local groups?

Did you refer the reader to any attachments? If so, keep a running list so you can double-check that they are in place.

Problem or needs statement

Did you write about

- ❑ The problem or need your proposed program or plan of operation will address?

- ❑ The research that proves the existence of the problem?

- ❑ The gloom, doom, drama, and trauma that justify the need for grant funds?

Did you refer the reader to any attachments? If so, list them for double-checking later.

Program design or plan of operation

Did you write about

- ❑ The purpose of the program?

- ❑ The goals and measurable objectives?

- ❑ The timeline for implementing the program?

- ❑ Significance and overall systemic change?

Did you refer the reader to any attachments? Remember to add to your running list.

Key personnel, organizational and partner resources, and equity statement

Did you write about

- ❑ The key personnel, including their qualifications and the time they will allocate to the project?

- ❑ The resources that your organization and its partners bring to the program?

- ❑ Have you demonstrated equity (fairness/equal opportunity for all) in hiring staff and recruiting program participants?

Remember that in the Common Grant Application format, key personnel information goes in the attachments, not the grant narrative. If you referred to any attachments, don't forget to add to the attachment checklist.

Evaluation and dissemination

Did you write about

❑ The methods your organization will use to evaluate the progress of your objectives?

❑ How you plan to share your findings with others? Remember that in the Common Grant Application, the evaluation goes in the attachments, not in the grant narrative.

Did you refer the reader to any attachments? Remember to update the attachments checklist.

Budget summary and detail

Did you remember to

❑ Double-check your budget summary totals?

❑ Write a detailed narrative to support the line-item figures in the budget summary?

As you've done before, note your references to any attachments so you can check to be sure that the attachments are in place.

Putting Your Attachments in Order

The attachments go in a specific order. For federal and state grants, the attachments are compiled in the order that you refer to them in the narrative. So, read through the narrative from front to back and put your attachments in correct order. Also in the narrative, you should have numbered each attachment when you referenced it — for example, *attachment 1, attachment 2,* and so on. Type the attachment number on each attachment. I like to type this in the upper right corner, as in Figure 17-1.

For foundation and corporate grant applications, use the NNG format for putting the attachments in the order shown in the following pages. (Chapter 1 has information on the NNG format.) Start with the evaluation plan — yes, in the NNG format, the evaluation is an attachment. Don't forget to add the resume of the lead evaluator or the credentials of the third party evaluator.

EVALUATION (all caps, bold face type, minimum 24-point size, centered on a page by itself, like Figure 17-2).

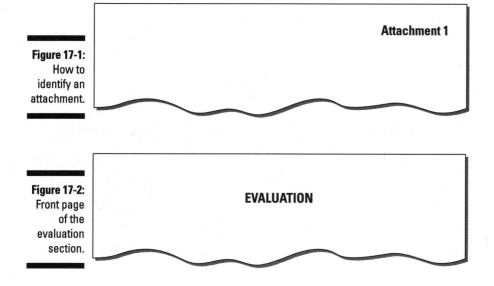

Figure 17-1:
How to
identify an
attachment.

Attachment 1

Figure 17-2:
Front page
of the
evaluation
section.

EVALUATION

ORGANIZATIONAL STRUCTURE/ADMINISTRATION (all caps, bold face type,
24 point or higher font, centered on a page by itself, like Figure 17-3).

Figure 17-3:
Front page
of the
section
where you
talk about
organiza-
tional
structure
and
administra-
tion.

**ORGANIZATIONAL STRUCTURE/
ADMINISTRATION**

The organizational structure/administration attachment is a brief description
of how your organization works, including responses to these questions:

✔ What are the responsibilities of the board, staff, volunteers, and (if a
membership organization) the members? Write a brief paragraph giving
the reader a one or two sentence description of each group's responsibilities. Sometimes for a new, nonprofit organization, I insert the by-laws
to fulfill this attachment requirement.

✔ How representative are these groups (the board, the staff, and so on) of the communities with which you work? What are the general demographics of the organization? For this attachment requirement, I usually provide a board roster that includes each board member's name, address, occupation, gender, ethnicity, and term on the board. I also attach a list of key staff positions and give gender and ethnicity.

✔ Who will be involved in carrying out the plans outlined in this request? Include a brief paragraph summarizing the qualifications of key individuals involved. For this attachment requirement, I just put in one-page resumes for each key staff person.

✔ How will the project be organized? Include an organizational chart showing the decision-making structure. Make sure the chart is up-to-date and includes a box for volunteers if your organization uses volunteers. Titles are more important than names, especially since the staff could change over the duration of the grant's funding period.

FINANCES (all caps, bold face type, 24 point or higher font, centered on a page by itself; see Figure 17-4).

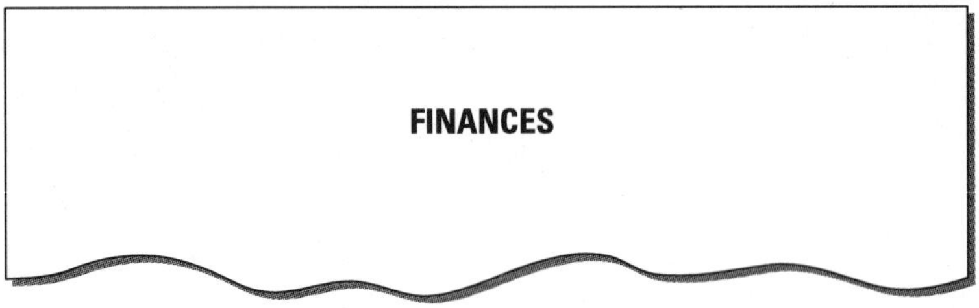

Figure 17-4:
Heading for the finance section.

FINANCES

In this section, you talk about

✔ The organization's current annual operating budget.

✔ The current project budget.

✔ A list of other funding sources for this request. Include amounts and whether received, committed, or projected/pending. I like to use a three-column table to list the source, amount requested, and status of request. (See Table 17-1 for an example.)

✔ The financial statement for the most recent complete year (expenses, revenue, and balance sheet), audited, if available. If your organization has one of those 20-pound financial reports, pull out the comments and breakout budgets for each department and just attach the overall organization expenses and revenue along with the balance sheet.

✔ A copy of your IRS 501(c)(3) letter. If you do not have 501(c)(3) status, check with the funder to see if it's willing to fund through your fiscal sponsor or is willing to exercise expenditure responsibility. You may need to submit additional information and change the portion of your grant narrative that introduces your organization to add information on your fiscal sponsor.

Table 17-1	Funding Sources Receiving the Request	
Source	*Amount Requested*	*Status*
ABC Foundation	$25,000	Committed
Jones Corporate Giving Program	$25,000	Pending
Smith Foundation	$25,000	Received

OTHER SUPPORTING MATERIAL (all caps, bold face type, 24 point or higher font, centered on a page by itself; see Figure 17-5).

Figure 17-5:
Front page
of the Other
section.

OTHER SUPPORTING MATERIAL

Other materials may include letters of support/commitment (up to three). It's okay to have some handwritten letters of support from your constituency. Don't correct spelling or grammar errors. Handwritten letters have a lot of impact on the reader.

Additional relevant materials include the most recent annual report (an original, not a photocopy), recent newsletters by your organization, newspaper clippings about your programs, and previous evaluations or reviews (up to three). *Note:* undated newspaper articles are useless.

Finally, the Other section is where I put supporting documentation that I have referenced throughout the grant application narrative that doesn't fit in any of the other attachment sections.

Using a Postcard to Track Your Application

When your federal grant application (both the original and the copies) is ready to mail, make sure to include a self-addressed, stamped postcard. On the front, write your name, your agency, and the agency's address. On the back, write your project name, the Catalog of Domestic and Federal Assistance number, the name of the federal initiative, the federal agency you are submitting the request to, and the specific federal department within the agency. Figure 17-6 gives an example of what you may write on the postcard.

When you receive it back from the funder, such a card provides enormous peace of mind. You know the grant has been delivered and you know the control number it has been assigned.

Post Card front side (don't forget to add the stamp!)

John L. Smith, Project Director
XYZ Organization
123 Folly Lane, Suite B
Tidewater, Florida 12345-0786

Post card back side (don't use a picture post card!)

The Zenith Project
CFDA 93.556 - Promoting Safe and Healthy Families
U.S. Department of Health and Human Services
Administration of Family and Children

Application Control Center number: _____

Figure 17-6:
Your peace-of-mind postcard.

Increasing Your Chances with a Few Finishing Touches

You can use some final touches to give your grant that extra edge — these techniques have helped me achieve my own funding success rate of 90 to 95 percent. Sharing these tips with you means that I want you to be successful in getting most, if not all, of your grant requests funded.

Imagine a BLT sandwich without the L and the T! Think about shoes that were meant to tie up . . . but don't have laces! Are you getting the point? Don't just type up 5 pages (the Common Grant Format limit) or 20 to 40 pages (the average length of federal or state grant applications), staple them together, and stick the package in the mail.

Bindings, staples, and clips

Federal grant application guidelines tell you how to secure your final grant application package (the cover forms, assurances, certifications, budget forms, narrative, and required attachments). Usually, you will be instructed not to staple or bind the finished document. The feds need numerous copies for the peer review process and it's easier to make copies of a document that hasn't been stapled together. Even if the federal grant guidelines state to mail one original and two copies, the funder will still make additional copies for the review process.

I always send two extra copies of a federal grant application. That's two over and above whatever number they ask for in the guidelines. Why? Just in case they need 'em!

Unless instructed otherwise, I use black binder clips. They're cheap and easy to find. They can also be removed easily when the feds want to make more copies. Some grant competitions at the federal level instruct you to prepare a cover with the project name and spiral bind all copies of the document.

Anything other than a simple clip looks (and is) wasteful. Unless instructed otherwise, stick with what's unobtrusive and effective.

Paper — the magic touch

For foundations and corporations, the type of paper that you submit your grant application on can be another way of communicating who you are, where you are, and your organizational philosophy. I'm a strong believer in using the subliminal approach to snatch my share of grant awards. Try some of these tips and see how they're received and the results of your efforts.

For environmental grant requests, always use recycled paper and recycled envelopes; use the region of the country to determine the color of the paper. For the East Coast and Midwest, I like pale blue; for the South and Southwest, any shade of peach or pink; for the North and Northwest, any shade of pale green; for the Central region, wheat colors.

For children and youth grant requests, always use bright, white paper. For the envelopes, have young children color white catalog-size envelopes with crayons. Give them bright colors to use and don't pick and choose from the budding artists. Even stick figures will catch the attention of the grant application intake person (usually a receptionist at the funding source), who, instead of removing the application and tossing the envelope, will clip a nicely decorated envelope to the grant application. The people reviewing the application will know you went that extra step. You can use a nice, clean, white mailing label to address the envelope.

I set up my mail merge fields for foundation and corporate funders when I write the cover letter and prepare the grant application cover forms. If you're not familiar with mail merges, get familiar with 'em! They can be one of your best friends in grant writing. Read one of the fine *For Dummies* books on word-processing programs for more information.

For corporate requests, do your homework. What are the corporation's colors? If you aren't familiar with the company's logo or products, pull up the company's Web site and see what colors it uses. Also look at the colors used in its annual report (which you requested with your initial letter of inquiry). Select paper for the grant application narrative and for the envelopes that reflects the corporation's colors. When your grant request arrives at the funder's office, you want it to strike a familiar chord! (Chapter 4 shows you how to write an initial letter of inquiry, and Chapter 5 shows you how to obtain information on corporate funders.)

For foundation requests that aren't for environmental programs or programs that benefit children, stick with plain white paper, no special weight or texture. Use any color envelope; just be sure that the envelope is catalog size. Using plain, stick-on mailing labels that have been printed from your mail merge program is okay. Foundations don't want to see anything fancy when it comes to paper.

Mail everything in catalog-size envelopes. Never, ever use a standard size envelope. Never fold anything, even letters of initial inquiry.

Handling specialized application forms like a pro

If the funding source requires that you submit the grant request on its application form, it doesn't want its form or required format altered. Follow its directions to the letter when filling out the forms. Having to use a form has its pros and cons.

Pros:

✔ You know exactly what the funder wants to read about.

✔ All you have to do is answer the questions, add the requested attachments, sign, and mail.

✔ The next time you request money from the same funder, you'll have the forms and most of the answers already in your computer.

Cons:

✔ You need a flatbed scanner in order to fill in the forms on your computer.

✔ You need a typewriter to prepare the forms if you do not have a scanner.

✔ If you decide to nix the typewriter and don't own a scanner, you can use your word processing software to type the responses, then shrink the type size to make them fit. Finish up by printing, cutting, and pasting your pieces of typed narrative into the allocated space.

✔ Your responses are limited to the space provided. If you write more, your grant request could be disqualified prior to being read.

✔ You need to find paper such that the scanned, then printed, form looks exactly like the original.

Funding sources that have their own form are very picky about not wanting it altered. I had a funder that required the information on 11- x 17-inch sheets of paper. These sheets don't fit on the average flatbed scanner or in a regular typewriter!

Pay special attention to the type of paper that the form is printed on if you have to replicate the paper. If it's recycled, then you use recycled. If it's a special color green or gray, then go find that color. Remember, this effort is all about meeting the funder's review criteria by following the grant guidelines and instructions. When the application that you mail in looks like the form it mailed out, you're on your way to getting reviewed and funded — the only goal for a grant writer.

 Set up the following merge fields for your funder information: *contact person, title, funder, address1, address1, city, state, zip,* and *amountreq.* You can insert the information into each data field, which allows you to mail merge into your cover form or cover letter, to print out a master funding source list for tracking purposes, and to print mailing labels.

Mailing the right way

The application must reach the funding source on time (if there is a deadline). Federal grant guidelines dictate that the application must be postmarked by a certain date. Personally, I don't work 25 to 100 hours on a federal grant application and then trust the application to regular mail. I prefer more of a guarantee than a mere postage stamp, so I use an express courier service and I always get the application to the courier two weekdays before the date by which the package must be postmarked. I treat state grant applications the same way. For foundation and corporate grants, I use regular mail, provided I'm not going to miss a due date.

Using an express mail service may cost a little more, but it assures that the grant will make it to its destination and have a chance to enter the review process.

By the way, the feds make no exceptions for late grant applications. Even natural disasters aren't a valid excuse. If the grant application is due on a specific date, then it had better be in the Application Control Center by that date. All the pleading, whining, or cajoling in the world, including calls to the funder from your congressional representatives, won't make a difference.

Chapter 18

Submitting Your Information Electronically

· ·

In This Chapter

▶ Working with online grant applications

▶ Summing up the pros and cons of electronic submissions

▶ Using online grants reporting systems

· ·

Many federal and state funding sources and private foundations have been testing the online transmission process for grant requests. Some of these funders are still fine-tuning this process and have been in the pilot phase for two or more years. Luckily for you, if they're in the pilot phase, you're usually given a choice of submitting your grant application the old way, on paper, or submitting it the new way, electronically. This chapter gives you the lowdown on the electronic grant submission process, covers some pluses and minuses of the process, and provides you with a look at the Federal Electronic Grants Management System.

Streamlining the Grant Seeking Process

Some foundations and corporate giving entities have created what they feel is a better idea when it comes to receiving grant applications. Rather than encouraging you to cut down more trees by using paper, they've created Web-based grant application programs. This means that you fill out an identifying form online (name, address, contact person, title, phone and fax, brief overview of what your agency does, check-off if you have a nonprofit status) and hit Submit. Once this is accepted, you're in their online tracking system and can access the full electronic grant application.

The application usually includes some language similar to this:

> Welcome to the American Animal Society's online grant application program. Please fill in all of the information on the cover sheet. Once you have submitted the completed cover sheet, you will be assigned a grant application identifier code. Filling out the cover sheet does not mean that an application has been filed. You still need to fill out the complete application online and send it in according to the rules of the program.

At this point, all the information you provide on the cover sheet is automatically added to the detailed grant application document before you download it.

Some online grant applications can be downloaded using an Adobe Acrobat Reader, which lets you view and print the document in PDF (Portable Document Format). This way, you can read the application carefully and make notes on what you want to enter into each section or create a word processing document for cutting and pasting sections into the online application. Remember that you can't spellcheck the content you're entering online in each of the information fields if you do not move data back and forth between the online form and a word processing program.

Submitting an online application full of typos or grammatical errors makes you look careless and can result in not getting funded.

Another online writing format is Rich Text Format (RTF). This is a basic format for saving a file in order to transfer complex documents between different types of word processing programs without loosing the bolding, underlining, italics, and other special touches that make your grant request more attractive to read.

Here are some selected sites with online applications:

- ✔ American Cancer Society Grant Application System: `www/w2c.com/gepps/about.cfm`
- ✔ U.S. Department of Justice: `www.ojp.usdoj.gov/vawo/contappkit/`
- ✔ Cystic Fibrosis Foundation: `www.foundationcommons.org/cff_docs.htm`

If you try the electronic grant submission process and fall in love with online grant writing, then I have the Web site for you. Log onto to `www.cybergrants.com` and get ready to pop open the bubbly and celebrate. This Web site is for grant seekers (nonprofits wanting money) and grantmakers (foundations and corporations giving away money). After you register for the first time, you are required to log in to the CyberGrants system in order to complete and submit a proposal. You need your federal tax identification number to complete this initial log-in process.

After you've logged in, you choose the state that you are looking for funding in and the area that your project falls into. Based on the information that you provide, a database screen comes up with the funding sources that match your location and interests. You can view grantmaking guidelines or other information on each funding source. Finally, you choose which funders you want to receive your proposal. You can select as many funding sources as you want.

Be prepared to enter contact information; organization information, mission, and history; project information (including the amount requested); and communities served information. Before the information you entered is sent to CyberGrants, you are given the chance to review everything you have written and make corrections. Once you hit Send or Done, CyberGrants sends an e-mail to the funding sources you selected, letting them know that they can view your grant application on the CyberGrants Web site.

How practical is this? Well, the site does not charge a fee for nonprofits registered with the Internal Revenue Service. So what do you have to lose?

A representative of the New York–based Bell Atlantic Foundation said CyberGrants has enabled it to become a more effective grantmaker by improving the quality of the applications and cutting down on administrative time and costs. Bell Atlantic has used the system for about five years. Bell Atlantic gives $38 million a year to nonprofits and receives about 20,000 grant applications a year!

One of the nice things about CyberGrants is that it also accepts public schools and allows them to register with their district and school identification numbers. Public schools don't have an IRS 501(c)(3) nonprofit status, but are treated as nonprofit organizations by funding sources.

I've done electronic grant applications for over a year. I like the ease of writing less, but I don't like the fact that some Web sites don't let you access their online process using Netscape. Microsoft Internet Explorer seems to be the program that the majority of online grantmakers have set up their access sites to be compatible with. A lot of bugs need to be to ironed out — that's evident from the number of times I have to reenter the information. For one funder, it took four tries and four telephone calls to the funding source's Management Information Systems department before the application was accepted. Some more pros and cons are in the list that follow.

Pros:

- ✔ You don't have paperwork, you just type and hit Send.
- ✔ The writing format is shorter (no lengthy narratives).
- ✔ You don't have to gather and copy attachments or supporting documentation (this only applies sometimes).
- ✔ Online applications save you time.

Cons:

- The organization may not have the type of application that allows a cut and paste or spellcheck.

- Once you push Send, you can't get it back.

- Hardware and software lock-ups mean you sometimes have to reenter your information.

- You have to deal with doubt about whether your grant application really reached the funding source.

- Some state and federal funders require you to print out the cover form, assurances, certifications, and budget forms and mail hard copies with original signatures to them within a certain time period after you file an online application.

Talking to the Feds after Your Grant Is Funded

The old way of doing business with the feds meant that once your grant was funded, you negotiated via a long and sweat-producing telephone call with the Office of Management and Budget. Sometimes it offered you what you asked for, but most of the time it offered you a lot less than you requested. The process of negotiation could last from one relatively short call to several calls over several days.

Once you actually received your first electronic transfer of grant funds, you had to have permission in writing to do virtually anything. Waiting for mail (and permission) from the feds took weeks. We're in the new millennium now, and the use of technology is making life a little easier for federal grant awardees.

From September of 1998 to March of 1999, the federal government piloted the U.S. Electronic Grants Project. To date, eight federal grantmaking agencies have agreed to work together to help bring the electronic grants process to grant seekers.

Why are the feds doing this?

- To enable real-time, interactive grant transactions and negotiations between grant seekers and federal agency personnel

- To facilitate data-sharing, reporting, and integration across federal agencies

- To eliminate the need for grant seekers to submit redundant data to the same federal agency or multiple agencies

The federal grantmaking agencies participating in the U.S. Electronic Grants Project are

- ✔ The Department of Education
- ✔ The Department of Energy
- ✔ The Environmental Protection Agency
- ✔ The Department of Interior
- ✔ The Department of Labor
- ✔ The Office of Naval Research
- ✔ The Small Business Administration
- ✔ The Department of Transportation

The minimum hardware requirements for the feds are

- ✔ 32MB RAM
- ✔ 133 MHz processor
- ✔ 20MB of free hard disk space
- ✔ 28.8 bps modem

The minimum software requirements for the feds are

- ✔ Windows 95, 98, or NT, or Sun Solaris
- ✔ Netscape Navigator or Internet Explorer (the latest versions)
- ✔ Java applet

Chapter 19

Cleaning Up and Following Up

In This Chapter

▶ Organizing the stacks

▶ Using grants-management software

▶ Keeping promises

▶ Locating your request after it's mailed

▶ Practicing patience

*Y*our grant application is in the mail! Whew, you're home free, right? Not quite. You've still got a lot of cleaning up and following up that needs your attention. From organizing your stacks of project information to keeping track of where your project went, tying up loose ends is a must for any well-organized grant writer. This chapter shows you how to take care of the housekeeping issues related to seeking grants.

Housekeeping 101

First, go out a buy a box of 100 manila folders. You're going to organize your grant application, funding sources, and project information so that you have a running start on finding grant-related information in the days, weeks, and months following the date you mail the proposal or application to the funders.

Some organizing tips:

✔ Put the completed grant application in a manila folder by itself. Put the title of the project on the folder tab.

✔ Put the background research, meeting notes, and other project-related information in a folder labeled *Background Information*.

✔ Put the funding source search results (the profiles of the funders receiving the grant request) in a folder and label it *Funding Search*. On the front of the funding search folder, print out and staple the alphabetized mail merge list of funding sources.

Mail mergers are lifesavers. If you're not mail-merge savvy, I strongly recommend that you get up to speed. To do so, check the user manual of your word processing program or consult the *...For Dummies* book that covers your program.

✔ Put all your folders in a hanging file folder with the project name and the month and year the project was mailed.

Note any communication you receive from the funding source on the database printout on the front of the funding folder. Try using *R* for rejection and enter the date of the rejection notice. Use *P* for pending and write *P* only when you receive a confirmation letter or postcard from the funder indicating that your grant request is under review and a decision will be made later. Use *F* for funders that decide to award a grant and make sure to note the amount of the award if it is different from the amount you requested.

You can expand your database to include the status of the request: Rejected, Pending a decision on (date), and Amount Funded. This way you can track your grant seeking efforts for each and every project under funding consideration.

I use this hard copy tracking process because I write anywhere from five to eight projects a month for an equal number of clients. However, if you work for one organization and submit only the occasional grant request, developing an electronic tracking process is probably going to make things easier for you (versus pen and pencil tracking).

Finding Tracking Software

Using a grants-management software program helps you keep track of the entire grant application process, from preplanning steps, partner information, funder information, the dates the fiscal reports and evaluation reports are due, and grant closeout. Commercial software programs are available to capture any segment of the grant seeking and record-keeping processes — or all of it.

This software can be costly, so always check to see if the vendor has a demo for downloading over the Internet. Make sure that the program you select to help you keep your sanity exceeds your needs and expectations before making a final purchasing decision. Software packages can range from $3,000 (for a single user) to $10,000 for multiuser systems.

The software is great for large organizations that plan to do a lot of grant writing — three or more requests going out every month, year-round.

Here are a couple of places to look for grants-management software reviews and advertisements:

✔ *The NonProfit Times:* www.nptimes.com

✔ *Philanthropy News Digest:* fdncenter.org/pnd/current/

Debriefing and Sharing with Your Lead Partners

Before you were able to write your grant request, you convened your staff, volunteers, community partners, and other interested parties to help plan the project design and provide the information needed for the needs statement.

Now, bring the stakeholders in your grants process back together for a debriefing. (Chapter 15 covers the stakeholders process if you need more information.)

Follow these debriefing steps:

1. **Bring each group of stakeholders in to review their efforts.**

2. **Give each person or agency a complete copy of the final grant request.**

3. **Answer questions and float some what-ifs (what if we are funded for less than we ask for? What if we're not funded at all? What if the needs of our constituents change before we're funded?).**

4. **Provide a general overview for the time frame in which the funding decision will be made by the funder.**

Remember that when you have a debriefing meeting, those individuals who may have written sections of your grant narrative see what you actually did with the final information. Some feelings may be hurt when a writing contributor sees massive changes in the final document. While you may have worked as a group putting together the narrative information, people present at the debriefing meeting may not have been present at the meeting for the document's final draft review.

Remind those who appear to be sulking of the ultimate goal — to get funded and to help a segment of the community.

Don't just share copies of the final grant request; also give your partners a list of the funding sources and the contact information. Why? Because someone may know a foundation trustee or a corporate giving officer personally. Sometimes a simple telephone call or e-mail to a connected friend can make the difference between getting funded and not getting funded. Share other critical information too. This is not the time to retreat and remain quiet. The open lines of communication that were established before you wrote the grant request must be kept open. Partnerships take work!

Information you should share includes

- ✔ A list of the funders
- ✔ Timelines for funder decisions
- ✔ A master list of partners with contact information
- ✔ Other projects or programs your organization has planned (this opens the door for future partnering opportunities)

What can partners do for you as a result of the sharing process? Partners can commit seed monies to begin program implementation on a small scale. Partners who know your needs can unexpectedly make donations of needed equipment, program space, or other items and services. Once a level of trust and openness has been established during the grant seeking and follow-up process, you've made friends for life with local businesses and other non-profit organizations. This ongoing dialogue can lead to your agency being asked to be a partner in its grant seeking efforts, resulting in your sharing a part of its grant award.

Partners can also give you leads on other funding sources for the project.

Tracking Your Request at the Funders

Your grant application is in the mail. You know the funder has received it, but you don't know if it is still in the envelope or on someone's desk for review and decision making — the decision to award your organization a grant. Here is the protocol of when to call, who to call, and when to just plain chill out and wait for the mail. The rules are different based on the type of funding source you sent your application to for consideration.

Foundation and corporate grant requests

Don't call, don't e-mail, and do not even stop by their offices if you applied to local funders for grant support. The key words here are *irritation* and *busy*. Foundations and corporate giving entities receive hundreds of requests daily and weekly and most are unsolicited. Unsolicited means they did not write or call you and say, "Hey, why don't you send us a proposal for your new program?"

When you call, you are considered a nuisance. When you e-mail, you are given the same title by the program staff. The rule of etiquette for grant seekers is to research the funding source thoroughly, write the request based on its grant application guidelines, make the required number of copies, and mail. At that point, the initiator in any further communication is the funder, not the grant seeker.

If your veteran colleagues advised you to visit with the funding source staff before you decided to apply for a grant, then one call to your inside contact is permissible. However, you don't need face-to-face meetings to win grants. I am living proof of that!

What to expect from foundation and corporate funders:

✔ Notification that the status of your request is pending

✔ Notification that your request has been rejected for funding

✔ Notification that your request has been awarded funding

The most desirable response from a funder:

> We recently received your request for funding. Our Regional Grants Committee meets on an annual basis. Our next meeting for your area is scheduled for November. If we need additional information, we will be sure to call you. Once we have had the opportunity to fully review your proposal, we will advise you of the Committee's decision. Sincerely . . .

This means you are still in the running for the money. Do not call this funder!

The least desired reply from a funder:

> Thank you for your recent correspondence requesting financial support from the ABC Foundation. Because of the large volume of proposals we receive on a regular basis, we are unable to send an individual response to each request. We are unable to fund your request, but recognize the value of the activities for which you are seeking funds and extend our best wishes for the success of your program. Sincerely . . .

This is why you send your grant request to more than one funder! Do not call this funder unless it's a community foundation or a bank trust fund. Community foundations and bank trust funds are local grantmakers. It's okay to call and find out specifically why your request was not funded.

After your first communication from the funder, expect a letter. The most desired letter from a funder:

> The ABC Foundation is pleased to approve for the XYZ organization a grant of $75,000. We ask that the money be spent exclusively to ensure that the goals and objectives of your project will be achieved. The grant will be paid to you in one payment and processing will begin as soon as the grant agreement is signed and returned to us. On behalf of the ABC Foundation, I wish you every success. Sincerely . . .

Some foundation and corporate funders, as well as state and federal funders, require that grant agreements be in place before the check is put in the mail. This is standard, but always have your legal department or attorney examine the language before you sign on the dotted line.

Not signing a grant agreement means no grant. Do call the funder when you have a question.

The second most desired letter from a funder:

> Thank you for your proposal requesting funding from the ABC Foundation. It is currently being reviewed by our staff. If more information is needed, you will hear from us within four weeks. If, however, you do not hear from us again, it means we have determined that your project does not fit our current program goals or strategies. The mission of our foundation is to . . . . Because the grantmaking is carefully focused to achieve certain goals and employ specific strategies, most grants are awarded through our initiated programs. However, we do accept unsolicited proposals and generally fund 10% of the requests we receive. Please do not be disappointed if your project doesn't get funded. Thank you again for taking the time to submit a proposal to our foundation. Sincerely . . .

At least you're still under consideration for funding. Just hold your breath for four weeks! Do not call this funder if you hear nothing after that period.

The least desired letter from a funder:

> Our staff has reviewed the inquiry you submitted about the possibility of funding from the ABC Foundation. We value the opportunity to learn about your efforts and appreciate the time you spent preparing the inquiry. Unfortunately, we are not able to fund your request. We receive numerous requests throughout the year, far

more than could possibly be funded. Although the ABC Foundation cannot be of assistance to you at this time, you have our best wishes for the success of your work. Sincerely . . .

Sometimes the rejection letter comes with a further stipulation that you do not submit another grant request for at least one year. Most rejection letters are sent to you within 90 days of the funder's receipt of your grant request.

Federal and state grant requests

Once you mail your grant application off to a state or federal funding agency, start the tracking process. The rules are different because the money you are requesting is public funds. Now is the time to make sure you've established great political contacts in your state's capitol and in Washington.

Political do's and don'ts:

- Do send a complete copy of the grant application to your elected officials.

- Do have any letters of support from elected officials that were written too late to submit with your grant application sent directly to the funding agency head (state or federal).

- Do call your senators' or representative's local and Washington offices to remind them that you need their assistance in tracking the grant application.

- Do ask for a face-to-face meeting with funding agency staff if your grant is rejected for funding.

- Don't scream and threaten elected officials. You really need their influence to help you get your grant funded, if not this time, then the next time it is submitted for funding consideration.

- Don't overlook elected officials when you convene the debriefing meeting.

- Don't count on always getting your grant funded just because you asked your elected officials to get involved in the tracking process.

- Do ask your elected officials to keep you posted on future grant opportunities if you are or are not funded. Get in the information loop for state and federal monies.

You're funded!

How will you know? At the state level, you receive a funding award letter. Monies are transferred electronically into your organization's bank account. Some monies are awarded and transferred in advance; other monies are released on a reimbursement basis.

At the federal level, you receive a telephone call from one of your elected officials in Washington. They notify you and issue the official press release to your local newspaper. Shortly after that, you receive a call from the Office of Management and Budget, known as the OMB. The OMB calls to negotiate the grant award. This means they may not offer you the amount you requested. (Chapter 18 gives you an overview of the OMB.)

If you agree to a lesser amount, you need to rewrite your goals, objectives, and timelines to match the reduced funding. (Chapter 13 gives details on goals, objectives, and timelines.)

You're not funded!

How will you know? At both the state and federal levels, you receive a rejection letter. No call, no advance warning. Just a cold, very disappointing rejection letter.

What can you do if you're not funded? Request a copy of the grant reviewers' comments. Contact your elected officials for assistance in getting a face-to-face meeting with funding agency personnel. And check out Chapter 20 for more on what to do after winning or losing your grant request.

The waiting is the hardest part

How much patience do you need to have when you're waiting for communication from a funding source?

- **Foundation.** Up to 12 months from the date the request was mailed. In once instance, I had a project funded 18 months after the request. One day, a $10,000 check just showed up at my client's office. The client even forgot what project the money was designated for!

- **Corporate.** Up to six months from the date the request was mailed. Corporate funders are the most likely to not let you know your grant request was not funded. Communication from a corporate funder means you have a check in the mail 80 percent of the time.

- **State.** Up to six months from the date the request was mailed. State agencies have rather quick turnarounds on decision-making.

- **Federal.** Six to nine months from the date you mailed the request. The length of time between the time you mailed in the grant application and the decision is made varies from agency to agency.

Chapter 20

Win or Lose — How to Play the Next Card

●●

In This Chapter

▶ Celebrating your success

▶ Getting more than you asked for

▶ Using the Freedom of Information Act

▶ Transferring rejection into new opportunities

●●

*W*hether you win or lose the grant seeking game, your work is not done. Once you know the status of your grant with a funding source, you need to attend to some tasks in order to wrap up loose ends. All too often, the grant writer drops the ball after finding out that a request for funding has been rejected. The inclination is to retreat, nurse some wounds, and wait until next year. And when grant writers find out that their request has been funded, they tend to want to celebrate and bask in the light of success.

Whether you get the bear or the bear gets you, you've still got work to do. This chapter guides you in the actions that should occur — win or lose.

Accepting Grant Monies

When you're notified of a funding award, shout and celebrate. But accepting the money means more than saying (or shouting) "Yes!" You must follow some steps to set up your role as the grant recipient. (The section following this one has more information on some of the terms that I use in the steps.)

1. **Notify all of your administrators, including the Chief Financial Officer (CFO).**

2. **Add "Accept grant funds" as an item on the agenda of your board of directors' next meeting.**

3. **Prepare an overview of the grant request (include the purpose, objectives, timelines for program implementation, project budget, and a copy of the official award letter from the funding source) for board review prior to the meeting.**

4. **Prepare a brief oral presentation to give to the board and draft resolution language.**

   The resolution will be to accept the grant award.

5. **If there is a grant agreement or contract to sign, have this document ready for the board.**

6. **Prepare a press release (providing the funder does not want anonymity) for board approval.**

7. **Create, purchase, or buy a certificate of appreciation for foundation and corporate funders, and get it signed by your board officers.**

8. **Meet with the CFO to discuss fiscal accountability, including creating a clear or single audit trail.**

I used some terms in the steps that the newcomer to grant seeking and grant writing may not be familiar with. So, I'm going to give you my shortcut definition for the terms that you hear frequently once your organization has been notified that it has been awarded a grant.

Chief Financial Officer (CFO). This individual is the person who makes the financial decisions for your organization. In smaller organizations, the CFO may be a bookkeeper working in concert with an executive director. In larger nonprofits, entire departments can handle the organization's finances, including fiscal reporting.

Resolution. Any agency with a board of directors or trustees or any government agency with a decision-making body (city council, town board, county board of supervisors) needs a resolution to apply for grant funds and to accept grant funds once an official letter has been received announcing a forthcoming grant award. Even if the funding source includes a check with the award announcement letter (foundations and corporations do so), you need a formal resolution before you deposit the check:

> The Emerson Township Board of Supervisors hereby resolves to accept $325,000 from the Kentucky Department of Transportation for the Chocktaw Bridge Project. These funds shall be used exclusively for this project. Any unexpended grant monies will be reported and returned to the state as required by Public Act 324.
>
> Approved unanimously on 7/21/2001.
>
> Signed by: Billy Jo McAllister, Emerson Township Clerk

Send the original resolution to the funding source. Do not send a copy. The funder needs to see the original signature.

Fiscal accountability. The obligation to insure that the funds are used correctly. Fiscal accountability is placed on the organization responsible for the management of grant funds. In most cases, this is the grant applicant. In some instances, it's the fiscal sponsor. (Chapter 16 explores what it means to be a fiscal sponsor.)

Clear or single audit trail. To create a clear or single audit trail, any grant funds received should be deposited into a separate account and tracked individually by using accounting practices that enable tracking the money from the award day by date, by expenditure, and by line-item allocation against the approved project budget (the budget approved by the funding source). Any auditor, internal or originating from the funding source, should be able to track the grant monies from the _money in_ to the _money out_ perspective without finding that these funds have been commingled with any other organizational funds.

In federal and state grants, the Office of Management and Budget (OMB) works cooperatively with the funding agencies to establish government-wide grants-management policies and guidelines. These guidelines are published through circulars and common rules. At the federal level, these documents are first introduced in the _Catalog of Federal and Domestic Assistance_ (CFDA). New circulars and common rules are published in the _Federal Register._ You can look at the federal OMB Web site at `www.whitehouse.gov/OMB/grants/index.html`. (Chapter 2 introduces the CFDA and _Federal Register._)

Here are the titles of federal grants-management OMB circulars:

- A-21: Cost principles for educational institutions
- A-87: Cost principles for state and local governments
- A-110: Uniform administrative requirements for grants and agreements with institutions of higher education, hospitals, and other nonprofit organizations
- A-122: Cost principles for nonprofit organizations
- A-133: Audits of states, local governments, and nonprofit organizations

The OMB Web site also has some of the grants management reporting forms on it, including the data collection form for reporting on A-133 single audits (SF-SAC).

The circular numbers are the keys to locating the document on the OMB Web site.

At the state funding level, the funding agency provides you with the funding stipulations, including the regulations for accessing, spending, reporting, and closing out grant funds.

Hitting the Grant Jackpot

Say that you've applied for a grant with five funding sources. One of the five funding sources funds you in full. The money is in, it's been deposited, and your project is up and running. But more mail comes in and guess what: Your project has received four more grants, totaling an amount equal to the full funding request. If your project is overfunded:

- ✔ Immediately contact each funder and explain your predicament.
- ✔ Ask their permission to keep the funds and expand your project's design.
- ✔ Ask their permission for grant monies to be carried over into another fiscal year.
- ✔ Be overly gracious and elevate the tone of your voice to one of ultimate surprise!

The worst scenario is that you will be asked to return the additional funding by all the funding sources after the first funder.

The best scenario is that you will be allowed to keep the funding and have a bigger and better project or program.

The best way to avoid the predicament of having too much money is to write a letter to each outstanding funding source (sources who have not communicated with you on their decision to fund your grant request) immediately after you know that you've reached full funding with the first funder or first group of funders. Be honest and quick. It's the right and ethical thing to do. (Chapter 16 talks more about the ethical approach to grant seeking.)

Knowing Your Rights When a Rejection Letter Arrives

If your grant application was rejected by a state or federal funding agency, then you're entitled to the grant reviewer's comments under the Freedom of Information Act (FOIA). If you're rejected by a foundation or corporate giving entity, you probably won't receive any reviewer's comments and you cannot use the FOIA as your trump card to get the comments. (Chapter 19 shows you the type of communication you can expect from a foundation or corporation when you are not funded.)

The FOIA provides access to all federal agency records (or portions of those records) except those that are protected from release by nine specific exemptions. Check out www.epic.org/open_gov/rights.html for the exemption list.

The FOIA does not apply to Congress or the courts, nor does it apply to records of state or local governments. However, nearly all state governments have their own FOIA-type statutes. You may request information about a state's law by writing the attorney general of the state.

When you use the FOIA, you receive the federal peer reviewers' actual written comments and scoring (the points that they bestowed on each narrative section in your grant application).

In order to invoke the FOIA, you must write a letter that includes the following information:

✔ The name of the agency that you're seeking the information from must be in the address and in the body of the letter.

✔ The application identifier code (at the federal level, the Application Control Center assigns an identifying number to your incoming grant application) must be included. This number is mailed to you on a postcard (you must include a self-addressed postcard in the final application for this purpose).

Chapters 8 and 17 provide insight on the federal peer review process. Chapter 17 also walks you through the postcard instructions for federal grant applications.

On the envelope, and at the top of the letter, write "Freedom of Information Act Request." Keep a copy of your request. You may need it in the event of an appeal or if your original request isn't answered. Federal agencies are required to answer your request for information within 10 working days of receipt. If you've not received a reply by the end of that time (be sure to allow for mailing time), you may write a follow-up letter or telephone the agency to ask about the delay.

Picking Up the Pieces and Starting Over

It's time to talk about salvaging your failed grant seeking efforts. This means finding another funding source and changing some of the narrative content to fit other types of funders. Here are some steps to get you started.

Transforming failed federal or state grant applications

First, order the peer review comments. Use them to find out what your peers found wrong with the narrative sections of the grant application. Fix the weaknesses. If parts of your sections were confusing or incomplete, write them over. Reconvene the grant writing team if others helped you put the application narrative together.

Why are you doing all this work on account of a failed grant?

- ✔ To get the grant ready for resubmission to the same federal grant competition when it cycles again, which is usually once per federal fiscal year.
- ✔ To have a *great* working document for cutting and pasting and reworking the narrative into state, foundation, and corporate grant application formats.

Face the facts. You went to the feds or the state government because you needed mega monies for your project. No other single funding source can fill the gap that would have been filled with a federal grant award. If you requested $1 million from the feds, you need to scale down your project design and project budget when you go to other funding sources. Identify any possible government monies (federal and state) and then look for foundation and corporate funding opportunities. Remember, you have to downscale your project narrative and your budget request based on each funding source's limitations.

Chapter 2 shows you how to get information on state-level grant opportunities. Chapter 5 covers how to find out about foundation and corporate funding sources.

Transforming failed foundation or corporate funding requests

Never, ever throw a rejected grant into your files, walk away, and give up.

- ✔ Go back and do another funding search to identify a new list of foundation and corporate funders that you can approach with your grant request.
- ✔ Convene your stakeholders' planning team to discuss the failed attempt with the first funder or funders (if you mailed the proposal to multiple funders). Sometimes, other people in the community have a funding lead to share with you. After all, they want to see you funded as much as you want to see your project funded.
- ✔ If you find a state or federal funding opportunity, you have to beef up your original foundation or corporate proposal to meet the requirements of the state or federal funder. This means writing more narrative and adding more research to support your needs statement. You also need a new project budget based on federal or state funding limitations.

Want more information? Chapters 7 and 8 walk you through the federal and state review criteria. Chapter 4 is about diversifying your funding options.

Chapter 21

Using a Letter to Ask for Goods or Services

· ·

In This Chapter

▶ Creating a wish list

▶ Selecting letter recipients

▶ Writing less for more

▶ Making the 30-day call to seal the deal

· ·

*W*hen your organization is in need of donated goods or services, you don't have to write a full grant application or proposal. Suppose you are planning to build a community playground and you already have volunteers lined up to level the ground and construct the equipment, but you don't have the funding in your budget for the equipment. A quick and easy letter can bring in lumber, bolts, paint, and other playground materials, or it can bring in ready-to-assemble manufactured equipment. Either way, a letter is simple and effective. This chapter shows you how to write a letter requesting donated goods or services.

Brainstorming the Possibilities

Using a letter to make a request opens endless possibilities. Take an inventory of your organization-level and project-level needs. You can use a letter to ask for either goods or services.

Goods that you may be able to obtain with a letter:

▸ **Equipment:** Copy machine, personal computers, laptops, notebooks, fax machine, typewriter, label maker machine, occupational training equipment, new or used vehicles, appliances, VCR players, televisions, digital cameras, video cameras, or other new and used capital equipment items.

> ✔ **Materials:** Cloth, needles, thread, model car kits, clay pots, assembly kits for all kinds of arts and crafts, or occupational training projects.
>
> ✔ **Supplies:** Copy paper, print or copy cartridges, standard office supplies or special project supplies. Special project supplies may be crayons, coloring books, day planners, or other age-specific or target group—specific supplies.

A letter may be able to obtain the services of a professional to assist with some of the following problems:

> ✔ Standard accounting procedures
>
> ✔ A strategic planning process
>
> ✔ Nonprofit management training
>
> ✔ Developing a human resources department
>
> ✔ Writing an evaluation plan for your grant-funded project
>
> ✔ Creating a marketing plan
>
> ✔ Creating a business plan for a low-interest loan (yes, nonprofits can apply for loans)
>
> ✔ Other areas where you need an experienced professional to provide guidance

Asking for Small Stuff in a Small Way

The letter format I'm about to introduce is easy to write and does the trick in getting you equipment, materials, and supplies, and even personnel to provide technical assistance to your organization. Before you start to write the letter, you need to do some homework.

> ✔ Research the companies that manufacture the items you need. Try using Hoover's Online to find some good leads on corporations that make what you need. You can log on to Hoovers at www.hoovers.com. Hoover's Online is a great resource. You can retrieve an overview of the company you're targeting, including its history, recent news articles, a list of officers, locations, subsidiaries (look for sites within a 100-mile radius of your project's location), competitors (other names to look up on Hoover's), and financials.
>
> The financials help you know the ability of the company to make a donation; look for a healthy profit line in the most recent fiscal year.

✔ Research the corporations that have *technical assistance* as an option under types of grants funded. Use the *Corporate Giving Directory* (Taft Publications) or log onto the Foundation Center's Web site at `www.fdncenter.org` and use the link to corporate funders on the Internet.

✔ Get vendor specifications on any needed equipment, materials, or supplies.

Do your homework and find out the name of the company official that you need to write to. I always write to the CEO for larger corporations and the owner of a small business. Even if they don't handle the actual request, they pass it down to the administrator who does. Always start at the top!

Approaching more than one corporation for the same item is okay. Remember, not everyone will say yes; if they do, celebrate and plan bigger and better. Now, it's time to look at what the letter should contain and how you should write it.

✔ Prepare a form letter that can be mail merged. This makes your letters look personalized and gives you the ability to print mailing labels.

✔ Open your letter by introducing yourself and your organization. Then state, specifically, what you're requesting from the company that you are writing to.

✔ Follow the first paragraph with the reason you need donated goods or services. What is the nature of the problem and why can't your organization purchase these goods or services outright?

✔ In the next paragraph, state what these goods or services will mean to your target population. Your target population is the people the goods or services will benefit. For example, if you're asking for a new copy machine to produce a community newsletter, the target population will be members of your community. What will the newsletter contain that will be of vital importance? How will their lives be better or change because of the information you provide?

✔ In the last paragraph, include a telephone number where you can be contacted if your letterhead does not include your specific number.

✔ Sign with a standard business closing (*Sincerely* or *Respectfully*).

✔ Add your typed name and title (leave room for your signature).

✔ Add the word *attachment* two spaces under your name and title.

✔ Attach an inventory list of the items that you are requesting. If you're requesting an employee on loan to assist in strategic planning or some other area of organizational deficiency, then list the specific tasks that you are asking the individual to assist with (sort of like a job description) so that the corporation lending the employee selects the right person. Also, indicate the length of time you're asking for technical assistance.

Keep this letter to less than two pages, not including the attached wish list.

Following Up after the Letter Is Mailed

After you mail your letter requesting goods or services, wait 30 calendar days and then call the individual you addressed in the letter. Ask her if she received your request and offer to answer any questions. This important courtesy can speed up her decision to help your organization.

Chapter 22

Exploring for International Funds

●●●

In This Chapter

▶ Identifying funders that are based outside the United States

▶ Finding resources for currency conversion

●●●

A grant writer who works in the United States is often given the charge of writing to funders that are based outside of the United States. Numerous agencies that have headquarters in the United States have their main operations in other countries. Some of these countries are in the European Union and some are in the developing areas of the world. The way you write to funders that are located in the United States is just a little different from the way you write to international funders seeking funding for projects that are not based in the United States. This chapter gives you some tips on how to succeed with international funding requests.

Gathering Information on International Funders

Even though I rely heavily on the Internet, I also use great, non-Internet funding tools that contain a wealth of international funding sources. Namely, funding directories from the European Foundation Centre (EFC). The EFC Web site address is www.efc.be, and you can order some terrific tools from the EFC.

Established in 1989 by seven of Europe's leading foundations, the EFC today has a membership of over 160 independent funders and serves a further 7,000 **organisations** linked through networking **centres** in 35 countries across Europe. (The boldfaced words above and below are spelled differently than you would spell them in the United States. Spelling is one of the adjustments you have to make when approaching European-based funding sources.) The EFC is located in Brussels, Belgium, and publishes numerous grant resources. Among the publications are the following:

✔ *European Foundation Fundamentals.* This publication attempts to define the work of independent funders and provides an overview of Europe's national-level independent funding community through a series of country reports. A section also gives you advice on seeking grants, from your initial research on the subject to writing your grant application.

✔ *Independent Funding.* This publication is a comprehensive directory aimed at providing foundations, corporate funders, governmental bodies, and grant seekers with a public record of the funding interests of the EFC members, both in Europe and elsewhere.

✔ *European Grants Index.* This publication lists almost 2,000 grants and **programmes** supported by nearly 100 foundations and corporate funders active in Europe. Grant listings are arranged alphabetically by funder, and indexes are provided by funder country and recipient country, as well as by grant subject focus, population focus, geographic focus, and types of support awarded.

Other publications include *Environmental Funding in Europe, Education Funding in Europe, Cultural Funding in Europe, Youth Funding in Europe,* the *Social Economy and Law Journal,* and the *Selected Bibliography on Foundations and Corporate Funders in Europe.* The prices listed on the Web site are in euros.

Knowing Application Protocol

Most of the members of the EFC require that you contact them personally to obtain grant application forms or guidelines for writing to them. Because the foundation landscape in Europe is varied, the legal and fiscal environments from one country to the next also vary.

Here are some sample entries to give you an idea of protocol in approaching these international funding sources.

Aga Khan Foundation. (Switzerland)

Geographical focus: International, Bangladesh, Canada, India, Kenya, Pakistan, Portugal, Switzerland, Tajikistan, Tanzania, Uganda, United Kingdom, and the USA.

Programme areas: Health, education, rural development, and NGO enhancement.

Applications: There are no formal application procedures. Before developing full proposals, **enquiries** should be made to the foundation office in the country where the proposal originates or where the projects would be executed. If there is no local AKF branch or affiliate, enquiries may be addressed to the foundation office in Geneva. Initial approach by letter.

Languages accepted: English.

Microtel — Bulgaria Foundation. (Bulgaria)

Geographical focus: Bulgaria, Central Europe, and Eastern Europe

Programme areas: Training, project and technologies, international, and information.

Applications: Application forms and conditions available. Initial approach by letter.

Languages accepted: Bulgarian and English.

Some of the EFC members have Web sites, but most only have e-mail addresses. Many do not accept applications in English.

You may want to consider using a translating service after you've written your letter of inquiry or grant application in English.

Keep in mind that

- ✔ The first contact should be via e-mail or fax correspondence.
- ✔ Before you start writing, do your homework and find out the preferred language.
- ✔ Become familiar with the four types of foundations: independent, corporate, governmentally supported or linked, and fundraising.

A corporate foundation is a nonprofit entity formed with the profits or proceeds from a company — a corporation. The corporate foundation awards grant monies just like a government funding agency.

Preparing Budgets in Euros

When you are going to mail your grant application to Europe, you need to first write it, in draft form, using U.S. currency for all the monetary figures. Then prepare a budget page and narrative in euros. A quick conversion service (dollars to euros) is available at the Web site www.xe.net/ucc. Make sure that your conversion is accurate, or you may be shortchanged if you win the grant.

Other currency conversion sites include

- finance.yahoo.com/m3?u
- www.oanda.com/converter/classic
- www.x-rates.com/calculator.html
- www.bloomberg.com/markets/currency/currcalc.cgi

Part V

The Part of Tens

In this part . . .

This part provides tips on a wide variety of grant writing topics. Surf through all these chapters if you really want to become a great grant writer! If you're writing just one or two grants and mostly want to keep out of trouble, be sure to read the chapter on grant writing no-no's. You definitely don't want to commit any one of these acts of grant suicide!

Chapter 23

Ten Ways to Personalize Your Request

. . . .

In This Chapter

▶ Using color for maximum effect

▶ Including photographs

▶ Mimicking the grant funder's language

. . . .

*I*f you think that grant writing is straight and narrow or cut and dried, then you are wrong! When I write grant applications, especially to foundations and corporations, I like to use the right side of my brain (I'm a lefty anyway) and be creative. Using some of the techniques that I show you in this chapter makes the project look like and read like a well-wrapped package, bows and all.

These are not finishing touches; these are ways to push your grant application from the edge of the grant reader's desk to the center. Experiment with each of these techniques and see for yourself what brings in the greatest grant awards and what gets rejected. Remember what you're trying to do: Make your grant request look like a personal invitation that calls, "Fund me, fund me!" to the grant reader.

Include Photographs

Use color or black and white pictures of your target population to capture the heart of the grant reader. If you're looking for funding for a project that benefits young children, then make a photo collage of children involved in various activities that your organization provides the funding for now. If you have an elderly target population, then include pictures of elderly men and women receiving services provided by your organization. Someone said that a picture is worth a thousand words. They hit this funding tip on the head.

Incorporate Color Graphics in Strategic Places

If your grant request is for computer or other word processing equipment, then don't use color printing. But for all of the other types of requests, using color can be fun and break the grant reader's doldrums. I like to use color shading in tables, import color charts, or insert a significant graphic in color in the header or footer. Using color gives life to a page of words. Color also gives the grant reader's eyes a respite from plain old narrative. When you're in doubt, think about what you like to read, what you're attracted to, and what makes you smile.

Make a Statement with Color

Creativity is appreciated in all circles of life. Remember to bring it to your grant writing. Try color-coordinating the paper you print the grant application on, the envelopes, and even the ink you use to sign the cover letter. When I've identified a group of funders in the southern part of the United States, for example, I print the grant application on salmon or peach copy paper. I then select a bright white catalog envelope for mailing the request to the funding source. I have the executive director of the nonprofit that is the grant applicant sign the cover letter using a brown, fine-point, felt-tip pin. The outsides of the envelopes are hand-addressed in the same shade of brown. Even the return addresses are handwritten in brown ink. The finishing touch is hand-selected stamps that carry a southern theme, like peaches, orange blossoms, a state bird, or another *just for you* stamp theme.

Include Handwritten Letters of Support

Each grant request should have at least three letters of support. These letters can be from parents, students, the elderly, or anyone else who is a part of your service population or who can vouch for the effectiveness of your program. If you have an animal shelter, then get letters from the veterinarians who volunteer their services or from individuals who have experienced successful animal adoptions.

What's great about the letters of support is that nonbusiness, nonprofessional writers can handwrite them. A parent can quickly write a letter to show her support for your proposed program. A student can write a letter on notebook paper. Anyone and everyone can use whatever paper and writing utensil they have at hand and put together a very personal, reader-attracting, handwritten letter of support. These letters are then attached to your grant application. I love to use letters from young children (about 3rd or 4th grade) that make a few grammatical errors. These kinds of support letters say to the funder, "We have real constituents that care."

Use Brightly Colored Envelopes

Pay attention to appearances! I said to do so earlier, but I'm saying it again because it is really an important strategic move in getting your grant request opened first, read first, and funded first!

Always use catalog-size envelopes. The envelopes can range in size from 8 ½ x 11 inches to 11 x 13 inches. Think carefully about the color of your envelopes.

If your target population is young children, give white envelopes to the children, along with several bright crayons, and let them draw and color to their heart's content. No receptionist at the funding source can pass up showing a unique envelope to his program officers. Hey, someone may just open it then and there to see what the request it about. Doesn't this beat having your plain brown or gray envelope sit in a pile waiting for weeks to be opened? I think so!

Use the Same Buzzwords That the Funder Uses

You've conducted a thorough funding search and found that a major corporation in your town is the best source to approach for $50,000 to build a community playground. The company you researched manufactures paper products. It prides itself on stamping *Made in America* on all of its products.

Here's how to take all this information and run with it — straight to the bank to deposit the big, fat check you're going to get. Not only do you write your request using some of their paper and their envelopes, but also, throughout the grant application narrative, you emphasize that the lumber, bolts, vinyl seats, chains (for the swings), and so on, are all products made in America. Go a step further to state that you plan to use community volunteers on a Saturday morning. Steeped in good old-fashioned work values, the volunteers will begin the morning with the Pledge of Allegiance and a prayer. Note that your town hall is just across from the new playground and the Boy Scouts will be on hand to play the national anthem as the flag is raised. Use words like *made in America, allegiance, loyalty,* and *old-fashioned* throughout your request. Remember that the only goal here is to get this project funded!

Mimic the Funder's Corporate Colors

Take a look at several corporate Web sites. What do you see? Color themes on each one. Look at any print materials you have gathered on each funding source, and what do you see? Color themes for each one. When you go to the grocery store, sometimes you can spot a favorite product by the color of the box or the color of the writing. Fortune 500 corporations spend an arm and a leg on advertising — getting the product's image to stick in your mind so that you will buy it.

Whether you choose a Fortune 500 funding source or a local business as your funder, look for their color themes. Use these same colors for the paper, the envelope, and even the ink with which you sign your grant cover letter. Colors are both subliminal and direct. We see them when we look at them, but what do the colors really say? Well, they say whatever you want them to say to the funder. I use this technique for all business requests, whether I'm writing a full-scale proposal or simply a two- to three-page letter request. It really works!

Use "We" instead of "It"

Use the word *we* throughout the narrative of the grant application when you refer to the applicant organization. Using *we* reminds the grant reader that real people are in need and asking for help (in the form of a grant award). Many grant writers have been conditioned through formal training to refer to the applicant agency as *it*. Don't buy that antiquated advice from anyone.

Use *we, our,* and *my* liberally. Doing so makes your application real; it breathes; it gets the money. This practical approach really helps your grant request get funded the first time you submit it to a funder for review.

Create a Watermark Theme

A *watermark* is a background image that prints on the paper in the background of the type. It's faded and subtle. It's a great way to carry a theme throughout the grant application narrative. When I write requests for fire departments, I like to use a pale yellow flame watermark on every page of the narrative. It makes a statement about the need to have dependable fire-fighting equipment; otherwise, flames will continue to consume property and lives in the grant applicant's community.

Grab Their Hearts with the Visual Results of Previous Grants

If your organization has been around for any length of time, then you or someone else has probably had to write monitoring and evaluation reports. Often, these reports include pictures. Senior citizens working in a computer lab or young children enjoying a new playground, for example.

Whatever the previous grants were awarded for, the agency should have pictures that capture the changes brought about by the grant. Save these pictures and put them in a photo album. I wrote several dozen grants for a nonprofit dance studio. All of them were funded. I asked the staff to start taking pictures of dance students practicing, at recitals, and in other reflective stances. When I needed to write a major grant application to the local community foundation, I replicated the photo album and included it with the grant application asking for $50,000. It worked!

Chapter 24

Ten Grant Writing No-No's

In This Chapter
▶ Following the rules
▶ Avoiding the most common mistakes
▶ Not resting on your laurels

*E*very profession has insider rules for succeeding or failing. Often, your grant-writing colleagues don't tell you the things to avoid — *your* failure somehow proves *their* competency. These rules are not posted on any walls or written in any academic guides for our profession.

I owe it to you to let you in on the down and dirty mistakes and just plain stupid errors that I have made. Unfortunately, these errors either cost me a well-paying client or earned a rejection letter. One foundation officer was kind enough to call me about my error in assuming that the foundation had a VCR to play the VHS tape I had enclosed with the grant application. It was a small foundation and simply chose to allocate its resources to awarding grants, not on frivolous office equipment that would not be used every day. Although the grant I submitted was not funded, I learned a valuable lesson about what not to do when finalizing a grant application package for the funder.

I've tried to think of everything I've done in an attempt to procure a grant over the years that I regret now. I refer to these mistakes as *grant suicide,* and I'm glad that you'll never make any of them.

Don't Forget to Get Permission and Input

Don't send out grant applications or proposals without board approval, community input, and thorough funding source research. You could lose your job; you won't have anyone rallying around acting excited when the grant award is announced; and after you spend 40 to 80 hours planning, researching, and writing a grant application, you want to send it to the funding source that perfectly matches your need.

Don't Look Stupid by Making Errors

Don't hastily prepare a proposal or grant application and mail it without someone else proofreading and editing the document at least twice. It's one thing to be a brand-new nonprofit without a lot of history and with very few attachments, but to mail typographical errors or grammatical errors is just plain dumb. Have a coworker, a colleague from another nonprofit, or someone else who is good with written English and able to review technical points read and reread your grant application. This includes the cover letter! Mistakes don't keep you from getting a grant award; they just make you look incompetent.

Don't Overlook the Importance of Stakeholders' Input

Don't assume that you know the needs of your constituency if you have no representatives from the constituency on your board or on an advisory committee. Your planning meetings should also include input from the target group. Funding sources look for evidence of input from the people you are proposing to serve. If they don't see it, you won't get funded.

Don't Include Audio or Visual Attachments

Don't include videos or cassette tapes with your proposals or grant applications unless the funding source specifically requests them. Don't include bulky attachments that are hard to view. Not all funding sources have VCRs or tape players as standard office equipment. Don't think that you're doing the funding source a favor by including a video or cassette tape that explains your proposed program.

Don't Do a Show-and-Tell Too Soon

Don't make copies of your full proposal or grant application for public reading; instead, provide a one-page overview of the proposal or grant application. Release full copies of your proposal or grant application only after it has been mailed to the funding source and the deadline has passed. Not everyone will understand the language you use in the needs statement. No one wants to read about the gloom, doom, drama, and trauma in their hometown. The last thing you want is to have your grant application censored.

Don't Submit a Rejected Grant Application without Making Major Changes

Don't take a proposal or grant application from a previously rejected funding attempt, dust it off, and resubmit it to a new funding source — or even to the same funding source! Doing so could get you a quick rejection letter. If your project didn't get the attention of the original funding source, something could be critically wrong with the program design or evaluation section. These two sections usually are weak in content and accountability from a grant review perspective. If you can't get a copy of the grant reviewer's comments, then ask a veteran grant writer to look at your failed proposal. Rewrite it, tweak it, beef it up, and dress it up. Then resubmit it.

Don't Assume the Funder Has No Changes from Year to Year

Don't use last year's funding source information to prepare a proposal or grant application this year. Personnel and priorities change constantly. Don't be lazy! Keep up-to-date publications at your fingertips or go online for the most recent information. You could waste a lot of your own and other people's time and energy if you don't stay informed of changes.

Don't Ignore the Printer

Remember that most funders don't get to see you. They don't get to see your building or your constituents. Although you may be able to include a few photographs, the main physical evidence that you even exist is your application. Make sure that it looks good!

Even if you don't have a laser printer, you can make do with an inkjet; they're cheap. Anything is better than a dot matrix printer or an old-fashioned typewriter! If you're stuck with a dot matrix and absolutely can't upgrade or print your document elsewhere, remember that dot matrix printers need frequent ribbon changes when large volumes of printing are done. Whatever type of printer you have, don't print your proposal with a worn-out ribbon or with the last bits of toner left in the cartridge.

Don't Get Caught by Murphy's Law — If It Can Happen, It Will

Don't just print your proposal or grant application, make multiple copies, and mail them. Look at every printed page. Look for lines that were bumped down, formatting flaws (such as the wrong font), missing page numbers, charts that didn't print fully, and other "but we were in a hurry to get it in the mail" types of errors.

I lost a grant award because the page with the goals and objectives was omitted from the final copy run. Don't ask me how it happened, but I do know that the copy machine did it and I didn't catch it. A grant reader at the state department of education found the error and wrote my school district a letter stating that the grant application would not be reviewed because it did not meet the technical criteria. Begging, crying, and kissing up won't convince a funder that your mistake should be overlooked. Your application will just be thrown out or sent back.

Don't Celebrate for Too Long; the Funding Ends Soon

Don't rest on your laurels once your grant request is funded. Running a project on grant money, also called *soft money,* means that you must be in constant pursuit of new soft monies to continue your project. Don't wait until the last quarter of funding to look for new money. Start searching for new grant monies at the end of the second quarter of current funding. Even without summative evaluation results, you can piece together enough data to seek continuation funding.

Chapter 25

Ten Data Collection Tips

In This Chapter

▶ Using government information

▶ Making smart use of the Internet

▶ Keeping your data current

*G*rant writers are bombarded with choices regarding where to obtain information. The choices are not just abundant because of the Internet, but they're also abundant due to the many professional, content-specific publications grant writers subscribe to and the newspaper articles we have clipped for years and neatly filed in topic-related folders.

When it's time to start collecting the data that you need to write the grant application — especially the needs statement — knowing where to start is often hard. This chapter gives you ten tips to help you with collecting data for your grant application's need statement.

Look at Data from the U.S. Census Bureau First

I like to use the Census Bureau's demographic data. The bureau's Web site is user-friendly, enabling you to choose which statistics you want to view from the zillions of databases. Knowing the zip code of the community you're trying to profile in your grant application narrative is helpful.

Another quick way to use the search mode on the Web site is to call your city, village, or town clerk. Give the clerk's office the street names or neighborhood names of the area that you're going to write about, and it will give you the census tract numbers. A *census tract* is an allocated geographic area, usually measured in blocks. Each tract has a six-digit number, like 0018.35. Once you have the numbers of the tracts that contain your target population, you can enter each one separately in the search window on the Web site. Just a reminder: Print your data tables and save them for future reference when you write about your organization's service area.

Look at Data from State and Local Government Agencies Second

All government agencies from the state level to the local level collect data on a regular basis about their service populations. You can use published and raw data from your state employment office, family independence agency (formerly known as the welfare office), public health department, state police, local school district, state department of education, county economic development department, city clerk, and other public data collecting agencies. The data is recent; it's probably more accurate than data collected at the federal government level.

By calling these agencies, you make new friends in high places — ones you can call or e-mail for updated reports every time you want to update the statistics you plan to include in your grant applications.

Use Data That Builds Credibility with the Funder

The reason I like to use government agencies for recent and accurate data is that they look great when you cite your data sources. For example, "According to a recent report released last month by the Fairview County Department of Public Health, the number of Hepatitis cases in the county has increased by 50 percent." If you're writing a grant application to conduct a prevention program for substance abusers, you now have relevant and startling data to share with your funding sources.

Always cite the source of the data in the narrative. Footnotes aren't necessary on foundation or corporate requests; they can be used in state and federal grant applications. I tend to shy away from using information collected by college students who have posted their findings on the Web. Credibility is the key, and I plan on keeping mine; you should do whatever it takes to keep yours, too!

Use Current Data

The hard part about researching a problem and looking for proven solutions is that the best information may be ten years old. This is my rule, and it works: If the data is over five years old, keep searching for information that's new. Remember: Things change every second of the day and will for infinity.

Most funding sources (foundations, corporations, and government agencies) have researchers on their staff. If the funder specializes in funding animal shelters, you can bet your socks that the funder has the most recent statistics on shelters, stray animals, occupancy trends, and euthanasia. The funders expect you to be up-to-date in your knowledge of the problem. Your vision for solving the problem should be consonant with (or at least take into account) the most recent thinking and statistics.

I can't think of anything that makes me angrier than when I am asked to be a federal grant reviewer (in other words, when I read grant applications) and I find that major, well-known nonprofit organizations have data that's over ten years old. The word we grant reviewers use to describe them is *lazy*. Well, lazy doesn't get the most review points, and lazy doesn't get funded!

Follow my advice on this one. Less than 10 percent of the grant applications that I write fail to get funding. Writing a winning grant application isn't easy — but it's definitely possible, even for a beginner. Just follow the guidelines that I present throughout this book and put in the time to make your grant shine.

Compare Statistics from the Same Family of Problems

Don't mix apples with oranges. Stay within data groups when doing comparisons.

Don't compare 8th-grade math scores from 1999 with 3rd-grade math scores from 1997. It seems like an idiotic mistake, but I've reviewed grant applications where the comparisons had no connection. If you make this mistake, *you won't get funded.*

Don't Ring if You Can Click

If you're writing a lot of grant applications (one or more per month), then use the Internet to collect relevant data from state and local agencies. Calling one or two times to request a data report is okay, but if you need different kinds of data from the same agency or department, then try the Internet first. Doing so will save you time, and no public sector employee will be thinking how annoying you and your repeated telephone calls are.

Organize Your Findings

Keep all data printouts in a folder in the project box. You may receive a telephone call from the funding source questioning your numbers or information. Going to the box and pulling the data to quote the date and source is easy. Yes, I did learn from experience, so I'm sharing this "don't look stupid to the funder" tip with you.

Look for Free Research Reports and Newsletters

Ask colleagues and search the Internet for free subscription services that publish research reports and newsletters with up-to-date data that's relevant to your organization and could be used in multiple other projects. I subscribe to just about everything free that each federal agency publishes. Get on their e-mail lists. I receive all grant announcements from the U.S. Department of Education, U.S. Department of Justice, U.S. Department of Commerce, and the Environmental Protection Agency. At the state level, I receive e-mail notices of grant announcements, available upon request from the departments of education, transportation, natural resources, commerce, public health, and housing. Even if I can't use the opportunity to apply for a specific grant, I pass the announcement on to my colleagues.

Share with Others and Experience the Bounty That Flows to You

Share data with other organizations in your community. A partnering organization may return the favor when a deadline is closing in and you're missing something. Don't be stingy with data sharing!

Allocate Time Daily to Search for Best Practices in Your Service Area

Every day I spend at least one hour searching the Internet for models (known as *best practices*) from nonprofit organizations around the globe. Remember, even when a program is in Sweden or Egypt, you can use relevant components or activities to create a program in the United States — especially if you can't find any domestic organization doing what you want to do for your target population.

Information has no boundaries. Whenever I find a successful program model in another state or country, I e-mail or write the program director and ask for an overview of the program or a copy of the most recent evaluation. Don't reinvent the wheel; just make the wheel run better with proven, experienced parts and knowledge.

Chapter 26

Ten Tips for Organizing Your Writing

In This Chapter

▶ Using your information

▶ Writing sequentially

▶ Using technology to speed the process

*E*very successful grant writer has well-honed organizational techniques when it comes to putting a grant application together. I can't speak for the others, but I have my own tips. I arrived at my system after years of having stacks and boxes of unsorted papers, journals, stick-on notes, and other paper clutter on my desk and all over my office. I just couldn't take it anymore.

These ten tips work well for me. They enable me to put my finger on any file or piece of information that I need for quickly writing the grant application narrative. This organizing system has contributed to my ability to write a foundation application in less than eight hours. You can write great grants just as quickly. Being organized is the first step.

Build a Mountain of Ideas to Write a Molehill

Brainstorm with others and make a list of buzz words, goals, objectives, and outcomes (what you want the constituency to have gained when the grant funding is over). Don't reject any ideas; just take notes. When you're confronted with writer's block, these notes will aid you immensely in moving on and writing the narrative.

Collect First, Write Second

Collect all the information to write the project before you write one word. Why? The writing process should flow smoothly and be uninterrupted. Writing one paragraph and then stopping to look for information to write the next paragraph is a bad scenario. If you have all the information you need in front of you, then you're ready to take off in first place and win the grants race.

Identify and Pull Attached or Appended Documents Early

Note what attachments you need before you start writing the narrative. Enlist the aid of a coworker to start collecting the attachments, requesting letters of support, and getting the tentative costs together so that you can attach documentation to support your project budget. If you're going to purchase equipment, have several vendors provide you with catalogs before you start writing. Tear out or copy pages with the specifications and prices for major equipment (meaning the cost is over $300).

Sort Information by Grant Application Narrative Sections

Sort the information you've gathered into file folders that correspond to each section of the narrative. I'm working on a project now. The folders are positioned upright so that I can see the tab. I arrange the manila folders in the order that the information will be written. Mine are in the following order:

Needs, problems, issues; history, mission, accomplishments, current programs and activities of the grant applicant; ideas and best practice models for the program design, plus copies of all evaluations on previously funded grant programs for this grant applicant (this helps me write realistic goals and attainable, measurable objectives for this project); constituency involvement in planning (meeting minutes, sign-in logs); partners and their roles (this also cues you in on who you need letters of support or letters of agreement from); evaluation ideas, including the resumé for the evaluator or credentials for the evaluation company; budget information and other supportive information.

Take Stock of What You Have and Don't Have

As I write each section, I note any missing information on the front of the folder. (I could have overlooked getting a really important piece of information in the rush to get started writing.) I make it a point to stop and look for the needed information before I move on to the next section.

Write Front to Back

Write each section in order. Begin with the needs statement and end with the budget summary and detailed narrative. The only exceptions to this writing order are the abstract or executive summary, the table of contents, and the cover letter. I write the abstract or executive summary after editing and proofing the grant application narrative. Of course, the table of contents is the next to last thing I write, and the cover letter is the finishing touch in writing the application, although it's what the reviewer sees first.

Write Like the Wind is Blowing You at 90 Miles an Hour

Write freely without doing your own editing and proofing. Write all that comes into your mind. Don't constantly cut and paste. Chances are the first thoughts on the screen are the best thoughts. The goal is to complete the entire narrative before you read it for clarity, focus, and continuity.

Make and Use Templates

Develop a template with federal, state, foundation/corporate grant section headings and questions. Pull up the template each time you start writing. It will be a reliable guide in helping you formulate responsive and competitive language.

Complete Each Section before Moving to the Next

When you come to a section for which you're missing needed information, don't write around the gap. Find something else to do or take a walk and recharge your mind and body. Don't write out of order. Wait until each piece falls into place. As a federal grant reviewer, I can tell immediately when someone has written his or her sections out of order. The thoughts just don't flow. Blatant errors jump off the page!

Save the Worst for Last

Prepare all forms last. I hate forms. I believe they were created to slow down the grant writing process for grant writers and to speed up the grant reading process for the funders. I always do forms last. A flatbed scanner and a great OCR (optical recognition) software program help ease the frustration of making corrections and staying within the lines. *Always* have someone else check your forms for completeness and accuracy.

Chapter 27

Ten Tips for Handling a Rejection Letter

· ·

In This Chapter

▶ Getting back on your feet

▶ Learning what you can from the rejection

▶ Using state and federal connections

· ·

*G*etting a rejection letter from a funding source after you've shed blood, sweat, and tears researching and writing your grant application can be a big letdown. Besides coping with your own personal disappointment, you also have to face your superiors, peers, and others in the community who rallied to your cause and helped you put the grant application together. The best way to handle a rejection letter is with your head up, hopes high, and a game plan for getting the funding through another source. In this chapter, I give you ten pointers on handling a rejection letter.

Don't Cry

This is not the time to fall apart. Shedding tears helps you feel better initially, but tears don't move your failed grant application to an award status. You need all the energy you can muster to keep chasing those dollars — you've got no time for tears.

Don't Give Up

I tell you to identify more than one funding source for your project for a reason: When one funder sends you a rejection letter, you still have numerous other chances to get the funding you need.

Open the Post-Rejection Discussion with Private Sector Funders

For foundation and corporate proposals: Contact the funder to see if discussion is possible. Maybe the funder just ran out of money. Maybe it didn't understand what you were trying to do, but because it receives so many grant requests, it just didn't have the time or staff to call you for further discussion at the time your grant application was reviewed.

Request the Grant Viewers' Comments for Public Sector Funders

For federal and state grant applications: First, call or write for reviewers' comments. You can use the Freedom of Information Act to request and receive copies of the grant reviewers' comments and scoring on each section of your grant application. Before you call the funding agency, have a copy of your rejection letter in front of you. On the letter, you should be able to find the name of the funding agency, the contact person, the telephone number, and maybe even the numerical tracking code that was assigned to your grant application when the funding agency first received it.

When you call the funding agency and request the reviewers' comments, more than likely you'll be told to request the comments in writing. Just write a normal letter, but at the top put the following header, in all caps: FREEDOM OF INFORMATION ACT REQUEST. Chapter 20 shows you how to write the rest of the letter.

Don't Take It as a Personal Rejection

You are just one more applicant with a grant application in the pile. Funding source staff are often overworked and underpaid. Sometimes you won't even get a standard rejection letter; instead, it's a standard rejection postcard. Not very original, but you have to be ready for it if you're submitting unsolicited proposals to foundations and corporations and submitting highly competitive grant applications to government agencies.

The reasons your grant didn't make it to the recommendation-for-funding stack could be any one of a dozen, none intended to be personal — from not enough money to fund all requests, to "Sorry, we just changed our funding priorities and haven't published or released this new information," to "No one was funded; we decided to suspend grantmaking for one year while we plan for new funding priorities."

Read the Letter Carefully and Look for a Window of Opportunity

Read the letter carefully. Some funders receive more requests than they can fund in a fiscal year, but they often invite applicants to reapply after a certain date.

Play Their Game and Win

Some funders automatically reject your grant request the first and second time it's submitted. They're looking for tenacity. So revamp the proposal and resubmit once a year or as often as the funders' guidelines permit. Don't be deterred by a rejection letter on the first try.

Track the Results of Your Efforts

Keep a copy of the letter in your project file. By filing rejection letters, you know the status of your requests, which sources are still pending, which sources have said no, and which sources have requested more information. Creating an electronic database isn't a bad idea, but always keep a hard copy as well.

Do It Again

Mark your calendar for the next open submission date, when you can resubmit a revamped proposal or grant application. Some funding sources accept only one proposal or grant application a year.

Use Your Connections — a Miracle Can Happen

If your federal or state grant application is rejected, contact your legislator for guidance and help in finding out the real reason it wasn't funded. All federal and state grants have to be awarded equally across geographic areas and split between rural and urban areas. The reviewers often factor in other equity indicators. These preferences are usually published in the application guidelines, but after receiving a rejection letter, it's still wise to ask your legislator to investigate. Even better, *demand* that your legislator investigate. His or her intervention may make the difference in getting your grant application funded in the next competitive cycle.

Appendix

Two Complete Examples of Grant Application Narratives

● ●

*T*his appendix contains the complete text of two grant application narratives that led to the award of funds. One is from an application for government funding and the other is addressed to a private foundation. My goal is to show you how various grant writing techniques — wording, formatting, highlighting, graphics — can work together in a successful document requesting grant monies.

To make sure you spot the many important features of each grant, I've dropped little notes into the text in a distinctive typeface and in parentheses.

1. Government Grant Narrative

The application that begins on the next page was written in response to an announcement of funding by a state department of education — an invitation to public school districts to apply for a Technology Literacy Challenge grant.

The abstract is written to fit on a form designed by the funding agency. The narrative is written in a free-flowing format but, as you can see, addresses certain grant review criteria. For a full discussion of review criteria, see Chapters 8 and 9.

PROPOSAL ABSTRACT

Applicant: <u>Montpelier Area Intermediate School District (MAISD)</u>

(Abstracts are one page and single-spaced.)

---

1) Goals of the Proposed Initiative

Goal #1 - Establish an effective and flexible technology infrastructure within the MAISD.

Goal #2 - Train Montpelier County educators, support staff, administrators, and classroom volunteers (parents, grandparents, retirees, and business persons) to effectively use and integrate technology into learning applications.

Goal #3 - Utilize current and new technologies for curriculum development and instructional strategies which will enhance student learning and lead to the improvement of VIMS and HSPT scores

2) Description of Proposed Initiative

Step 1: **Frame Relay.** Forty-six buildings (including central offices, transportation centers, and all other separate buildings on each of the seven LEA campuses, including the MAISD) will be connected by a 128K frame relay connection. The frame relay will facilitate multiuser access within the MAISD network to student management record programs (LEA and MAISD teachers and administration), transportation routing information (LEA and MAISD teachers, administration, and transportation personnel), and word processing programs, spreadsheet applications, and curriculum software packages (mathematics and reading related to VIMS and HSPT preparation, science, social studies, and language arts). Via the frame relay, each LEA will have access to the MAISD Web server and inter- and intra-district E-mail.

Step 2: **Training Lab.** The MAISD will install a training lab at its offices in Shelburne. This centralized professional development site for Montpelier County teachers and administration will have 16 learning stations. The lab will facilitate the training of more than 800 teachers and 700 support staff in the MAISD service area. A cadre composed of postsecondary education community trainers, MAISD consultants, and LEA technology personnel will provide the training for the 1,500-plus personnel.

Step 3: **Technology Support.** In Year 1, a full-time technical support specialist will be hired to assist set-up of the system in all 46 buildings.

Step 4: **Professional Development.** Six experienced technology trainers from the MAISD partners will provide 25 half-day, full-day, and multi-day lab-based and on-site (at LEAs) sessions to K-12 and ISD teachers, administrators, paraprofessionals, secretaries, community college staff, public librarians, and students.

3) Benefits to Students

Accessing core curricula-related software programs in each LEA's classrooms will enable 13,971 Montpelier County students to **benefit** from the Wide Area Network (WAN) offerings intended to assist them in applying knowledge, materials (tools), and skills to solve practical problems, in school and in the world. The WAN will result in teachers who are technology literate, who will, in turn, transfer their technology skills into each and every classroom. Students who understand the role and impact of technology, learn to identify when to use technology to solve a problem or accomplish a task, and can obtain, organize, and manipulate information will perform better on the VIMS and HSPT. The improvement in scores will not be instantaneous, but over the long haul, in alignment with the five-year, long-range technology plan that encompasses the needs of Montpelier County learners, an upturn will occur.

TECHNOLOGY LITERACY CHALLENGE GRANT APPLICATION

MONTPELIER AREA INTERMEDIATE SCHOOL DISTRICT

(Government grants start with the grant name and applicant name.)

1. Proposed Initiative: A clear description of the proposed initiative, its connectedness to the applicant's strategic long-range technology plan, and how it will foster the use of technology in the classroom.

Description of the proposed initiative - The proposed initiative of the Montpelier Area Intermediate School District (MAISD) is to **bring connectivity into Montpelier County**.

(Subsections stand out with italics.)

Step 1: **Frame Relay.** Forty-six buildings (including central offices, transportation centers, and all other separate buildings on each of the seven LEA campuses, including the MAISD) will be connected by a 128K frame relay connection. The major advantage of installing a frame relay is that only a single connection will be required from the MAISD to the multiplexers, reducing line costs for each LEA after grant funds are expended, yet providing a high-speed interface to facilitate information exchanges between the MAISD and each LEA. The frame relay will facilitate multiuser access within the MAISD network to student management record programs (LEA and MAISD teachers and administration), transportation routing information (LEA and MAISD teachers, administration, and transportation personnel), and word processing programs, spreadsheet applications, and curriculum software packages (mathematics and reading related to VIMS and HSPT preparation, science, social studies, and language arts). Via the frame relay, each LEA will have access to the MAISD Web server and inter- and intra-district E-mail. **Priority will be given to creating a network that serves the needs of students first; staff, second.**

(Key words and sentences are highlighted in bold.)

Step 2: **Training Lab.** The MAISD will install a training lab at its offices in Shelburne. This centralized professional development site for Montpelier County teachers and administration will have 16 learning stations. Eight stations will be with Apple platform and eight stations will be PC/ Pentium platform. The lab will have printers, a video/computer projector, a scanner, a 3-D projector/ imaging device, a digital camera, a color Quick cam, an overhead projector, a videodisk player, a large-screen data monitor, an electronic print board with computer interface, a VCR, tables, chairs, a wall screen, bookshelves, and a resource library. The lab will also have a file server and a wide variety of software (ClarisWorks, Microsoft Office, Hyper Studio, and several dozen other programs) to serve the educational and informational needs of the end users (students and staff). In addition, MAISD will also subscribe to electronic information services (Proquest, First Search, etc.). The lab will facilitate the training of more than 800 teachers and 700 support staff in the MAISD service area. A cadre composed of postsecondary education community trainers, MAISD consultants, and LEA technology personnel will provide the training for the 1,500-plus personnel.

Step 3: **Technology Support.** In Year 1, a full-time technical support specialist will be hired to assist set-up of the system in all 46 buildings. This individual will be responsible for supporting the frame relay; consulting with LEAs for planning (technology plans); conducting a district technology needs assessment; resolving the integration of technology into existing curricula; recommending hardware, software, and materials purchases for each LEA and coordinating districtwide purchasing (bulk ordering for cost-effectiveness); acting as a technology liaison for MAISD, the LEAs, Montpelier Community College, the Middle Vermont Education Network Consortium, and the Coalition of Greater Grafton (which encompasses a wide range of public human and social service agencies and businesses within Montpelier County); and providing basic technology troubleshooting for the network.

Step 4: **Professional Development.** Six experienced technology trainers from the MAISD partners will provide 25 half-day, full-day, and multi-day lab-based and on-site (at LEAs) sessions to K-12 and ISD teachers, administrators, paraprofessionals, secretaries, community college staff, public librarians, and students. Topics will include, but will not be limited to: Basic Computers and Technology, District/Building Level Technology Planning, Multimedia Using Hyper Studio, Basic Macintosh, Windows 2000, ClarisWorks, Advanced ClarisWorks, Basic Microsoft Office, Advanced Microsoft Office, Curriculum and Technology Connections (Social Studies, Science, Language Arts, and Mathematics that synchronize with VIMS and HSPT preparation), Technology in Lower Elementary, Technology in Upper Elementary, Thematic Instruction and Technology, Web Page Design, Basic Internet (World Wide Web), Advanced Internet (Gopher, Telnet, newsgroups, etc.), Desktop Publishing for the Elementary Teacher, Desktop

Publishing for the Secondary Teacher, Computer/Network/Technology Troubleshooting, Technology in the Workplace, Applied Technology, and Using Technology for Research. A partnership developed with Mountain Ridge State University and Central Vermont University will award graduate credits to educators and continuing education units to non-educators completing the training.

Connectedness to Montpelier ISD's strategic long-range technology plan - The goals of MAISD's long-range technology plan are:

(Bullets shout!)

- To facilitate long-range technology planning for the LEAs.

- To actively monitor technology/media trends, information, and equipment districtwide. To involve business and community agencies in using technology for improving communication and program development.

- To showcase technology/media, information, and equipment for a variety of applications.

- To train personnel to effectively use and integrate technology into instruction.

- To establish an effective and flexible technology infrastructure within the MAISD.

- To utilize current and new technologies for curriculum development and instructional strategies which will enhance student learning and lead to the improvement of VIMS and HSPT scores.

(Each of the four steps moves toward achievement of the long-range technology plan.)

How implementing this initiative will foster the use of technology in the classroom - Each LEA already has computers in classrooms, at least one computer lab, and a multimedia center in their library. Every building has Internet access via at least one modem-equipped workstation. In most districts, these technology purchases have been part of the general fund budget. In two of the districts, the general fund money was enhanced by successful bond issues. MAISD's four-step initiative is centered on getting information technologies into the classrooms across the county and making sure they are used. Teachers will be well trained, given technical support, and continually monitored for their effective use of these new technologies. As a result, students will be less dependent on the traditional roles of teachers and will rely more on teachers as resource coaches who can help them electronically navigate through a vast array of educational resources and learning opportunities. Via the network, beginning at kindergarten and continuing through 12th grade, Montpelier County students will have full and equal access to learning applications that link them with the outside world and prepare them for the world of work.

2. Impact on Student Learning: A description of how the proposed initiative will benefit students and result in increased student learning.

Accessing core curricula-related software programs in each LEA's classrooms will enable 13,971 Montpelier County students to **benefit** from the Wide Area Network (WAN) offerings intended to assist them in applying knowledge, materials (tools), and skills to solve practical problems, in school and in the world. While the applicant was not able to secure any longitudinal research to prove or disprove that Vermont students that have had access to technology since 1992 (first year of the state's technology plan) have scored significantly higher than their technology deficient peers, the State's Technology Outcomes do provide a substantial base for building the connection between technology access and the possibility of improved learning outcomes. Currently, only one of the seven LEAs has students who exceed the state percentages for *satisfactory* on the VIMS. The remaining districts have noticeable trouble spots. Statewide *satisfactory* scores for 4th and 7th grade math are 60.5% and 51.4%, respectively; for reading, 49.0% and 40.4%.

(Careful presentation of statistics helps build a strong argument for the proposal.)

	1999 VIMS Results for *Satisfactory*			
District	**Math** **4th Grade** **Percent**	**Math** **7th Grade** **Percent**	**Reading 4th Grade** **Percent**	**Reading** **7th Grade** **Percent**
Chester Area Schools	61.2	**42.4**	52.9	**32.6**
Central Montpelier Public Schools	**50.3**	55.2	55.2	**35.3**
Grafton Public Schools	66.7	**50.0**	50.6	**31.2**

1999 VIMS Results for *Satisfactory*				
District	**Math** **4th Grade** **Percent**	**Math** **7th Grade** **Percent**	**Reading 4th** **Grade** **Percent**	**Reading** **7th Grade** **Percent**
Ludlow Community Schools	**44.9**	63.2	**39.7**	46.8
Middlebury Community Schools	**50.0**	52.1	**38.1**	**39.7**
Troy Area Schools	64.6	**39.6**	**40.5**	**26.1**
Vergennes Community Schools	72.5	67.3	52.9	41.8

When technology outcomes are effectively integrated across curricular areas, the result is a technologically literate individual. The WAN will result in teachers who are technology literate, who will, in turn, transfer their technology skills into each and every classroom. Students who understand the role and impact of technology, learn to identify when to use technology to solve a problem or accomplish a task, and can obtain, organize, and manipulate information will perform better on the VIMS and HSPT. The improvement in scores will not be instantaneous, but over the long haul, in alignment with the five-year, long-range technology plan that encompasses the needs of Montpelier County learners, an upturn will occur.

Educational reform and the integration of technology into learning share a profound symbiosis: technology requires the rich learning environments envisioned by reformers; reform demands the power of technology to put students at the center of their own learning. MAISD's systematic adoption of reform will mean a critical mass of rural and virtually isolated educators and support staff will participate in countywide collaborative professional growth. This important step, professional development, will make the difference in how effective the WAN and its offerings will be for Montpelier County students.

Establishing a WAN throughout Montpelier County that links each LEA to the ISD's server for numerous educational and informational software applications will result in **increased student learning** by:

- Providing teachers with training to enable them to make optimal use of technology in their classrooms, libraries, and computer labs.

- Integrating technology into instruction.

- Wiring all public schools to provide them with access to the *information Superhighway*.

- Developing the ability for each school to communicate with other schools and outside organizations to support classroom learning activities.

- Ensuring that each building has appropriate educational software.

- Enabling schools to take advantage of future technological innovations as they become available.

- Developing instructional standards for technology.

- Preparing students to meet and exceed statewide VIMS and HSPT scores and the National Education Goals.

   Funding under this grant will enable the MAISD to provide access and connectivity, a training lab, staff development, technical support, and content resources countywide.

   3. Plan of Action: A plan which includes clearly defined goals and objectives for what is to be accomplished during the grant period, indicators of success, activities to be undertaken, and a timeframe.

(Notice how the numbers below clearly outline the plan of action. Impressive!)

   The MAISD plan of action addresses the needs of seven LEAs enrolling 13,791 students; 14 private/parochial/denominational schools enrolling 954 students; and three facilities serving 181 special education pupils. In addition, 215 students who are the children of seasonal migrant workers will also benefit from the technology literacy initiative in Montpelier County. With funding from the Vermont

Department of Education, MAISD will be able to achieve the following goals and objectives from its long-range technology plan.

(Multiple goals stand out better within framed sections.)

Goal #1	Establish an effective and flexible technology infrastructure within the MAISD.
Objective	Connect the MAISD to 46 buildings in seven LEAs in Montpelier County.
Activity	Install a 128K frame relay connection.
Indicators of Success	Every LEA will provide 50 percent in-kind support for the connectivity infrastructure in order to have access to educational and informational software applications, including student management record programs, and will incorporate daily technology usage into their classroom and building-level activities.
Timeframe	Fall 2000 through Spring 2001

(Futuristic goals!)

Goal #2	Train Montpelier County educators, support staff, administrators, and classroom volunteers (parents, grandparents, retirees, and business persons) to effectively use and integrate technology into learning applications.
Objectives	Develop one, 16-station learning lab at the MAISD to facilitate countywide training and house the WAN.
	Train a minimum of 1,500 districtwide personnel and one volunteer per building site.
Activity	Purchase and install all hardware and software to accommodate full on-site and end user interface.
	Meet with educational partners and plan technology professional development. Provide initial and ongoing training in the lab and on-site to support instructional, administrative, and support applications.

Indicators of Success	Full participation in training. Demonstration of trainee knowledge and application abilities in the lab and in the classroom. Transfer of knowledge and skills into improved and enhanced core curricula applications that impact student achievement.
Timeframe	Fall 2000 to Summer 2001

(Measurable objectives!)

Goal #3	Utilize current and new technologies for curriculum development and instructional strategies which will enhance student learning and lead to the improvement of VIMS and HSPT scores.
Objective	Hire one full-time technical support specialist to provide technology-related services to the seven LEAs, as well as the buildings on the MAISD campus. Note: 50 percent local match for this position in Year 1 and 100 percent local match in succeeding years.
Activity	Provide support for the frame relay; consult with LEAs for planning (technology plans); conduct a district technology needs assessment; resolve the integration of technology into existing curricula; recommend hardware, software, and materials purchases for each LEA and coordinate districtwide purchasing (bulk ordering for cost-effectiveness); act as a technology liaison for MAISD, the LEAs, Montpelier Community College, the Middle Vermont Education Network Consortium, and the Coalition of Greater Greenville (which encompasses a wide range of public human and social service agencies and businesses within Montpelier County); and provide basic technology troubleshooting for the network.
Indicators of Success	Attainment of Goals 1, 2, and 3 of the MAISD long-range technology plan. Improved VIMS and HSPT scores for Montpelier County students by the 2001/2001 school year, demonstrating that the students and staff of the MAISD have met the technology literacy challenge and are on the way to meeting and exceeding the National Education Goals.
Timeframe	Fall 2000 through Summer 2001

(Reasonable timeframes!)

4. Parent and Community Involvement: A description of how parents, public libraries, business leaders, and community leaders have been involved in the development of the strategic long-range technology plan.

The MAISD School Improvement Committee has 17 members, including parents, business owners and managers, community leaders, and Montpelier County residents-at-large, who consider themselves stakeholders in the education process. Parents make up at least 30 percent of each LEA's school improvement team. Area libraries and businesses, along with almost a dozen human and social service agencies, join the MAISD staff on the Montpelier Area Alliance, which has a technology subcommittee. This subcommittee worked to develop and support board adoption of the MAISD long-range technology plan.

(Notice the inclusion of stakeholders--parents, libraries, businesses, human and social service agencies. Stakeholders are important throughout the narrative.)

5. Equitable Access: A description of how the acquired technologies will help promote equity in education and provide access for teachers, parents, and students to the best teaching practices and curriculum resources, including students enrolled in private schools, their teachers, and other educational personnel.

(Standard advice for narratives: Amplify project equity.)

Equitable Access Target	Tactics for Inclusion
Public school teachers	Initial and ongoing lab and on-site training, ongoing observation of applications in the classroom by LEA administrator and ISD personnel, and ongoing technical support.
Parents of public school students	LEA newsletters detailing the WAN, classroom enhancements, lab and on-site training times open to parents.
Public school students	WAN connected to 46 LEA and MAISD buildings.
Private school teachers	Letters sent to the 14 private schools inviting teachers to the initial and ongoing lab training. On a fee-for-linkage basis,

Equitable Access Target	Tactics for Inclusion
	private schools will be invited to become a part of the WAN via the frame relay. Upon notification of state funding, letters will be sent and followed up with telephone calls.
Private school students	Ability to access the same programs as public school students through any LEA school library or adult education class using the network.
Other public school educational personnel	Included in initial and ongoing training.
Other interested parties including, but not limited to, home schools, business owners and managers, personnel from members of the Montpelier Area Alliance	LEA newsletters mailed to home schools, business owners and managers, personnel from members of the Alliance, and other interested parties. The county's home schools teach a total of 21 students.

6. Performance Evaluation: The process for ongoing evaluation of how technologies will: 1) be integrated into the school curriculum, 2) improve student learning, and 3) meet the National Education Goals and any challenging content or student performance standards.

(Complete narratives cover all evaluation bases.)

Evaluation standards for how technologies will be integrated into school curriculum - The Vermont Department of Education's Five-Year Technology Plan outlines the planning and coordination for supporting the integration of technology-based programs in curriculum. A short-term formative evaluation and a longitudinal three-year (2002-2005) summative evaluation will be developed by MAISD with technical assistance from the Middle Vermont Education Network Consortium and Central Vermont University. The stakeholders' evaluation team will include teachers, parents, students, experts in the field of technology integration into the classroom, and ISD personnel. Together, the evaluation team will develop standards based on the state's recommendations as they apply to this area. The district technology needs assessment will be conducted immediately upon notification of a grant award. This assessment will provide the needed LEA inventory data and knowledge levels to assess the hardware, software, and information skills needed to create a technology literate teaching and student body in Montpelier County. The school improvement plan is a product of ongoing educational reform in each LEA and at the ISD. The MAISD long-range technology plan has been written to incorporate the known needs of the LEAs that relate to educational reform, i.e., school improvement through the integration of technology into curricula. Achievable and quantifiable benchmarks will be set for each LEA by grade level based on the K-12 Standards of Quality document for technology outcomes. MAISD will prove to its stakeholders that the ongoing investment of public monies to install technology infrastructure will, in fact, provide Montpelier County students with the opportunity to understand what technology can and cannot do in our complex society. The technology will serve as the interdisciplinary link between mathematics, science, social studies, language arts, and other areas of education. Close monitoring by LEA administrators, ISD staff, the stakeholders' evaluation team, school improvement committees, and technology subcommittees will ensure that any monetary investment is resulting in improved academic performance, improved state and national assessment scores, and improved learning environments—with the return on taxpayer investment being students who graduate from high school meeting and exceeding the National Education Goals.

How the proposed four-step initiative will improve student learning - As new curricula applications are accessed by the 13,971 students enrolled at the LEAs and MAISD, they will:

- Learn on an individualized basis how to master basic skills.

- Be given tutorial assistance via computer, with teachers and/or volunteers aiding learners with special needs to meet the benchmark standards for core curriculum and technology outcomes.

- Develop critical-thinking skills, problem solving abilities, and cooperative-learning skills that will further facilitate classroom achievement, academically and socially.

- Understand the link between technology applications, inquiry-centered instruction, assessment scores, and workforce readiness as it relates to graduation, seeking employment, entering college, and finding one's place in the world.

- Be driven to excel even further because inquiry-centered instruction breeds curiosity, tenacity—proving to one's self that one can do better than in the past.

(Notice the use of state and national standards.)

How Montpelier County students will meet the National Education Goals and any challenging content or student performance standards - This four-step implementation of MAISD's long-range technology plan will challenge each student's learning style and address it with flexible but proven software applications designed to support curricular outcomes. The three MAISD technology goals addressed in this grant application and the resources already available, but isolated across districts in this very rural county, address the four goals of the National Plan for Technology in Education:

- **All teachers in the Nation will have the training and support they need to help students learn through computers and the information superhighway.** [Extensive professional development and ongoing on-site technical support will be provided to Montpelier County teachers.]

- **All teachers and students will have modern computers in their classrooms.** [Each LEA and ISD special learning center has already demonstrated a local investment in technology.]

- **Every classroom will be connected to the information superhighway.** [Every student has access, either in the classroom, the library, or in a computer lab, to a computer station. There is at least one connection site in each LEA to the Internet. The difficulty lies in the local dial-up barriers, which will be addressed in the last section of this grant application.]

- **Effective and engaging software and online learning resources will be an integral part of every school curriculum.** [Via the WAN, literally dozens of effective and engaging software programs will be accessible to every Montpelier County student.]

This four-step initiative addresses Goals 3, 4, 5, 6, and 8 of the National Education Goals. Meeting the four goals of the National Plan for Technology in Education and five of the eight national education goals can only be achieved when local and state-required standards of academic measurement are achieved districtwide within each LEA. Our students will use what they have learned via the WAN and through their academic and life experiences to score higher on the ACT and SAT as they seek to climb yet another rung of the educational ladder.

7. Budget: Evidence of reasonableness and cost-effectiveness of the budget, including a detailed explanation of the projected costs under the requested standard price quotations, as appropriate, to

support the funding request. Applicants should also provide an overview of the budgetary projections for implementing each phase of the long-range plan and clearly delineate which phase of the overall plan would be accomplished with the requested grant.

The MAISD will apply to the Universal Service Fund which gives a significant discount for collaborative purchasing efforts for the 128K frame relay connection and the technology lab components. Factoring in the discounts, it will cost $150,000 for the frame relay connection; $100,000 for line costs (with a 50% local match); $100,000 for the training lab (25% match by ISD); and $45,000 for the lab's hardware and software (includes E-mail and Web server). The total cost for connectivity is $395,000, with $320,000 being requested in this grant application and $75,000 coming from the LEAs and ISD. Professional development will cost $35,000, and the technical support specialist position will add $40,000 (50% local match from the LEAs) to the budget. The total cost for training and support is $75,000, with $55,000 being requested in this grant application and $20,000 coming from the LEAs.

(Justify the cost!)

The cost to **implement three of the long-range technology plan's 12 goals** is $470,000; a total of $375,000 is being requested in this grant application for goal implementation.

8. Management Plan: A management plan identifying key personnel and the time commitment of each.

The project director will be Louann Madison. She is currently in a dual position between the MAISD in Shelburne and the Lake Fontana Regional Education Service District in Lakeville. Ms. Madison's MAISD title is Director of Career Technical Education and Administrative Assistant to the Superintendent. She will be responsible for hiring the technical support specialist, providing administrative oversight, and reporting to the superintendent at MAISD on grant-funded activities. She will also be responsible for putting together the evaluation team. Ms. Madison will be assigned to this grant at 0.10 FTE. **Her resume is attached.**

(Show the line of responsibility!)

The technical support specialist position will be 1.0 FTE. This individual will report directly to Louann Madison. He or she will be responsible for the following: supporting the frame relay; consulting with LEAs for planning (technology plans); conducting a district technology needs assessment; resolving the integration of technology into existing curricula; recommending hardware, software, and materials purchases for each LEA and coordinating districtwide purchasing (bulk ordering for cost-effectiveness); acting as a technology liaison for MAISD, the LEAs, Montpelier Community College, the Middle Vermont Education Network Consortium, and the Coalition of Greater Grafton (which encompasses a wide range of public human and social service agencies and businesses within Montpelier County); and providing basic technology troubleshooting for the network. **A list of other ISD personnel and their time commitment is attached.**

(Address funding priorities!)

Special Consideration: Some 22.5 percent of **school-age children in Montpelier County are below the poverty level** (Kids Count, 1999). Montpelier County ranks 17 out of 22 counties in poverty. **Local dial-up access is across two LATAs,** making it costly for 50 percent of the LEAs (the three largest in the county) to access the Internet cost-effectively. The WAN will resolve this issue, as technology sites will be able to access the Internet via the ISD's grant-funded toll-free number for out-of-LATA users. The **free and reduced lunch count for each LEA individual school building ranges from 7.9 percent to 95.7 percent.** The state average is 31.39 percent. Of the 46 buildings to be connected via the WAN, 20 buildings exceed the state average. Vermont State University rates Montpelier County as an **8 in rurality**, with 9 being the most rural rating. The county has a high migrant worker population each summer and early fall.

2. Foundation Grant Narrative

The narrative beginning on the next page is addressed to a private foundation — a request for a planning grant. Because a planning grant is meant to give an organization the time and money to figure out its purpose and direction, the plan of operation or project design area of the narrative does not have measurable objectives. That rarely occurs in grant writing and explains, in part, why the narrative is shorter than the proposal to a government funder that appears earlier in this appendix.

The following narrative example also shows how to present a project by a religious organization. Only about 30 percent of foundation and corporate funders have an interest in funding a project of this nature. The writing is directed specifically to funders that have awarded grants to projects closely linked to a church body.

PROPOSAL NARRATIVE

<u>Description of Kansas Methodist Children's Services (KMCS)</u>

➤ Problems, needs, and issues addressed by KMCS

The applicant, an IRS recognized 501(c)(3) nonprofit organization, offers help and hope to hurting children through foster care, counseling services, and treatment programs. The caring staff works with children of all ages, on a nondenominational basis, to heal the hurts of the past and provide hope for the future. KMCS isn't just about children, it's also about families. Many of the children served have parents who love them but who simply have never really learned *how* to be parents. Through innovative methods of counseling and training for the entire family, the family unit is kept intact whenever possible.

(Word choice and phrasing are crucial matters in effective proposals. Notice, above, "help and hope to hurting children," "caring staff," "heal the hurts of the past and provide hope for the future," and "parents who love them but who simply have never really learned to be parents." For more about words and phrasing, see Chapter 9.)

(Use current stats, as below.)

The 1999 Kids Count state profile for Kansas provides indicators for at-risk children in the state and compares them to U.S. statistics.

National Indicators (1998)	Kansas	U.S.
Child death rate, ages 1-14 (deaths per 100,000 children)	37	30
Teen violent death rate, ages 15-19 (deaths per 100,000 children)	87	69
Juvenile violent crime arrest rate, ages 10-17 (arrests per 100,000 youths)	522	506
Percent of children in poverty	22	21
Percent of poor families with children receiving welfare assistance	86	85

In Kansas, all but one of these alarming trends have increased over the last decade. The status of all children, rich or poor, minority or nonminority, with one parent or two parents, Christian or atheist, have become the primary concern at KMCS. Our board believes that major intervention from the private and public sectors is critically needed to plan pilot projects for Kansas families that will grow into major publicly and privately supported systemic programs to *make* CHILDREN FIRST.

(Emphasize inclusion of all.)

• KMCS history and major accomplishments

KMCS began in 1976 with a dozen children who needed a temporary home away from their families. The children's home, then a small shelter on five acres of land in northwest Dodge City, had been a long time coming. For some 20 years, a determined group of Methodists had devoted money and effort into a home for needy children before the dream at last became a reality. In the last 24 years, KMCS has grown into a multifaceted child care ministry serving well over 1,000 children and families each year. Originally a home for children who simply needed a temporary home, KMCS shifted its focus to abused and neglected children in the 1980s when the demands of society shifted. Today, as the number of troubled children continues to rise, the dedicated staff of KMCS helps children find love and security--many for the first time in their lives. The number of children helped in KMCS programs over the past five years follow.

(Show the track record.)

Program	94-95	95-96	96-97	97-98	98-99
Residential Treatment Center	76	76	89	89	92
Therapeutic Foster Care	45	164	293	253	257
Independent Living Preparation	22	18	29	21	25
Counseling	867	931	830	842	1,197
Therapeutic Group Homes	23	29	24	31	21
Comprehensive Group Homes				38	74
Total	**1,283**	**1,595**	**1,719**	**1,511**	**1,666**

Program

Residential Treatment

Center

Therapeutic Foster Care

Independent Living

Preparation

Counseling

Therapeutic Group Homes

Comprehensive Group

Homes

Total

- Current programs and activities

    Residential Treatment Center - Medicine Lodge Center, in Dodge City, provides psychiatric treatment for girls ages 6 to 18. The program combines intensive individual therapy with family counseling, with the goal of reuniting the family whenever possible. A team of mental health professionals develop an individualized treatment plan for each resident. An on-campus special education program is included in the treatment program for students who are not emotionally able to attend public school.

    Comprehensive Foster Care - Foster parents provide temporary care and treatment in a home setting for children from birth to 18 years with the ultimate goal being the reunification of the children with parents, placement with other family members, or transition into an adoptive home. Foster parents receive training before a child is placed in their home, and support from an KMCS social worker during placement. Foster families are reimbursed for costs involved in caring for the child. The KMCS foster program is currently limited to Lucas County, but plans are in process to provide this service statewide.

    Independent Living Program - Independent living skills are crucial for young people, especially for the girls ages 14 to 18 who are placed in the KMCS Wrangler Program. Most will be living on their own when they are 18 years of age. This program focuses on teaching the skills necessary for self-sufficiency. The girls receive educational and vocational training which prepares them for adult life. The program also includes survival skills development, with training in money management, cooking and nutrition, household appliance usage, personal hygiene, and consumer awareness. All residents are evaluated upon admission, and a specialized treatment plan is developed for each. The Wrangler House is located in Olathe.

    Counseling Services - Services are available for people of all ages through the KMCS counseling program. Staff specialize in addressing a variety of problem areas, with special emphasis on working with the whole family. Services are provided by trained staff who integrate mental health principles with spiritual values. KMCS offers psychiatric services to children under 18 years of age. At-risk children in seven school districts receive help through KMCS's school-based group therapy program. An intensive family preservation program is another innovative service offered to children and families. The program's goal is to avoid the need for placement of the child outside the home. KMCS has two counseling offices in Lucas County.

    Therapeutic Group Homes - Emotionally troubled girls ages 8 to 15 receive care in two treatment-oriented group homes. Pathways, an eight-bed facility, is located in Dodge City, and Our House, with six beds, is located in Minneola. Program staff work to reduce the symptoms that necessitated out-of-home placement and to reunite the family. Involvement of family members is essential to the success of the program.

    Comprehensive Group Homes - Two group homes for girl's ages 10 to 16 provide long-term care for children who are either awaiting reunification with their families, placement in foster homes, or transition to independent living. Destiny is a six-bed home for 10- to 13-year-old girls. Sharing Place is a 10-bed home for 13- to 16-year-old girls. Behavioral health technicians are trained and act as surrogate parents to group home residents, focusing on nurturing, supporting, and guiding the children in developing social and coping skills.

(The comprehensive list of programs and activities shows that the applicant is able to manage a planning grant.)

The KMCS board of trustees has approved a five-year strategic plan, "Building A Future For Children." The plan began this year and will take the agency into the year 2000. It calls for upgrading all facilities, strengthening family reunification efforts, and establishing regional centers in Pratt, Yates Center, Fredonia, Southeastern Kansas, and the Smith Buttes area. It also mandates that KMCS provide technical assistance to churches in their efforts to develop family ministries. In addition, KMCS will venture into providing other needed services to schools and homes. This grant application seeks funds for planning a pilot project in south central Dodge City that will develop the skills of mothers who are on welfare to become professional foster parents, thus removing them from the welfare rolls and, at the same time, providing a resource for children.

(Widespread impact is critical.)

Description of Request

- Professional Parents Partnering Project

    The Professional Parents Partnering Project is a new initiative that KMCS will undertake in 2001 to identify and train welfare mothers residing in District 7 of Lucas County (the Rockhurst-College Park neighborhood in south central Dodge City) to become foster parents who derive most or all of their income through providing foster care. In order to build the base for a successful pilot and what will later become a full-scale welfare reform program, KMCS is seeking a one-year planning grant from your organization.

(A slightly longer purpose statement above, but effectively focused.)

- Purpose and constituency, goals, objective, and timeline

    The purpose of KMCS's request is to seek grant funds to develop a written conceptual model that will select and train AFDC and other low-income families in the Eden Project area to provide permanency-focused professional foster parenting to children from the Eden Project area. Those selected will be trained to provide short-term foster care and to mentor to the families of children in their care.

    Goals of the partnership

1. To remove families from AFDC or economically strengthen under-employed families capable of becoming licensed foster parents.

2. To provide short-term, permanency-focused foster care to children in their own community.

3. To mentor families whose children are at risk of being removed or who must be removed for reasons of health or safety.

4. To bring to bear the resources of a community to strengthen families and support those who provide direct care to families through an interlocking network of community and professional programs.

(The grant will pay for a plan encompassing four end-goals.)

    Objective and timeline for the planning period

    KMCS will have a written conceptual model in place for pilot and eventual full implementation of the Professional Parents Partnering Project by the end of the 12-month funding period.

(The objective and timeline above is very short statement--a variation from most proposals--because the whole idea of the project is to plan.)

Result of the Professional Parents Partnering Project's Planning Grant

In Phase II, KMCS will be prepared to identify, train, and enable five low-income, welfare-dependent families to become state licensed professional foster care providers in a pilot program that will test the parameters of the state's welfare and foster home programs and the abilities of the selected families. This 12-month phase will begin immediately following the planning period and will require new funding for start-up.

(Above, planting the seeds for the next grant!)

Strategy

Hire a 1.0 FTE project planner

Write a detailed program design which includes pilot and implementation budgets, identification of sources of support, and identification of partners.

Obtain a commitment from the partners to participate in this initiative.

Complete a feasibility study of the Eden Project area. This study will determine the possible number of families who could be trained as professional foster parents. It will include the number of children who are in foster care already whose families live in the area and the number of licensed foster care providers in the area as well as other statistics.

Develop an instrument/process to screen and assess potential foster parents.

Obtain a waiver from the state to allow foster parents to derive their sole source of support from foster care income.

Obtain a waiver from the state to allow families currently receiving   welfare to become foster parents and still receive Medicaid and/or food stamps while in paid training and for a specified number of days after becoming licensed foster parents until their foster care income exceeds their state welfare grant amount.

Finalize model and desirable roles of the various partners.

Secure funding for pilot phase.

(Showing how grant funds will be used effectively.)

- Project's constituency

Target neighborhood demographics

The target neighborhood is in the heart of the Rockhurst-College Park neighborhood. It is home to 1,511 households. Bordered by Haven Avenue to the east, Brooklyn Drive to the west, Lincoln Avenue to the north, and Jackson to the south, the residents are predominately Native American (67 percent), followed by Anglo (25 percent), African American (4 percent), Hispanic (4 percent), and other (1 percent. Thirty-three percent of the residents are under the age of 18, while 59 percent of those over the age of 25 never completed high school. There is a great deal of unemployment in the neighborhood. Of the total population of 3,974 residents, 3,119 households receive food stamps and 2,009 adults and children are on welfare. Of those who are employed, the median household income is $11,893. The neighborhood ranks 15th among Dodge City's top 100 high crime communities.

(A portrait of gloom. But the funder can make it go away.)

> *Urban poverty and its impact on the neighborhood*
>
> The economic dynamics of urban America, including south central Dodge City, are of increasing importance as the U.S. workforce shifts from mostly Anglo males to minorities and women. By the year 2000, urban areas will provide a crucial portion of consumers and employees. The deterioration of inner-city neighborhoods over the past 20 years is slowing as many cities, including Dodge City, receive community development block grant funds, become a designated empowerment zone or enterprise community, and are the benefactors of private neighborhood revitalization efforts. According to a national report published by the Committee for Economic Development, a research group headquartered in New York City, "The millions of people living in distressed inner-city communities do not live up to their potential due to joblessness and inadequate job preparation, crime, social disorganization, and deficient housing, among other ills."

(Translation: This neighborhood is teetering on the edge of doom. Effective proposals do not let the funder's imagination wander.)

> *Hopelessness giving rise to integrated, communitywide actions*
>
> Since 1996, the target neighborhood, known locally as the Eden Project, has been experiencing metamorphic change due in part to the Rockhurst-College Park Neighborhood Association, the Church on the Avenue, Neighborhood Housing Development Corporation, and the City of Dodge City's myriad federally funded neighborhood development initiatives. Badly needed human and social service resources are gradually falling into place via a church-based resource center. A crime watch diligently deters incidences of crime, although gangs continue to thrive. Most importantly, following a neighborhoodwide clean-up effort, which included minor repairs on selected homes, recent federal and local grants are enabling the Eden Project area to benefit from new multifamily housing for the elderly and major rehabbing of block after block of deteriorated housing stock. Local funders have taken notice and are supporting the revival of an area that was once considered a desirable neighborhood for raising a family.

(Drama!)

> *Welfare reform - a problem handed down to the states*
>
> The term "welfare reform" is not new. Job training has been around for as long as the desire to reform welfare has been an initiative of our government. Workfare programs have come, been criticized, and faded. The current federally funded initiative is under scrutiny for only taking the best candidates for job skills training and overlooking the hard-to-serve. Unfortunately, it is the hard-to-serve that will never leave the ranks of welfare. For many families, welfare has been generational, a way of life. Simply planning to eject families from welfare after a specific period of time does not address the preservation of families, nor does it address long-term self-sufficiency for the post-welfare, single female head of household. Coupling poverty with a limited understanding of English takes these struggling families beyond the definition of "hard-to-serve." In other words, single mothers in the Eden Project area will be left out of the kind of jobs needed to provide food and shelter for their children.

(Trauma!)

> *Facing reality*
>
> The KMCS is a long-established, holistically focused agency that believes in addressing issues that others consider too difficult to address. The family unit is a complex kaleidoscope of changing circumstances. KMCS is seeking to team with other organizations already working in the Eden Project area and bring new partners into the effort to provide family support services. This effort means getting homes rehabbed so they will pass state inspection and qualify as suitable for the foster home designation. It also means identifying families, English speaking and non-English speaking, and getting them trained to qualify as state licensed

foster home providers. It means asking the Kansas Department of Economic Security to waive some of its stringent licensing requirements that would automatically eliminate Eden Project single-parent, female-headed families. It does not mean that health or safety issues will be overlooked; it means that families with the greatest hardships to overcome will be given a chance to succeed.

The state's child-welfare system has become so overburdened that abused children are being placed in hospitals and commercial day-care centers because there is not enough foster care available. As child abuse and neglect cases continue to rise in Lucas County, the demand for foster homes has reached an all-time high. There are over 2,300 children in 1,787 foster-parent homes, and over 200 children in emergency shelters waiting for foster homes. (Kansas Statesman, February 3, 2000)

(Nailing down the needs.)

KMCS believes that welfare reform is the right direction for the nation, but that simply leaving the states to solve the dilemma of cutting welfare budgets by cutting families is not the Christian solution. KMCS believes that the welfare reform drive and improving child welfare can and should go hand-in-hand, synergistically supporting each other. We all have a stake in lending a hand, but first we must be capable of garnering the resources necessary to extend that hand. With your funding support, the Professional Parents Partnering Project can conduct research and develop a model for moving families from welfare to work in south central Dodge City. This model will encompass more than simply providing job training, as the families trained will become licensed foster care providers. They will become the life-linking resource for at-risk children now living in circumstances equal to or worse than those from which these families will rise from.

(The promise to make a difference.)

- Constituency representation during the planning process

    Organizations that will be asked to participate in the planning process include, but are not limited to:

    Rockhurst-College Park Neighborhood Association (RCPNA) - The mission of the RCPNA is (1) to create a safe, clean, and crime-free community and (2) to establish an environment that will encourage the active participation of children, families, the members of the community, and community agencies in community activities. Every resident of the neighborhood--homeowner or renter--is a member of the association, as are nonresident property owners who support the mission of RCPNA.

    The Church on the Avenue - Fifteen percent of the neighborhood residents attend the Church on the Avenue. Eighty percent of the church's ministries are within the Eden Project area, located in the heart of the Rockhurst-College Park neighborhood. For the Professional Parents Partnering Project, the church is committing to provide space for community meetings, classrooms for family training, and actively supporting programs that seek to break the cycle of poverty for neighborhood residents. The church regularly provides food and clothing to needy residents of the area as well as low-income housing for the elderly.

    Neighborhood Housing Development Corporation (RHDC) - This affiliate of the Methodist Foundation of Kansas has aligned itself with the Eden Project's neighborhood association (RCPNA) and residents to understand the needs of the neighborhood and begin working with residents to obtain the currently lacking social support services. RHDC is committing to assist families selected for the partnership pilot in bringing their homes up to foster care home licensing requirements by using funds from a recent City of Dodge City grant for minor rehabilitation of single-family, owner-occupied homes. Through its numerous neighborhood revitalization projects (biannual neighborhoodwide clean-up, new multifamily housing for the elderly, new single-family homes, rehabilitation of selected single-family homes), RHDC is seeking to break down the barriers and stigma associated with inner-city neighborhoods.

KanCare - This company coordinates Lucas County's mental health services. It is funded with state and federal money and contracts with residential treatment facilities for behavioral services.

Kansas Department of Economic Security, Division of Children and Family Services - This mammoth umbrella agency manages the state's child welfare system. It has been under continual scrutiny by the state legislature for an alarming turnover rate among administration and staff. Public accusations have been made about children languishing in foster care too long, foster parents becoming frustrated and resigning, and the steadily increasing number of abused and neglected children overloading an already fragile system. (Kansas Statesman, October 24, 1999)

(Proof of input at every stakeholder level.)

- Systemic change KMCS is trying to achieve

    As the issue of the separation of church and state continues to be debated across the nation, it is clear that the *state* alone cannot continue operating under the business as usual paradigm. Funds are scarce, public scrutiny is brutal in revealing gaps in services, and the real stakeholders are being shortchanged. The *church* and the many service entities that have grown out of the church have been heading in the direction of providing what were once considered *state* services. Housing used to be a word synonymous with the Department of Housing and Urban Development; now Habitat For Humanity with its Christian-based sweat equity program is touching all corners of urban and rural America, building homes without *state* funds. One Church One Child has taken the lead in *church*-based adoptions, working hand-in-hand with *state* children's services agencies to expedite what was traditionally a prolonged, tedious process by placing hard-to-adopt children with one family in each *church* across America.

(Privatization makes a strong argument.)

    The family is a prime focus of the KMCS ministry."

    While nationally the secular community and church leaders struggle with confusing and burdensome Supreme Court rulings, those out in the "trenches" of human need and spiritual despair, witnessing the deterioration of family life and its most precious part--children--work silently. KMCS dreams and does planning, collaboration, and creating of models to harness the resources and unique strengths of both church and state to work synergistically toward the reunification of the family--America's greatest asset.

(Sharing the vision.)

ATTACHMENTS

Evaluation Section

Organizational Structure/Administration Section

Finance Section

Other Supporting Material Section

Index

• *Numbers & Symbols* •

424 Form, 42
501(c)(3) nonprofit status, 72, 80, 190, 203
8734 Form, 191
990PF Form, 70, 191

• *A* •

abstracts
  checking, 198
  described, 76
  example, 263
  importance of, 113
  table of contents and, 120
  writing, 119
accomplishments, writing about, 76, 124–126
accuracy standards, evaluations, 169
activities, writing about, 74, 76, 78, 142
Adobe Acrobat Reader, 210
advanced ruling period, 191
Aga Khan Foundation, 234
allocation, line item, 179–180
Always Dream Foundation, 16
American Association of Grant
      Professionals, 173
American Cancer Society Grant Application
      System, 210
American National Standards Institute, 168
annual campaigns, 13
annual reports, 203
appendices, 122
Application Control Center, 227
application kits. *See* federal grant application
      kits
applications. *See* grant applications
Arthur Vining Davis Foundations, 16
Arts Midwest, 16
assurance forms, 44, 47
AT&T, 17
attachments
  board of directors, 80
  corporations, 21
  Evaluation section, 200
  Finances section, 202–203
  foundations, 19, 20
  funding sources, 202–203
  key personnel, 199
  NYRAG format, 21
  online applications and, 211

order of, 200–203, 256
organization information, 80
Organizational Structure/Administration
      section, 201–202
Other section, 203
audit trails, 225
audits, 33, 191
authorizing legislation, 30
authorizing statute, 76

• *B* •

bank trust funds, contacting funder about, 219
Bell Atlantic Foundation, 211
Ben & Jerry's Foundation, 17
benchmarks, 78, 110, 144
best practices, 253
bids, construction, 183
BJA (Bureau of Justice Assistance), 171–172
board of directors, 80
bold font, in grant applications, 128–129,
      137, 139
brick and mortar projects, 13, 146
budget detail, 80, 180
budget information forms, 44
budget period, 87
budget worksheets, 99
budgets
  current operating, 72
  developing, 186–187
  direct costs, 184
  ethics and, 191, 193
  federal grants, 99
  indirect costs, 184–185
  inflation and, 189
  international, 235–236
  line-item changes, 33
  matching funds and, 187–188
  multi-year, 189
  narrative, 80
  project cost, 75
  salaries, 78
  summaries, 80, 179–180, 200
  supporting documentation, 192
  terminology, 179–185
  time interval for, 87
building funds, 13
bulleted lists, in grant applications, 137
bulletins, federal program, 100
Bureau of Justice Assistance (BJA), 171–172

• C •

Call for Public Comments announcement, 30
capital equipment, 182–183
capital support, 13
cash contributions, 88–89
cash-match monies, 89
cassette tapes, including with grant application, 246
Catalog of Federal and Domestic Assistance. *See* CFDA
Census Bureau, 249–250
census information, 135, 249–250
census tract, 249
CEO (Chief Executive Officer), 75
certificate of appreciation, 224
certification forms, 44, 47
CFDA (Catalog of Federal and Domestic Assistance)
  described, 15, 25
  policies and guidelines, 225
  searching for federal grants, 27–29
  state-level contact and, 91
CFDA number, 43, 91
CFO (Chief Financial Officer), 75, 162, 223–224
CGA (Common Grant Application), 19, 116
challenge monies, 13
charts, 129, 134, 136
checklists, 197,–200
Chief Executive Officer (CEO), 75
Chief Financial Officer (CFO), 75, 162, 223–224
Chronicle of Philanthropy, 66
codirectors, program, 159
collaborative partners, 88
colonias area, federal grants and, 91
color charts, 135
color graphics, 129
color, use of, 129, 135, 206–207, 240–242
Common Grant Application (CGA), 19, 116
community foundations, 219
community partners, 77, 88, 130–131, 160
community, description of, 77
competitive grants, 24
Computers For Learning Program, 39
conferences, funding for, 13
congressional districts, 73
congressional legislators, 32
construction
  grant funds, 175, 183
  in-kind contributions and, 188
consulting services, 13
contact person information, 73
continuation grants, 13
continuing support grants, 13

contracted services, 183, 188
contractual line, 183
contributions
  cash, 88–89
  employee matching, 13
  in-kind, 87–89, 185, 188
corporate foundations, 235
corporate funders
  activities, 68
  application due-dates, 69
  application forms, 69
  color themes and, 206, 242
  cover letters and, 114
  described, 16
  evaluation stakeholders, 90
  fields of interest, 68
  Form 990PF, 70, 191
  initial approach, 58
  letter of inquiry, 58
  mailing lists, 69
  notification of award, 220
  paper and, 205–206
  previous grants, 68
  prioritizing, 69–70
  purpose statement, 68
  rejection letters, 220–221, 260–261
  researching, 63–69
  response time, 222
  resubmitting funding requests, 228
  searching for, 57
  tracking grant requests, 218, 220–221
  Web sites, 16
Corporate Giving Directory, 231
corporate grant applications
  attachments, 200
  example, 21
  guidelines, 21
  mailing guidelines, 208
  management plan and, 163
  organization history, 126
  personnel, 162
  writing, 21
corporate grants, 10
corporate responsibility, 16
corporations
  donated goods and services, 229–232
  employee matching gifts, 13
  finding addresses and contacts, 65
  news about, 64
  requesting information, 64
  social responsibility Web pages, 65
  technical assistance, 231
cost justifications, 80
cost summaries, 80

cost-effective programs, 91, 108
Council of New Jersey Grantmakers, 20
cover forms
  Common Grant Application, 116
  example, 116
  federal grant applications, 36, 42–43, 118
  ink color and, 43
cover letters
  CGA format, 19
  checking, 198
  contents of, 114
  example, 116
  foundations, 19
  government grant applications and, 114
  importance of, 113
  tone of, 114
cover sheets, 19, 21
currency, foreign, 235–236
CyberGrants system, 210–211
Cystic Fibrosis Foundation, 210

● *D* ●

data
  analysis, 168
  collection, 168, 249–252, 256
  defined, 168
databases, mailing, 216
debriefing meetings, 217–218
demographic data, 76, 249–250
Department of Health and Human Services
    (HHS), 39
direct costs, 184
direct grants, 24–26
direct purpose statement, 142
Disclosure of Lobbying Activities form, 47
dissemination, 79, 177–178
donated goods and services, 229–232

● *E* ●

e-mail
  communication with funders, 73
  grant application followups and, 218
  submitting grant requests, 209–213
e-mail lists, 252
EEO (Equal Employment Opportunity) language,
    79
EFC (European Foundation Centre), 66, 233–234
electronic tracking process, 216
employee matching gifts, 13
employer identification number, 72
Empowerment Zone, 91
endowments, 13
Energy-Related Laboratory Equipment
    Program, 39

Enterprise Community, 91
Enterprise Foundation, 16
envelopes, for grant requests, 206, 240–241
environmental grant requests, 206
EPA (U.S. Environmental Protection Agency), 41
Equal Employment Opportunity (EEO)
    language, 79
Equipment Donations Program, 39
equipment, nonprofit organizations
  cost of, 192
  donated, 39, 229
  grant funds for, 182–183
  soft cash and, 188
equitable access, 79
equity statement, 166
equity, government grants, 142, 165–166
ethnic statistics, 129
European Foundation Centre (EFC), 66, 233–234
European Foundation Fundamentals, 234
European Grants Index, 234
Evaluation Center at Western Michigan
    University, 173
evaluation plans
  contents of, 97–98, 168
  examples, 171–172, 174–176
  resources, 170, 172–173
  terminology, 167–170
  third-party evaluators and, 174
evaluation teams, 169, 172–173
evaluations
  attachments, 200
  conducting, 79
  defined, 167
  external, 173–174, 176–177
  final, 98
  formative, 169
  interim, 98
  internal, 169, 172–174, 176
  outcome, 98, 170
  process, 98
  sharing findings, 79
  stakeholder, 79, 90, 172–174, 176
  standards for, 168–169
  summation, 170
  tools, 170
evaluators
  defined, 169
  identifying, 90
  third-party, 90, 98–99, 170, 173–174, 176–177
executive directors, 73
executive summaries
  checking, 198
  described, 76
  importance of, 113
  table of contents and, 120
  writing, 119

expenses
  general, 14
  miscellaneous, 184, 189
  operating, 14
external evaluations, 173–174, 176–177
Exxon Mobil, 17

• F •

fact sheets, 100
Fannie Mae Foundation, 17
FC-Search, 57
feasibility standards, evaluations, 168
federal agencies, 99, 100, 212–213
federal congressional districts, 73
Federal Emergency Management Administration
    (FEMA), 36
federal grant application kits, 8, 35
federal grant applications. *See also* government
    grant applications; grant applications; state
    grant applications
  approval of, 221
  assurance forms, 44, 47
  budget forms, 44, 99
  certification forms, 44, 47
  closing date, 86
  contact names, 73
  cover forms, 36, 42–43, 118
  cover letters and, 114
  described, 10, 35
  electronic, 209–210, 212–213
  equity section, 142, 165–166
  errors and omissions on, 41
  forms, 35–36, 41–44, 47
  goals and objectives, 97
  guidelines, 85–87, 95–99
  indirect cost line, 184–185
  late, 208
  lobbying-activity disclosure form, 47
  mailing guidelines, 208
  numerical scores, 94
  order of, 200
  organization history, 126
  organizing, 41–42, 197, 198
  page limits, 18
  peer-review process, 94
  pre-review process, 93–94
  rejection letters, 222, 226–227, 260–262
  resources, 164–165
  response time, 95, 222
  resubmitting, 227
  review criteria, 93–100
  review process, 47
  reviewers' comments, 226, 260
  securing, 205
  tracking, 204, 221–222
  type of applicant category, 72
federal grant competitions, 24, 26, 30
federal grant monies, 24–25
federal grants. *See also* government grants;
    grants; state grants
  announcements, 30–32, 86–88
  award size, 31
  calculating chances, 88
  calculating grant award, 88
  competitive, 24
  contributions, 87–89
  deadlines, 31
  described, 35
  eligibility criteria, 33, 86, 88
  eligible applicants, 31
  evaluating, 86–88
  federally designated areas, 91
  finding, 24, 26, 28–30
  funding considerations, 33
  funding options, 32–34
  funding programs, 37–41
  gathering research, 89–90
  legislative authority, 86, 88
  length of, 32
  line-item changes, 33
  notification of acceptance, 221
  number of, 32
  number of years needed, 33
  preparing for, 31, 32
  review criteria, 33, 85–91
  sample table of contents, 18
  third parties and, 87
  total funds needed, 33
  Web sites, 37–41
Federal Register
  described, 15, 25
  federal grant announcements, 86
  federal grant application kits, 35
  federal grant forms, 36
  grant competitions, 95
  searching for federal grants, 29–30
  tracking grant announcements, 31–32
fellowships, funding for, 13
FEMA (Federal Emergency Management
    Administration), 36
Finances section, 202–203
financial statement, 73, 80, 202
fiscal accountability, 225
fiscal sponsors, 190–191, 225
fiscal year, 73
flow charts, 78, 163
FOIA (Freedom of Information Act), 226–227, 260

for-profit organizations, 72, 163
formative evaluations, 169
forms
    assurance, 44, 47
    budget, 44
    certification, 44, 47
    color of, 207
    cover, 42–43
    examples, 263
    federal grant applications, 35–36, 41–44, 47
    federally mandated, 122
    Form 424, 42
    Form 8734, 191
    Form 990PF, 191
    foundation grant narrative, 279
    government grant narrative, 263
    guidelines, 207
    lobbying-activity disclosure, 47
    pros and cons, 207
    specialized, 207
    working with, 258
formula grants, 24, 28
Foundation Center, 15, 57, 65–66
Foundation Directory, 66
foundation funding, 17, 19, 57
Foundation Grants Index, 66
foundations
    activities, 68
    application due-dates, 69
    application forms, 69
    attachments and, 19, 200
    community, 219
    corporate, 235
    cover letters and, 114
    evaluation stakeholders, 90
    fields of interest, 68
    Form 990PF, 70, 191
    grant applications, 19, 20
    initial approach, 58
    letter of inquiry, 58
    mailing guidelines, 208
    mailing lists, 69
    management plan and, 163
    narrative example, 279
    news about, 64
    notification of award, 220
    paper and, 205–206
    personnel, 162
    previous grants, 68
    prioritizing, 69–70
    private, 16, 191
    public, 16
    purpose statement, 68

rejection letters, 220–221, 260–261
requesting information, 64
researching, 63–69
response time, 222
resubmitting funding requests, 228
sources, 16
tracking grant requests, 218, 220–221
Freedom of Information Act (FOIA), 226–227, 260
fringe benefits, as soft cash source, 188
full-time equivalent (FTE), 162
Funders Online, 66
funding. *See also* grant funds
    corporate, 16
    foundation, 17, 19
    government, 15
    matching, 187–188
    multiple sources, 56–58, 61
    steps for, 56–58
Funding $ourcebook, 67
funding plan
    action plan for, 55
    assessing needs, 52–53
    creating, 49, 52–55
    described, 12, 50
    goals, 54
    objectives, 54
    prioritizing funders, 70
    structure, 50–51
    SWOT analysis, 52–53
funding publications, 66
funding sources
    amount requested, 75
    attachments, 202–203
    future, 110
    international, 233–236
    listing, 202–203
    mailing databases, 216
    organizing, 215–216
    qualifications and, 71–73
    researching, 17
    response time, 222
    writing format for, 17
fundraising, 10–12, 193
Fundsnet Services site, 66

● *G* ●

GEAR UP (Gaining Early Awareness and
    Readiness for Undergraduate Programs), 28
General Services Administration (GSA), 28
gifts, employee matching, 13
goal statements, 143

goals
  described, 77, 141
  federal funding, 95
  objectives and, 147–148
  writing, 77, 97, 110, 142–143
government
  fiscal year, 73
  U.S. Electronic Grants Project, 212–213
  Web sites, 65
government agencies, 17, 212, 250. *See also*
      state agencies
government grant applications. *See also* federal
      grant applications; grant applications; state
      grant applications
  contents, 19
  deadlines, 31
  described, 10
  example, 263
  format, 18
  guidelines, 33
  online, 209–210, 212–213
  organization history, 126
  retrieving, 30
  state forms, 42
government grant monies, 23
government grants. *See also* federal grants;
      grants; state grants
  application kits, 17
  audits and, 33
  direct, 24–26
  format, 18–19
  formula, 24
  information on, 23
  passthrough, 24, 26
  review criteria, 85–91
  searching for, 15
  state level, 23
  third-party evaluators and, 90
Government Printing Office (GPO), 29
government publications, 15, 29, 99, 100
GPO (Government Printing Office), 29
grant announcements, 94, 97, 252
grant application forms
  cover forms, 116, 118
  filling in, 74–75
  international funders, 234
grant applications. *See also* corporate grant
      applications; federal grant applications;
      state grant applications
  analyzing, 89–90
  appendices, 122
  attachments, 80–81
  budget section, 179–187
  buzzwords and, 241
  cassette tapes, 246

checklist for, 197–200
children and youth, 206
closing date, 69, 86
color use, 240–242
complex, 10
cover letter, 114
data collection, 249–252, 256
defined, 8
envelopes, 240–241
environmental, 206
errors in, 246, 248
finishing touches, 197, 205–206, 208
foundations, 19, 20
goals and objectives, 142–145, 147, 148
graphics, 240
guidelines, 33, 85–87, 208
international, 235
length, 8
letters of support, 81, 203, 240–241
mail merge feature, 198
mailing, 208
matching funds, 187–188
multiple, 56–58, 61
notification of acceptance, 220
online, 209–213
opening section, 101–103
order of items in, 113–114
organizing, 197–198, 215–216, 255–258
PDF format, 210
permissions, 245
personalizing, 239–243
photographs, 239, 243
qualifications, 71–73
regional forms, 20
rejection letters, 220–222, 226–227, 259–262
releasing, 246
releasing copies, 247
request section, 107–108, 110
response time, 222
resubmitting, 227–228
securing, 205
signatures, 75
stakeholder input, 246
submitting electronically, 209–213
table of contents, 120–122
templates, 257
tracking, 58, 204, 216–222
unsolicited, 37
video tapes, 246
watermark themes, 242
wrapping up, 80–81
grant competitions, 95
grant funds. *See also* funding
  accepting, 223–225
  amount requested, 75

audit trails, 225
building, 13
certificate of appreciation, 224
conveying need for, 133–136, 138–139
equipment, 182–183
fiscal accountability, 225
for-profit organizations and, 72, 163
funding stipulations, 225
individuals and, 163
matching, 14
multiple awards, 226
need for, 107–108, 110
notification of award, 220–221
overfunded projects, 226
plan of action, 77
preparing for review criteria, 86–91
print resources, 66–67
purpose of, 74, 77, 87, 142
qualifications, 71, 72, 73
regulations, 225
renovation, 13
return of, 191
review criteria, 85
scholarship, 14
sources of, 14, 15
spreading cost of, 107
successful grant seeking, 64
tracking, 225
Web sites, 64–67
winning, 63–64, 101–108, 110
grant proposals, 8. *See also* grant applications
grant writers, 8–9
grant writing
  becoming proficient, 10
  brainstorming, 255
  buzzwords and, 241
  capturing reader attention, 139
  data collection, 249–252
  freelance, 9
  generalizing, 10
  Groups of Three tactic, 102
  learning about, 1
  no-no's, 245–248
  occupation, 1, 7
  organizational techniques, 255–258
  skills required, 10
  success rate, 7
  terminology, 12–14, 71–79, 81, 87–88
  versus fundraising, 10–12
  words that work, 101–108, 110
grant writing consultants, 9
grants. *See also* federal grants; government
    grants; state grants
  approved but not funded, 95
  construction, 175

continuation, 13
continuing support, 13
contributions, 87–89
corporate, 10
defined, 7
diversifying sources, 56–58, 61
eligibility criteria, 33
funding considerations, 33
gathering research, 89–90
number of years needed, 33
organizing information, 215–216
planning for, 12, 49, 52–55
return of money, 191
review criteria, 33
sources of, 14–15
third parties and, 87
total funds needed, 33
grants-management software, 216–217
graphics, 129, 131, 134, 136, 240
graphs, 129
GSA (General Services Administration), 28

• *H* •

hard matching funds, 185, 187–188
Hazardous Materials Emergency Preparedness
    program, 40
Henry Luce Foundation, 16
history, 76, 124–126
Hoover's Online site, 65, 230
HUD (U.S. Department of Housing and Urban
    Development), 40

• *I* •

icons, in this book, 4
IMLS (Institute of Museum and Library
    Services), 37
impact statement, 151
implementation strategy, 148, 150
in-kind contributions, 87–89, 185, 188
income, program, 193
Independent Funding, 234
Independent Television Service, 16
indirect charges, 189
indirect costs, 183–185
indirect purpose statement, 142
initiatives, 76–77
Institute of Museum and Library Services
    (IMLS), 37
interest income, 193
internal evaluations, 169, 172–174, 176
international funds, 233–236

Internet. *See also* Web sites
  data collection, 252
  government publications, 29
  grant seeking and, 65
  newsletters, 252
  online grant applications, 209–213
  research reports, 252
  salary information on, 192
  submitting grant applications, 209–213
  target population information, 134
Internet Explorer browser, 211
IRS (Internal Revenue Service)
  501(c)(3) classification, 72
  501(c)(3) letter, 203
  501(c)(3) nonprofit status, 80
  advanced ruling period, 191
  employer identification number, 72
  fiscal sponsors and, 190–191
  Form 8734, 191
  Form 990PF, 191
  nonprofit status, 191
  tax-exempt status, 72, 80
italics, in grant applications, 137

• J •

journals, 100

• K •

Kellogg Company, 17
Kellogg Foundation, 173, 190
key personnel, 78, 98, 156–163, 199

• L •

LEAs (Local Education Agencies), 160
leased equipment, 183
Legal Services Corporation (LSC), 37
legislative authority, 86, 88
legislators, 32, 73, 95, 221, 262
letter of inquiry, 58
letters
  of support, 81, 203, 240–241
  rejection, 220–222, 226–227, 259–262
  requesting goods and services, 229–232
library, public. *See* public library
line of accountability, 158, 160
lobbyists, disclosing use of, 47
Local Education Agencies (LEAs), 160
local government, 18–19, 250
Local Initiatives Support Corporation, 16

• M •

mail merge feature, 198, 206–207
mailing databases, 216
mailing guidelines, 208
management plan, 78, 160–163
maps, 136
matching funds, 14, 182, 185, 187–188
materials, project, 183, 192, 230
measurement tools, 170
measurements, data collection, 176
membership fees, 193
memorandum of agreement, 160
Metropolitan Life Insurance Company, 17
Metropolitan Statistical Area (MSA), 90
Microtel, Bulgaria Foundation, 235
mileage reimbursement, 181–182
milestones, nonprofit organization, 125, 144
mission statement, 74
MSA (Metropolitan Statistical Area), 90

• N •

naming projects, 74
narratives
  analyzing, 227
  attachments and, 200
  budget, 80
  charts, 134
  checking, 198
  community partnerships, 130–131
  content requirements, 95–99
  defining parts of, 76–79
  defining problems, 96
  dissemination and, 178
  examples, 263, 279
  foundation grant, 279
  government grant, 263
  graphics, 131
  indirect costs, 185
  introduction, 76
  key personnel, 156–163
  numerical scores, 96
  objectives, 96
  online applications and, 211
  order of information in, 256
  organization information, 76, 124–131
  page limits, 93–94, 137
  tables, 130–131, 134
NASA (National Aeronautics and Space
    Administration), 37
National Center for Urban Partnership, 66
National Directory of Corporate Gift Giving, 66

National Endowment for the Arts (NEA), 37
National Endowment for the Humanities
  (NEH), 38
National Network of Grantmakers (NNG), 19, 69
National Science Foundation (NSF), 38
NEA (National Endowment for the Arts), 37
needs statement, 77, 133
NEH (National Endowment for the
  Humanities), 38
Netscape browser, 211
New York Regional Association of Grantmakers
  (NYRAG), 20
newsletters, including in grant requests, 81, 203
newspaper articles, including in grant requests,
  81, 203
NNG (National Network of Grantmakers), 19, 69
nondiscriminatory policies, 79
Nonprofit Facilities Fund, 16
nonprofit organizations
  accomplishments, 76, 124–126
  action plans, 55
  annual report, 203
  background, 76
  best practices, 253
  budget summary, 80
  contact names, 73
  current operating budget, 72
  defined, 87
  describing, 104
  donated goods and services, 229–232
  employee matching gifts, 13
  federal congressional districts, 73
  financial statement, 80, 202
  fiscal sponsors, 190–191
  fiscal year, 73
  Form 990PF, 191
  funding goals/objectives, 54
  geographic area served, 75
  goals, 77
  history, 76, 124–126
  identifying opportunities, 53
  identifying problems, 52–53
  identifying strengths, 52
  information about, 80, 198
  legal name, 72
  mailing address, 73
  milestones, 125
  mission statement, 74
  narrative information, 124–131
  organizational structure, 201
  planning for grants, 12, 49, 52–55
  programs, 127–128
  public schools as, 211
  purpose statement, 142

SWOT analysis, 52–53
tax-exempt status, 72
technical assistance, 14
year founded, 72
nonprofit status, 8, 80, 191
NonProfit Times, 64, 217
notices of funding availability, 31
NSF (National Science Foundation), 38
NYRAG (New York Regional Association of
  Grantmakers), 20

objectives
  described, 141, 143
  evaluating, 97–98
  goals and, 147–148
  measurable, 78, 108, 110, 170, 176
  narrative, 96
  outcome, 144, 146–147
  plans for reaching, 78
  process, 144–145
  third-party evaluations, 176
  writing, 78, 97, 110, 142, 144
Office of Management and Budget (OMB), 44, 47,
  212, 222, 225
office supplies, 183
OMB (Office of Management and Budget), 44, 47,
  212, 222, 225
OMB circulars, 225
Online Evaluation Resource Library, 172
Ontario Trillium Foundation, 190
operating expenses, 14, 192
Organizational Structure/Administration
  section, 201–202
organizational charts, 163
Other section, 184, 189, 203
outcome evaluations, 98, 170
outcome objectives, 144, 146–147
overhead, 184–185

paper, used in grant requests, 205–206
participants, program. *See* target population
partners, grant program
  collaborative, 88
  community, 88
  debriefing, 217–218
  described, 130
  responsibilities, 201
  sharing information, 217–218
  writing about, 130–131

passthrough grants, 24, 26
passthrough monies, 24
PDF (Portable Document Format), 210
peer review panel, 94
peer-review comments, 227
peer-review process, 94
per diem, 181
performance outcomes, 150
permissions, grant applications, 245
personnel line, 181
personnel, program
  considerations, 158–159
  contracted, 183, 188
  determining salary, 192
  education, 158–159
  equal opportunity, 79
  equity and, 142, 165–166
  example, 157
  fringe benefits, 188
  hours, 158
  in-kind contributions and, 188
  inflation and, 189
  key, 78, 98, 156–163
  management plan and, 160–163
  nondiscriminatory policies, 79
  projects, 156–163, 181, 183
  rules for selecting, 157
  salaries, 78, 158
  selection process, 157–159
Pew Charitable Trusts, 16
PGA Foundations, 16
Philanthropic Reform Committee, 19
Philanthropy News Digest, 64, 217
Philanthropy News Network, 64
Philip Morris, 17
photographs, including in grant requests,
  239, 243
plan of action
  contents, 141
  described, 77
  goals, 142–145, 147–148
  impact statement, 151
  objectives, 142–145, 147–148
  strategies, 148, 150
  timeline, 150–151
  workplan, 152–153
plan of operation, 97, 141, 152–153
planning grants, 279
Portable Document Format (PDF), 210
post office boxes, 73
postcards, 204
postscript, 21
pre-review process, 93–94
print resources, 66–67
private foundations, 16, 191

private sector funding. *See* corporate funders;
  foundations
problem definition, 96
problem solution, 21, 77
problem statement
  described, 21, 133, 199
  writing, 77, 104–107, 136
problems
  defining, 96
  writing about, 133–134, 136
process evaluations, 98
process objectives, 144–145
Program Evaluation Standards, The, 168
programs
  cost of, 108
  current, 76
  describing, 127, 128
  design, 77, 141, 145, 147
  development, 14
  income, 193
  objectives, 96
  responsibility for, 78
  systematic changes, 78
project administrator, 157
project director, 98, 157
project grants, 28
projects
  acronyms and, 74
  cost of, 75, 91, 108, 179–180
  dates, 75
  design, 97
  developing budgets, 186–187
  duration of, 87
  evaluating, 167–170, 172–177
  failed, 169
  flow charts, 163
  geographic area, 75
  goals, 170
  impact of, 151
  implementation strategy, 148, 150
  improving, 169
  income, 193
  management, 98
  model, 177–178
  naming, 74
  organizational charts, 163
  organizing, 202, 215–216, 252, 256
  overfunded, 226
  performance outcomes, 150
  personnel, 156–163, 181, 183
  resources, 164–165
  significance of, 78
  third parties and, 87
  timelines, 142, 150–151
  total cost, 75
  workplans, 152–153

proof of tax-exempt status, 80
proposals, 8. *See also* grant applications
propriety standards, evaluations, 169
public charities, 191
public foundations, 16
public library
   government publications, 29
   viewing grant announcements, 86
   Web research, 65
public schools, 160, 211
public sector funding. *See* government funding
publications, government, 99–100
purchasing cooperatives, 192
purpose statement, 87, 142

qualitative approach, 170
quantitative approach, 170

Regional Associations of Grantmakers
   (RAGs), 20
regional forms, 20
rejection letters
   corporate funders, 220–221
   foundations, 220–221
   government funders, 222
   grant reviewer's comments, 226–227
   handling, 259–262
renovation funds, 13
reporting number, 72
reports, government, 100
research findings, 100
resolution language, drafting, 224–225
resources, identifying, 165
review criteria
   preparing for, 85–91
   writing for, 93–100
review points, 96
Rich Text Format (RTF), 210

Sage Publications, 172
salaries, 78
salary surveys, 192
SBA (Small Business Administration), 38
scholarship funds, 14
seed money, 14, 218
seminars, funding for, 13
Senate districts, 73

services, donated, 230
single audit trail, 225
Single Point of Contact (SPOC), 91
Small Business Administration (SBA), 38
soft matching funds, 185, 188
soft money, 187, 248. *See also* in-kind
   contributions
software, grants-management, 216–217
SPOC (Single Point of Contact), 91
stakeholders, 169–170, 217, 246
stakeholders evaluation, 79, 90, 172–174, 176
standards, 175
state agencies. *See also* government agencies
   data collection, 250
   examples, 15
   funding projects and, 75
   online grant applications, 209
   Single Point of Contact (SPOC), 91
state grant applications. *See also* federal grant
   applications; grant applications
   approval of, 221
   budget forms, 99
   contact names, 73
   contents, 19
   cover letters and, 114
   described, 10
   equity section, 142, 165–166
   example, 263
   format, 18
   forms, 42
   goals and objectives, 97
   guidelines, 95–99
   indirect cost line, 184–185
   mailing guidelines, 208
   numerical scores, 94
   order of, 200
   organization history, 126
   peer-review process, 94
   pre-review process, 93–94
   rejection letters, 222, 226–227, 260–262
   resources, 164–165
   response time, 95, 222
   resubmitting, 227
   review criteria, 93–100
   reviewers' comments, 226, 260
   tracking, 221–222
   type of applicant category, 72
state grants. *See also* federal grants;
   government grants; grants
   described, 15
   direct, 24–26
   finding, 23
   formula, 24
   notification of acceptance, 221
   passthrough grants and, 26

statement of diversity, 79
statistics, data collection, 251
strategies, writing about, 78, 142, 148, 150
summation evaluation, 170
supplies, project, 183, 188, 230
Sustainable Development Grant Program, 41
SWOT analysis, 52–53

• T •

table of contents
  checking, 198
  described, 120
  example, 121
  format, 121
  importance of, 113
  items included in, 120, 122
tables, 78, 130–131, 134, 136
Taft Group publications, 67
target population
  census information, 135
  charts and graphs, 136
  defining, 76, 128–129
  demographic data, 76, 90
  equity and, 142, 165–166
  ethnic statistics, 129
  evaluations and, 79
  goals for, 77
  programs for, 127–128
  project impact on, 78
  researching, 134
  tables, 134
  writing about, 142
tax-exempt status, 72, 80
taxes, 14. *See also* IRS
taxpayer identification number, 72
technical assistance, 14, 231
Technology Opportunity Program (TOP), 39
templates, 257
terminology, grant-related
  budgets, 179–185
  common terms, 12–14
  evaluation plans, 167–170
  general terms, 87
  government terms, 88
  grant writing, 71–79, 81
  program-specific terms, 87
third parties
  cash contributions, 88–89
  defined, 87
  in-kind contributions, 87–89
third-party agreement, 87
third-party evaluators, 90, 98–99, 170, 173–174, 176–177

ticket sales, planned events, 193
timelines, 78, 142, 150–151
TOP (Technology Opportunity Program), 39
Touch'em All Foundation, 16
Toyota USA Foundation, 17
travel expenses, 181–182, 188
tuition income, budget and, 193
Turner Foundation, 16

• U •

U.S. Census Bureau, 249–250
U.S. Department of Agriculture (USDA), 38
U.S. Department of Commerce (DOC), 39
U.S. Department of Education (DOED), 39
U.S. Department of Energy (DOE), 39
U.S. Department of Housing and Urban Development (HUD), 40
U.S. Department of Human Services Partner Gateway Web site, 65
U.S. Department of Justice (DOJ), 40, 171, 210
U.S. Department of Labor (DOL), 40
U.S. Department of the Interior (DOI), 40
U.S. Department of Transportation (DOT), 40
U.S. Electronic Grants Project, 212–213
U.S. Environmental Protection Agency (EPA), 41
U.S. Institute of Peace (USIP), 41
unallowable costs, 182
United Way, 192
unsolicited proposals, 37
USDA (U.S. Department of Agriculture), 38
USIP (U.S. Institute of Peace), 41
utility standards, evaluations, 168

• V •

videos, including with grant applications, 246
volunteers
  debriefing, 217–218
  involvement of, 103
  responsibilities, 201
  sharing information, 217, 218

• W •

watermark themes, 242
Web browsers, 211
Web sites. *See also* Internet
  American Cancer Society Grant Application System, 210
  Arthur Vining Davis Foundations, 16
  Arts Midwest, 16
  AT&T, 17

Ben & Jerry's Foundation, 17
Bureau of Justice Assistance, 171–172
CFDA, 27, 29
Chronicle of Philanthropy, 66
corporate funders, 16
corporate social responsibility, 65
currency conversion sites, 236
CyberGrants, 210–211
Cystic Fibrosis Foundation, 210
Enterprise Foundation, 16
European Foundation Centre, 233
evaluation plans, 170, 172
Exxon Mobil, 17
Fannie Mae Foundation, 17
federal funding programs, 37–41
federal grant application kits, 35
Federal Register, 29
Foundation Center, 15, 57, 65–66
Funding $ourcebook, 67
Fundsnet Services, 66
GPO, 29
grant seeking resources, 64–67
Henry Luce Foundation, 16
Hoover's Online, 65, 230
Independent Television Service, 16
Kellogg Company, 17
Kellogg Foundation, 173, 190
Kristi Yamaguchi's Always Dream
    Foundation, 16

Local Initiatives Support Corporation, 16
Metropolitan Life Insurance Company, 17
National Center for Urban Partnership, 66
NNG, 19
Nonprofit Facilities Fund, 16
OMG, 225
Online Evaluation Resource Library, 172
online grant applications, 210–211
Ontario Trillium Foundation, 190
Pew Charitable Trusts, 16
PGA Foundations, 16
Philip Morris, 17
private foundations, 16
public foundations, 16
regional form example, 20
Sage Publications, 172
Taft Group publications, 67
third-party evaluators, 173
Touch'em All Foundation, 16
Toyota USA Foundation, 17
Turner Foundation, 16
U.S. Census Bureau, 249–250
U.S. Department of Justice, 210
William Randolph Hearst Foundations, 16
workplans, 141, 152–153
worksheets, 80

Notes

Notes

Notes

Notes

Notes

Notes

Notes

Notes